True Prayer

TRUE PRAYER

An Invitation to Christian Spirituality

KENNETH LEECH

'A theologian is one whose prayer is true.'
EVAGRIUS OF PONTUS (Fourth century)

Harper & Row, Publishers, San Francisco

New York, Grand Rapids, Philadelphia, St. Louis
London, Singapore, Sydney, Tokyo, Toronto

FIRST HARPER & ROW PAPERBACK EDITION PUBLISHED 1986.

Library of Congress Cataloging in Publication Data

Leech, Kenneth.
True prayer.

1. Prayer. I. Title.
BV215.L38 1980 248.3′2 80-8358
ISBN 0–06–065227–6
ISBN 0–06–065232–2 (pbk.)

89 90 MPC 10 9 8 7 6 5 4 3

Contents

Preface

In my book *Soul Friend* (Sheldon Press 1977) I examined the Christian tradition of spiritual direction and guidance. The present book is a more general one, and is in some respects a companion volume to *Soul Friend*, although it assumes less knowledge of Christian belief and practice. I have attempted to approach the questions of prayer and the spiritual life with the needs of the ordinary, intelligent Christian in mind. I have assumed little background knowledge, only a desire to pray and to understand what Christian spirituality is about. For the sake of simplicity I have avoided detailed references, since these are accessible in other more detailed studies. Most quotations are from the great spiritual classics, references to other contemporary works being, for the most part, reserved for the Bibliography.

1

Prayer and God

> Our Father in heaven. (Matt. 6.9)
>
> If you have a false idea of God, the more religious you are, the worse it is for you—it were better for you to be an atheist.
>
> WILLIAM TEMPLE

In prayer we open ourselves out to God, and this process is one of liberation and awakening. This is how the tenth-century Byzantine mystic St Symeon described it:

> Imagine a man standing at night inside his house with all the doors closed: and then suppose that he opens a window just at the moment when there is a sudden flash of lightning. Unable to bear its brightness, at once he protects himself by closing his eyes and drawing back from the window. So it is with the soul that is enclosed in the realm of the senses: if ever she peeps out through the window of the mind, she is overwhelmed by the brightness, like lightning, of the pledge of the Holy Spirit that is within her. Unable to bear the splendour of unveiled light, at once she is bewildered in her mind, and she draws back entirely upon herself, taking refuge as in a house, among sensory and human things.

So God breaks out like light breaking forth at morning (Isa. 58.8), and the human experience of God has often been described as an awakening, a heightening of consciousness and perception. We move from darkness to light, from shadows to reality. To know God is to know one's own true Self, the ground of one's being. So prayer is an intensely human experience in which our eyes are opened and we begin to see more clearly our own true nature. Julian of Norwich, in the fourteenth century, speaks for the whole mystical tradition.

> Then our Lord opened my spiritual eyes and showed me the soul in the middle of my heart. The soul was as large as if it were an eternal world, and a blessed kingdom as well. Its condition showed it to be a most glorious city. In the midst of it sat our Lord Jesus, God and Man, beautiful in person, most majestic of kings, and most worshipful Lord. And I saw him arrayed in solemn state. Most gloriously is he seated within the soul, in rightful peace and rest. His Godhead rules and upholds both heaven and earth, and all that is, and is supreme in might, wisdom and goodness. Nor will he quit the place he holds in our soul for ever—as I see it. For in us is he completely at home, and has his eternal dwelling.

It is the human experience which is the starting point of prayer: a process of growing awareness of why people love us and forgive us, and of openness to the wonder and glory of the creation, of nature, and of the elements. Frequently, in that endless search for peace and stillness, we look towards big, old established parts of the creation—the sea, the mountains, the countryside. Here we discover great beauty, natural stillness, and the constant reassuring motion of a life-giving force behind things. Within nature, death is more acceptable than within humanity. A dead tree can look very beautiful. The idea of a sunken ship, with its skeletons and its treasure, is exciting. Equally exciting is the sense of natural awe which may be the beginnings of a sense of God.

> The heavens are telling the glory of God; and the firmament proclaims his handiwork.
> Day to day pours forth speech, and night to night declares knowledge.
> There is no speech, nor are there words: their voice is not heard.
> (Ps. 19.1–3)

So prayer may begin with the experience of sheer wonder and amazement at the natural world. There is a close link between the experience of peace and inner calm which comes through looking at a starry night, and that which comes through encountering someone of great holiness and spiritual perception. We may find ourselves filled with awe, and this involves both fear, and reassurance that, deep down, the universe is filled with glory. This experience is captured best by poets and artists. So we read the well-known words of Wordsworth.

And I have felt
A presence that disturbs me with the joy
Of elevated thoughts; a sense sublime
Of something far more deeply interfused,
Whose dwelling is the light of setting suns,
And the round ocean and the living air,
And the blue sky, and in the mind of man:
A motion and a spirit that impels
All thinking things, all objects of all thought,
And rolls through all things.

'Lines Composed a Few Miles Above
Tintern Abbey 13 July 1798'

Or, more recently, Gerard Manley Hopkins.

The world is charged with the grandeur of God.
It will flame out, like shining from shook foil;
It gathers to a greatness, like the ooze of oil
Crushed. Why do men then now not reck his rod?
Generations have trod, have trod, have trod;
And all is seared with trade; bleared, smeared with toil;
And wears man's smudge and shares man's smell: the soil
Is bare now, nor can foot feel, being shod.

And for all this, nature is never spent:
There lives the dearest freshness deep down things;
And though the last lights off the black West went
Oh, morning, at the brown brink eastward, springs—
Because the Holy Ghost over the bent
World broods with warm breast and with ah! bright wings.

'God's Grandeur'

In the writings of the mystics, it is the sea which, over and over again, is the symbol of God's immensity. Yet the wildness and terror of the sea is also seen as a hostile force as well as a symbol of renewal. In the Old Testament the sea is hostile to God, and

God's victory over the primordial ocean is celebrated in song. So in Psalm 74 God divides the sea by his power, breaks the heads of the dragons, and crushes Leviathan. In Isaiah 51, God cuts Rahab in pieces, pierces the dragon, and dries up the sea. God is seen as triumphant over the sea in the work of creation when the Spirit breathes over the waters and brings peace out of chaos. So the Flood, the Red Sea, the Waters of Babylon, all symbolize God's power over and through water. So too in the New Testament, Christ's kingship is seen in his calming of the sea, while in the vision of the new order in Revelation 21, there is no more sea but the river of the water of life flows through the city.

It is in this mingling of terror and peace that the sea becomes a powerful symbol of the activity of God. The troubled sea stands for disorder and confusion in the cosmic order. So the coming of peace to the sea is a sign of the Kingdom of God. In the sea, as in the desert, were evil forces. Behemoth, the great serpent or dragon, lived in the waters, and the conquest of the demons in the waters was an important image in the early liturgies of Christian Baptism. The conquest of the waters is the conquest of the monsters who destroy humanity, the conquest of the depths of evil.

Yet the sea is also the symbol of God's infinite love. The mystics speak of losing themselves in the ocean of God's love, of being drowned in union with God, of the abyss of wonder. And this theme is reflected in many hymns.

> Till in the ocean of thy love
> We lose ourselves in heaven above.
>
> There's a wideness in God's mercy,
> Like the wideness of the sea.

The peace of the sea is seen as a sign of the peace of God; the vastness of the sea as a sign of eternity; the 'self-loss' which comes through drowning as a sign of self-transcendence. Yet often it is precisely this self-loss that we fear, and we hide ourselves in a cave, sheltered from the powerful force of open sea. Fear of the consequences of self-giving drive us into isolation.

At heart prayer is a process of self-giving and of being set free from isolation. To pray is to enter into a relationship with God and to be transformed in him. And this relationship is close to the relationships we have with human beings. Many people however see prayer merely as asking God for things, pleading with a remote Being about the needs and crises of earth. Sometimes these pleas produce a response: often they do not. So prayer is seen in essentially functional terms—is it effective or not? does it produce results? It is hardly surprising that we see prayer in this way, since we live within a social order which is geared to the notion of efficiency and production as the supreme end of existence. But in order to pray well we need to disengage ourselves from this way of thinking.

So what is prayer? It is a 'sharing in the divine nature', a 'taking of manhood into God'. So we can say, in the words of the eastern teacher St Gregory of Sinai, 'Prayer is God'. When we think about prayer, we are thinking about God, and about human consciousness of God. I am not suggesting that asking is not appropriate or unimportant. In fact, the teaching of Jesus places asking as a central element in prayer. But this depends upon the kind of relationship we have with God, and upon the kind of God we believe in. Beginning to think about prayer then is beginning to think about God, for the Christian faith knows nothing of God apart from the fact of relationship.

In this book I will be concerned with Christian prayer. Not all prayer is Christian, and not all prayer is to God. Prayer in itself is a human activity, something which we all do. At its simplest, prayer is longing, desire, the expression of our deepest aspirations, joys, or sorrows. We may pray *to* other people. We often pray to an unknown force in the universe. The prayer of Christians is not something essentially different from this basic human prayer, but it builds upon it and moves beyond it. Julian of Norwich, the fourteenth-century mystic, believed that prayer was a natural experience and should be a common one. 'It seems to me', she wrote in her *Revelations of Divine Love* (Chapter 10), 'that this should be and is an experience common to us all.' But Christian prayer is a specific kind of prayer: it is prayer *in Christ*. And this prayer is rooted in, and arises out of, the Christian understanding of God.

It is often said 'We all worship the same God'. But this is not so. The god of much conventional religion is a being who dwells, if he exists at all, above and beyond the world. He may express 'interest' in it and in us from time to time, but he is essentially uninvolved. The graffiti which says 'God is not dead—he just doesn't want to get involved' sums up this view of God well. But such a remote god is far removed from the God of Christian faith, and when the atheist rejects such a god, he is absolutely justified. Indeed the protest of atheism against such a god is essential. The God of Christian prayer is an involved God, a social God. Involvement and society are among the essential marks of Christian prayer because this prayer is actually a participation in God. God is involved in humanity, and so prayer is an involvement in humanity. God is social and not isolated, and so prayer is a social, not an isolated, activity. There is a fundamental solidarity about prayer which is central to the Christian understanding. The taking of manhood into God embraces spirituality and politics, the inner and outer worlds, in one process. Or, as St Paul puts it, 'If anyone is in Christ, there is a new creation' (2 Cor. 5.17). The quest for union with God and the quest for the unity of mankind is one quest. Prayer needs always to be seen within this social context, for there is no such thing as *private* prayer. The word private comes from the Latin *privatio* which means robbery. To the Christian, nothing is private, least of all prayer. God is not private, but personal and social, Being in relationship. That is the meaning of the symbol of the Trinity: that in God there is social life, community, sharing. To share in God is to share in that life. As the Athanasian Creed says of the Trinity: 'None is afore or after other, none is greater or less than another.'

Prayer is God. It is the movement of God to man, and of man to God, the rhythm of encounter and response. In this sense, all Christian life, all discipleship, is prayer. But this continuous 'practice of the presence of God' depends upon cultivation. The disciplines of regular times and concentration points in the life of prayer are intended to provide a framework for cultivating a life which becomes all prayer, a life in which the division between 'prayer' and 'work' becomes blurred and unreal. For prayer is a living encounter with a living God. In prayer we are seeking to achieve a continuous state of recollection of and wakefulness to the reality and presence of God. Prayer then is closely linked with knowledge. But this knowledge is not a cold, intellectual knowledge. It is what the Greek Fathers called *theoria*: a passionate, contemplative insight, involving communion and sharing. Prayer is closely linked with, and inseparable from, theology. So Evagrius in the fourth century defines a theologian as 'one whose prayer is true'. Growth in prayer and growth in theology always go together.

Prayer and theology are concerned with the experience of God, with the point at which time and eternity meet. T. S. Eliot expressed it thus:

> to apprehend
> The point of intersection of the timeless
> With time, is an occupation for the saint—
> No occupation either, but something given
> And taken, in a lifetime's death in love,
> Ardour and selflessness and self-surrender.
> For most of us, there is only the unattended
> Moment, the moment in and out of time,
> The distraction fit, lost in a shaft of sunlight,
> The wild thyme unseen, or the winter lightning
> Or the waterfall, or music heard so deeply
> That it is not heard at all, but you are the music
> While the music lasts . . .
>
> 'The Dry Salvages'

It is at moments of disclosure such as these that men and women may be led to speak of their experiences of God. But Christian life is more than a series of such moments; it is a life in which God is seen and known through the actual process of living and being. 'Blessed are the pure in heart, for they shall see God' (Matt. 5.8). St Irenaeus (second century) insists that the life of man is the glory of God. So the aim and goal of Christian life and prayer is to see God.

To see God calls for a real change in us, the renewal of our minds (Rom. 12.2), in which the world of conventional waking consciousness is transcended. Many recent writers have described our western culture as deprived, undernourished, suffering from a flawed consciousness, and lacking experience of transcendence. What we call sanity is in effect deprivation. True sanity involves the transcendence of the normal ego, or conscious self, in order to find the true deepest self. But the search for transcendence is itself alien to our technological culture which makes efficiency and technique the criterion. To pray is to reject this way of looking at reality as narrow and inadequate.

It is this narrowness which William Blake warned us of when he attacked 'single vision', seeing *with* the eye rather than *through* it.

> We are led to believe a lie
> When we see with, not through, the eye
> Which was born in a night to perish in a night
> While the soul slept in beams of light.

Blake goes on:

> Unless the eye catch fire
> The God will not be seen.
> Unless the ear catch fire
> The God will not be heard.
> Unless the tongue catch fire
> The God will not be named.
> Unless the heart catch fire
> The God will not be loved.
> Unless the mind catch fire
> The God will not be known.

Prayer then is closely allied with vision and insight. To pray is to make the most of our moments of perception, and this means giving time, approaching time in a new way. There is no need to rush around feverishly looking for a prayer life: we need to slow down and look deeply within. What is the point of complaining that God is absent if it is we who are absent from God, and from ourselves, by our lack of awareness?

This book is addressed to people who are trying to follow the Christian way of prayer and to deepen their awareness of life in the Spirit. I have avoided many references to other contemporary writers, and most quotations are from Scripture, the Fathers and the great spiritual classics. But each Christian needs to personalize his or her prayer resources, and readers may be led to build up their own resource book of prayers and themes. This volume has arisen out of my prayer, and I hope it will lead into prayer.

It is often thought that the God of Christian belief is a being who exists above and beyond the world. Hegel accused Christians of propagating a 'dull and killing belief in a superior being, altogether alien to man'. When Yuri Gagarin returned to the USSR from his space flight, and reported that he had not seen God, a Russian Orthodox priest remarked 'If you haven't seen him on earth, you will never see him in heaven.' In fact, the experience of God in Jewish and Christian history is that of a God who is known in the midst of the turmoil of human struggle. The Bible teaching about God is that he is revealed in storm and cloud, in fire, in thick darkness, in crises and conflicts, in political upheavals and in the tragedies of individuals and nations. God is a consuming fire (Deut. 9.24) who comes to judge and purge the earth. The approach to God is therefore marked by awe and terror, and it is fraught with danger. How can this be? It is not because God expresses his anger in a personal vendetta, a kind of cosmic tantrum, but simply because to open oneself up to the eternal splendour is to open oneself to the risk of being consumed. Orthodoxy is about being consumed by glory: the word means not 'right belief' (as dictionaries tell us) but right *doxa*, right glory. To be orthodox is to be set alight by the fire of God. The Psalms speak of the God of glory whose voice and power are upon the waters (Ps. 29.3), of his glory which is shown in cloud and darkness (Ps. 97.2–6). We are warned in the Old Testament that no person can see the face of God and live (Exod. 33.20. Cf. Judg. 6.22, 13.22; Gen. 32.30; Exod. 19.21; Isa. 6.5). Yet Jacob saw God face to face and lived (Gen. 32.30) as did Moses (Exod. 33.11), while Isaiah, Amos, Micah, and Ezekiel all, in some sense, saw the Lord (Isa. 6.1; Amos 7.7; 9.1; Mic. 1.1–3; Ezek. 10.18–19, etc). In the New Testament, God is said to dwell in unapproachable light (1 Tim. 6.16), and no man has seen him or can see him. No one has ever seen God (John 1.18; 1 John 4.12), but Jesus has seen him (John 6.46) and revealed him (John 1.18).

In our relationship with God, therefore, we need to hold together these two Biblical emphases: that God cannot be seen, and yet a relationship of knowledge and intimacy is possible. God is at the same time both unapproachable and close, beyond our vision and within our hearts. The mystics, who above all are absorbed in the intimacy of union with God, are unanimous that the knowledge of God involves an entering into mystery. In the words of St Gregory of Nyssa (330–95), it 'transcends all knowledge and is everywhere cut off from us by the darkness of incomprehensibility'. Or, as the fourteenth-century mystic, Jan van Ruysbroeck expressed it, God is 'simplicity and one-foldness, inaccessible height, and fathomless depth, incomprehensible breadth and eternal length, a dim silence and a wild desert'. Neither mystics nor theologians—and the eastern Christian tradition knows no distinction for all theology is mystical theology—in the orthodox Catholic tradition are very much concerned with the notion of God's existence. So St John of Damascus (675–749), one of the greatest theologians of the eastern church, wrote:

> God then is infinite and incomprehensible, and all that is comprehensible about him is his infinity and incomprehensibility. All that we can say cataphatically concerning God does not show forth his nature but the things that relate to his nature ... God does not belong to the class of existing things ... not that he has no existence but that he is above all existing things, nay even above existence itself.

Similarly in the west St Thomas Aquinas (1225–74) speaks of the hidden nature of God:

> What God is always remains hidden from us. And this is the highest knowledge one can have of God in this life, that we know him to be above every thought we are able to think of him.

It is this hidden God, beyond thought and concept of man, who, in Christian belief, took to himself human nature. The great God of heaven became small, humbled himself, to assume the form of a slave (Phil. 2.7). God, sang St Ephrem the Syrian in the fourth century, is the Great One who became small.

> The Mighty One entered and put on insecurity from Mary's womb; the Provisioner of all entered—and experienced hunger; he who gives drink to all entered—and experienced thirst; naked and stripped there came forth from Mary he who clothes all.

'The Word became flesh'; that is the central Christian claim about God's relationship to humanity, and it is the basis of Christian prayer. The Word is God's self-expression, who was with God in the beginning, and through whom all things were made. He is the source of life, and the light which enlightens all humanity. It is this Word who became flesh and dwelt among us (John 1.1–14, Cf. 1 John 1.1–3).

But the Incarnation of Christ in time must become a personal reality in us, there needs to be a taking flesh in us if our prayer in Christ is to grow. This is brought out strongly in a Christmas Day sermon by Meister Eckhart in the fourteenth century:

> We are celebrating the feast of the Eternal Birth which God the Father has borne and never ceases to bear in all Eternity: whilst this Birth also comes to pass in Time and in human nature . . . But if it takes not place in me, what avails it? Everything lies in this, that it should take place in me.

Prayer then is the interiorizing of the Incarnation. The Word is to become enfleshed in me. Bethlehem is here. So Christmas Day is to become all days, and the adoration of Emmanuel, God with us, must be a daily and continuous event.

There is far more however to the Christian teaching about Incarnation. For the purpose of the Incarnation was to raise humanity to share the Divine life. So Origen (185–254) speaks of our divinization (*theopoiesis*) through contemplation, while St Irenaeus (130–200) speaks of our participation (*metochē*) in God. 'The Word became man', he says, 'in order to make us what he is himself.' Again, St Athanasius (296–373) writes that 'he became man that we might become divine'. In the seventh century, St Maximus the Confessor says: 'A firm and trustworthy basis for hope of the deification of human nature is God's Incarnation which makes of man a god in the same measure as God himself became man.' However unfamiliar this kind of language may be to those brought up on conventional western Christianity, it is an integral part of orthodox Christian teaching. St Thomas Aquinas repeats it: 'The only begotten Son of God, wishing to enable us to share in his divinity, assumed our nature, so that by becoming man, he might make men gods.' But perhaps the most widespread and uninterrupted witness to this truth occurs in the prayer at the mixing of water and wine, recited every day in the Roman Mass: 'By the mystery of this water and wine, may we come to share in the divinity of Christ who humbled himself to share in our humanity.'

So the goal of prayer, grounded in the Incarnation, is the union of man with God. But, the Christian mystic emphasizes, this union does not abolish the separate identities of divine and human. Ruysbroeck compares the relationship between God and man to an iron in the fire.

> That measureless love which is God himself dwells in the pure deeps of our spirit, like a burning brazier of coals. And it throws forth brilliant and fiery sparks which stir and enkindle heart and senses, will and desire, and all the powers of the soul, with a fire of love ... As air is penetrated by the brightness and heat of the sun, and iron is penetrated by fire, so that it works through fire the works of fire, since it burns and shines like the fire ... yet each of these keeps its own nature—the fire does not become iron, and the iron does not become fire. So likewise is God in the being of the soul ... The creature never becomes God, nor does God ever become the creature.

So our path is one of 'exploration *into* God', an exploration which involves a real transformation of the personality. Such a transformation is the goal of human history, and it must include both the personal and the political. There can be no genuine transformation in the political order without a profound change in the individual consciousness. But equally there can be no personal change which does not also carry with it the demand for radical change in society.

If we look at the earthly life of Jesus, we see how it was surrounded and shaped by prayer, and how this prayer was essentially linked with the coming of the Kingdom of God. The public ministry of Jesus begins with prayer at his Baptism (Luke 3.21; Matt. 3.13–17; Mark 1.9–11), and ends with prayer on the Cross (Matt. 27.46; Mark 15.34; Luke 23.46). In addition, we have records of two actual prayers in the first three gospels. These are the cry of jubilation that the divine mysteries have been revealed to the simple (Matt. 11.23ff.), and the prayer of agony in Gethsemane (Mark 14.36). In John there are three more: one in the story of Lazarus (11.41f), one in the Temple forecourt (12.27), and the great High Priestly Prayer (17). We are told that Jesus prayed in solitude (Mark 1.35; 6.46; Matt. 14.23; Luke 3.21; 5.16; 6.12; 9.18; 18f). We know too that he prayed 'a great while before day' (Mark 1.35) and also in the evening (Mark 6.46), and sometimes all night (Luke 6.12). It is probable that he observed the Jewish tradition of praying every morning, afternoon, and evening.

But the prayer of Jesus continued and culminated at the Cross. The heart of the atonement was prayer, for what Jesus achieved at Calvary was the union of mankind with God. It is this union which is the goal and climax of Christian prayer. By his death Christ has overcome hostile powers and brought to an end the alienation of humanity. Through his Cross he had brought unity and peace (see Eph. 2.11–17; Col. 1.15–23.) Prayer in Christ is a sharing in the mystery of his Cross and Resurrection. We pray as limbs and organs in his crucified and risen Body. The whole activity of prayer takes place within the context of the life, death, and resurrection of Jesus, within the context of a life outpoured and renewed.

Christians hold that Jesus died, rose again, and ascended, and to many people, the doctrine of Ascension spells remoteness—Jesus goes away into a remote heaven. The Ascension becomes a spatial removal of Jesus from the sphere of human contact. There is a dreadful and notorious passage in the Book of Common Prayer of the Church of England called the 'Black Rubric' in which this view is expressed. Having denied the real presence of Christ in the bread and wine, the rubric continues '. . . the natural Body and Blood of Our Saviour Christ are in Heaven and not here, it being against the truth of Christ's natural Body to be at one time in more places than one.'

So the ascended Christ becomes the unrelated, unrelatable Saviour. In fact the whole point of the Ascension is missed here. Heaven and earth become crude geographical entities. But the New Testament teaches that Christ ascended so that he might be *closer* to us in his risen body, and that he might fill all things (Eph. 4.10). So Paul can say that Christ is in us (Rom. 8.9ff; 2 Cor. 13.5; Col. 1.27). Christians are joined to the risen and ascended Body of Christ, and indeed are described as the Body of Christ itself. We are raised, assumed, into Christ's nature, and it is through this assuming that healing comes. 'What is not assumed', wrote St Gregory of Nazianzus (329–89), 'is not healed.'

The Ascension of Jesus then is the glorifying of humanity. 'It was not merely one man but the whole world that entered', wrote St Ambrose (339–97) while his contemporary St John Chrysostom

(347–407) taught that 'we have scaled the heavens' and that 'the universal nature was brought into heaven through the first fruits'. And it is because of this that the Holy Spirit has come upon the human race in power. 'Being therefore exalted at the right hand of God, and having received from the Father the promise of the Holy Spirit, he has poured out this which you see and hear' (Acts 2.33). It is only through the Spirit that we pray at all. All prayer is the work of the Spirit, and we only pray because God gives us prayer. The Spirit prays within us in groanings that cannot be uttered, pleading with God on behalf of his people (Rom. 8.26–7). The life of prayer is a life in the Spirit, a life of great variety, for, as St John of the Cross stressed, no two people can travel more than half way on the same route to God.

The mystics see the path to God as an adventure. As we saw earlier, the symbol of the sea is a constantly recurring one. So St Symeon the New Theologian (949–1022) writes of the ocean of God's glory.

> A man standing on the sea shore sees the limitless ocean of the waters, but his gaze cannot reach as far as its edge, and he looks upon only a small part. So it is with the man who is counted worthy to gaze through contemplation upon the limitless ocean of God's glory and to look upon it with his mind: he does not see it as it is, but only so far as it is accessible to the inner eyes of his soul.
>
> A man standing on the sea shore, not content with merely looking at the waters, may also wade into them as far as he chooses. So it is with spiritual men: according to the intensity of their desire, they can enter consciously into the light of God, both participating in it and contemplating it.
>
> A man standing on the sea shore, so long as he remains on dry land, can look around on everything and gaze out across the ocean of the waters. But when he begins to enter into the waters and to immerse himself beneath them, the further he advances the less he sees of things outside. So it is with those who become sharers in the divine light: the further they advance into the knowledge of God, the more deeply they plunge into unknowing.
>
> A man who wades into the waters of the sea up to his knees or his waist can see clearly everything that is outside the waters.

> But when he plunges into the depths and becomes wholly submerged under the waters, he can no longer see anything outside and he knows only one thing, that he is entirely immersed in the deep. So it is with those who progress spiritually and ascend towards perfect knowledge and contemplation.

If prayer is to be true, it is essential to be aware of the danger of false paths. So St John, whose First Epistle begins with a proclamation of the Word made flesh, ends the same Epistle with the warning 'Little children, keep yourself from idols' (1 John 5.21). Idolatry is, in its essence, a narrowing of vision, a distorted perception. In William Blake's words,

> The Visions of Eternity, by reason of narrowed perception
> Are become weak Visions of Time and Space,
> fix'd into furrows of death.

This narrowing of perception brings us to a condition where vision ends and the sun goes down on prophecy. We become imprisoned in what St Paul calls the 'carnal mind'. For the essential feature of an idol is that it can be seen, unlike the true God, whom no one has seen at any time.

The Biblical attack on idolatry is a byproduct of concern for the truth of the mystery of God. The Old Testament forbade the making of all images of God, even images in the mind. God is known in his activity, and we can enjoy communion with him. But to seek to represent God in his essence is forbidden. For this reason Judaism was seen as atheistic in the Graeco-Roman world. The Jews themselves found the ban difficult, and they were constantly reverting to idols. From the story of the golden calf down to the time of the Maccabees, the prohibition on making images aroused fierce arguments. The prohibition was not due to the belief that the image would be mistaken for, and identified with, the deity. This was not in fact the case in the cults with which Israel came into contact. The pagans knew, as well as Israel, that God is invisible and cannot be captured in any form. The image is simply a medium of the spirit. It is the Book of Deuteronomy, a late document, which gives a detailed rationale for the prohibition.

> And you came near and stood at the foot of the mountain, while the mountain burned with fire to the heart of heaven, wrapped in

> darkness, cloud and gloom. Then the Lord spoke to you out of the midst of the fire; you heard the sound of words, but saw no form; there was only a voice ... Therefore take good heed to yourselves.
>
> Since you saw no form on the day that the Lord spoke to you at Horeb out of the midst of the fire, beware lest you act corruptly by making a graven image for yourselves, in the form of any figure, the likeness of male or female, the likeness of any beast that is on the earth, the likeness of any winged bird that flies in the air, the likeness of anything that creeps on the ground, the likeness of any fish that is in the water under the earth. And beware lest you lift up your eyes to heaven, and when you see the sun and the moon and the stars, all the host of heaven, you be drawn away and worship them and serve them, things which the Lord your God has allotted to all the people under the whole heaven. But the Lord has taken you, and brought you forth out of the iron furnace, out of Egypt, to be a people of his own possession, as at this day. (Deut. 4.11,12,15–20)

The fact that Israel saw no visible form of God at Sinai but only heard a voice is here presented as the reason why images are not allowed. The transcendence and mystery of God must be preserved. And this attack on idolatry was carried on by the early Fathers of the Christian Church. St Gregory of Nyssa (330–95) insisted that all concepts of God were false likenesses and therefore idols. God himself was beyond concept and image.

Yet in spite of this attack on idols, the church has both accepted and even encouraged the use of images, icons and symbols of God's activity. Churches in the east and west contain pictures or statues of Christ, Mary, and the saints, and people burn candles before them. In fact, these images play a very major part in the actual prayer life of millions of ordinary Christians. The use of images in worship and prayer has been controversial for many centuries. In 787, the Second Council of Nicea—the seventh of the General Councils of the Church—condemned the iconoclasts or breakers of sacred pictures. During the first four centuries, when the church was a persecuted minority in a pagan empire, pictures were used sparingly, but when the persecution came to an end, they became widespread. In 725 the Roman Emperor Leo III opened his attack on sacred pictures and ordered their removal from public places. There followed the 'iconoclastic controversy' which culminated in the Second Council of Nicea. The argument of the iconoclasts was that the use of sacred pictures (icons) was idolatry in the Biblical sense of the word. For Scripture condemned not only the worship of images of false gods (Exod. 20.45) but also that of images of the true God, such as Jeroboam's golden calves (1 Kings 12.28).

To this argument St John of Damascus (675–749) replied that since Old Testament times the Word had become man. It was therefore legitimate to make an image of the Incarnate Christ. He also distinguished between the veneration given to men and angels (*proskunēsis*) and the worship given to God alone (*latreia*). *Proskunēsis* is the eastern practice of prostrating oneself before a superior, as Abraham did to Ephron (Gen. 23.12) and the Amalekite to David (2 Sam. 1.2). St John of Damascus stressed that while *proskunēsis* can be offered to God or man, *latreia* can be offered only to God. Idolatry is defined as *latreia* offered to an idol.

So, in the second stage of the debate, the iconoclasts changed their ground, and argued that God is incomprehensible (*aperigraptos*, literally uncircumscribed). Because Christ is God, he cannot therefore be represented in a picture. But the Council replied that Christ *as man* was not uncircumscribed, and that the iconoclasts were denying his true humanity. So St Theodore the Studite (759–826) justified the painting of icons of Christ by insisting on his human characteristics: 'An indescribable Christ would be an incorporeal Christ, but Isaiah (8.3) describes him as a male being, and only the forms of the body can make man and woman distinct from one another.' It is because God became material and entered into matter that we are able to use matter as a means of grace and a way to God.

At the same time, the danger of idolatry is ever present, and we need to beware that the 'things of God' can actually cut us off from God. The Old Testament prophets condemned the Temple cultus as an evasion of the problem of justice. So Jeremiah: 'Do not trust in these deceptive words: "This is the Temple of the Lord, the Temple of the Lord, the Temple of the Lord."' (7.4) For God, unlike the idols, is known in and through our brothers and sisters in the human family. For the prophets, therefore, the actual existence of idols is irrelevant: God is not known on that abstract level of existence, but in the active work of love, compassion and justice. The Temple can be an alienating force, preventing the true worship and service of God.

> The God who made the world and everything in it, being Lord of heaven and earth, does not live in shrines made by man, nor is he served by human hands, as though he needed anything, since he himself gives to all men life and breath and everything. (Acts 17.24–25)

The God we serve is beyond the limitations of cult and concept. We come to him by *agnosia*, unknowing. The knowledge of God is not an intellectual knowledge, even of the purified intellect. It demands a radical transformation of our actual way of knowing. What is theology but the testimony to mystery? As Pseudo-Dionysius (*c*.500) wrote, 'The mysteries of theology, simple, unconditional, invariable, are laid bare in a darkness of silence beyond the light.' St Augustine speaks of 'the region of unlikeness'. One of the favourite illustrations used by the fathers and mystics is the vision of God given to Moses through the cloud. So St Gregory of Nyssa (330–95) explains in his *Life of Moses:*

> What now is the meaning of Moses' entry into the darkness and of the vision of God that he enjoyed in it? ... The sacred text is here teaching us that ... as the soul makes progress, and by a greater and more perfect concentration comes to appreciate what the knowledge of truth is, the more it approaches the vision, and so much the more does it see that the divine nature is invisible. It thus leaves all surface appearances, not only those that can be grasped by the senses, but also those which the mind itself seems to see, and it keeps on going deeper until by the operation of the Spirit it penetrates the invisible and incomprehensible, and it is there that it sees God. The true vision and the true knowledge of what we seek consists precisely in not seeing, in an awareness that our goal transcends all knowledge and is everywhere cut off from us by the darkness of incomprehensibility.

This stress on knowledge which 'consists precisely in not seeing' is central to the eastern Christian spiritual tradition. In a strikingly similar passage Pseudo-Dionysius in his *Mystical Theology* speaks of Moses who only sees the place where God is.

> And then Moses is cut off from both things seen and those who see, and enters into the darkness of unknowing, a truly hidden darkness, according to which he shuts his eyes to all apprehensions that convey knowledge, for he has passed into a realm quite beyond any feeling or seeing. Now, belonging wholly to that which is beyond all, and yet to nothing at all, and being neither himself nor another, and united in his highest part in passivity with him who is completely unknowable, he knows by not knowing in a manner that transcends understanding.

The knowledge of God, which comes through prayer, is therefore a 'dark knowledge', 'knowing by not knowing'. So the mystics speak of God in the language of depth and of the abyss. Ruysbroeck in the fourteenth century refers to 'the deep Quiet of the Godhead' and the 'dim silence', 'the fathomless Abyss that is the Being of God', 'the unconditional Dark'. In the same period, the author of *The Cloud of Unknowing* is concerned particularly with the unknowability of God by the mind.

> But now you ask me and say, 'How shall I think about him, and what is he?' and to this I cannot answer you except in this way, 'I do not know'. For you have brought me with your question into that same darkness and into that same cloud of unknowing that I would that you were in yourself. For of all other creatures and their works, yes, and of the works of God's self, a man may, through grace, have full knowledge, and he can think well about them: but of God himself no man can think. And therefore I would leave all that thing which I can think, and choose to my love that thing which I cannot think. Why? He may well be loved, but not thought. By love he may be gotten and holden; but by thought never. And therefore, although it is good sometimes to think of the kindness and the worthiness of God specially, and although it is a light and a part of contemplation: nevertheless, in this work it shall be cast down and covered with a cloud of forgetting. And you shall step above it stalwartly but lustily, with a devout and a pleasing

> striving of love, and try to pierce that darkness above you. And smite upon that thick cloud of unknowing with a sharp dart of longing love.

To learn to pray is to learn a knowledge through love rather than through the intellect, it is to enter the 'cloud of unknowing', the darkness of faith.

However, in Christian understanding there is no knowledge of God except through communion with people, and in prayer we communicate not only with God but with each other at the deepest possible level of our beings. There is a solidarity in prayer, an inner centre, a point beneath words and actions, where we meet as children in the presence of our Father. So our prayer begins '*Our* Father' for all prayer is social prayer. St Cyprian (died 258) put it well in his treatise *On the Lord's Prayer*:

> Our prayer is public and for all, and when we pray, we pray not for a single person, but for the whole people, because we are all one. The God of peace, the teacher of harmony, who taught unity, willed that each should pray for all, according as he carried us all in himself alone.

Moreover the eastern teacher St Nilus in the fifth century held that it was impossible for hardness of heart and cruelty to others to coexist with prayer. 'If you wish to pray in the right way, do not cause another soul to sorrow; otherwise you run in vain.' There is therefore the closest link between prayer and human relationships.

Jesus teaches us to approach God as 'Father'. In the Old Testament God is not often spoken of as 'Father': in fact, there are only fourteen places where it occurs. They refer to God as the Creator with a unique relationship to Israel his first-born (Deut. 14.1). In the prophets, there is a sharp contrast made between God's fatherhood and human faithlessness. But it is the whole community which addresses God in this way. There is no evidence that anyone in Judaism addressed God as '*My* Father'. Yet this is precisely what Jesus did in all his prayers—some twenty-one times. Altogether we find the word Father used for God in the mouth of Jesus one hundred and seventy times in the Gospels. There is only one prayer of Jesus, the cry of dereliction from the cross, in which 'My Father' is missing. Also Jesus used the Aramaic word 'Abba'. Thus in Gethsemane he prays: 'Abba, Father, all things are possible to thee; remove this cup from me; yet not what I will but what thou wilt' (Mark 14.36). 'Abba' was a very familiar form of address, rather like 'Daddy', a childlike form. In the Gospels then 'Father' is *the* description of God. Jesus is clearly encouraging a relationship with God which is marked by childlikeness.

The most important use of 'Abba' by Jesus occurs in the 'Lord's Prayer' (Luke 11.2–4; Matt. 6.9–13). And the early Christian church used the cry 'Abba, Father' (Rom. 8.15; Gal. 4.6) as a Spirit-inspired echo of Jesus' own prayer. They came, through it, to share in Jesus' own intimate relationship with God. So Paul can say that this prayer is the proof of the fact that we are children of God. In fact we know from the writings of St Cyril of Jerusalem that in the fourth-century Jerusalem church the Lord's Prayer was always used immediately before the Communion—that is, it belonged to that part of the Liturgy to which only the baptized were admitted. The Lord's Prayer therefore was reserved for full members of the church. The candidates for Baptism were taught the Lord's Prayer as part of their catechesis, or instruction, and they prayed it for the first time when they made their first Holy Communion. It was through Baptism that they were brought into a relationship of intimacy in which they could say 'Abba'.

But why should one address God as 'Father' and not as 'Mother'? What is the justification for using only male images for God? The theme of the 'motherhood of God' was not taken very seriously in the west until St Teresa of Lisieux in the nineteenth century, but there are biblical sources for the idea. God is compared to a mother in Second Isaiah (49.5; 66.13). Human beings, male and female, are said to be made in God's image (Gen. 1.26–7; 5.1–2), and, while the text does not emphasize the point, the implication is that God is male *and* female. In the Gospels, Jesus compares himself to a mother hen (Matt. 23.37), and the woman in labour is a resurrection symbol (John 16.21). The feminine element in the Holy Spirit is particularly brought out in the Syrian writers. Clement of Alexandria speaks of Christians feeding from the breast of the Logos, while St John Chrysostom lists many names for God, including not only Father but also Spouse, Sister and Mother.

In the prayers of St Anselm (1033–1109) Jesus is addressed as the Mother who gives birth to new Christians.

> And thou, Jesus, sweet Lord,
> art thou not also a mother?
> Truly, thou art a mother,
> the mother of all mothers,
> who tasted death, in thy
> desire to give life to thy
> children.

It is however in Julian of Norwich in the fourteenth century—significantly one of the first female theologians and spiritual writers—that we find most clearly the feminine naming of God: 'But our true Mother, Jesus, he alone bears us to joy and to endless living' (*Revelations of Divine Love*, Chapter 60). God, says Julian, is as truly a Mother as a Father, for 'we owe our being to him, and this is the essence of Motherhood'. Our growth in experience of God needs to go hand in hand with our experience of the human community in which men and women live and work together in equality and harmony: human experience and divine revelation need to illuminate each other.

Again, as in the human community, to ask is an essential element in the relationship of prayer. We ask as members of a family, not in the spirit of selfish individualism. The Lord's Prayer in fact is entirely a prayer of petition—asking that God's name be hallowed, that his Kingdom may come, that we may be nourished, forgiven, preserved from temptation, and delivered from evil. The teaching on prayer in the Gospels centres around petition. 'Ask and it shall be given you; seek, and you shall find; knock, and it shall be opened to you' (Matt. 7.7). Jesus' own prayer included a core of petition—for forgiveness of his murderers, for the increase of Peter's faith, for the sanctifying of his disciples, for the unity of the church, and for his own faithfulness to God's will.

To pray for people and for the needs of the world is called *intercession*. For many people it is a particularly difficult aspect of prayer. If God knows what is going to happen anyway, what is the point of asking? The important point to grasp is the fact of co-operation. In ordinary daily life God works through our co-operation. The fact that God knows whether we should be wet or dry does not prevent us from taking an umbrella. Clearly God is allowing us to influence the course of events. For we are not robots, and the world is not a machine. What if the same applies to prayer? Intercessory prayer is not a technique for changing God's mind, but it is a releasing of God's power through placing ourselves in a relationship of co-operation with God. It is an act. Prayer and action should not be opposed to each other, for prayer *is* action. Intercession means literally to stand between, to become involved in the conflict.

In the Old Testament the prayer of intercession is a redemptive work, a priestly act of identifying oneself with the sufferings of the people. So Abraham intercedes for Sodom (Gen. 18.16–32), Moses lifts up his hands to intercede for Israel (Exod. 17.11–12), and prays that God would be with his people (34.9). In Ezekiel, the oppression and falsehood cause God to say 'I sought for a man among them who should build up the wall and stand in the breach before me for the land that I should not destroy it: but I found none' (Ezek. 22.30). Similarly in Second Isaiah, 'he saw that there was no man and wondered that there was no intercessor' (Isa. 59.16). Again, the work of intercession is closely linked with the theme of redemptive suffering: '... he poured out his soul to death, and was numbered with the transgressors; yet he bore the sin of many, and *made intercession* for the transgressors' (Isa. 53.12).

On the other hand, it is wrong to restrict our 'special' intercession to those who are sick and suffering, as we often tend to do, and to ignore other needs and calls for guidance. Maybe by focusing only on the physically sick, we are really thinking of God as a kind of superior magic-man, rather than opening up all human life to the grace and direction of God. Intercession is simply our co-operation with God in the work of reconciliation. It is, like all prayer, God-centred, but in intercession this fact needs to be stressed more strongly, in view of the danger of focusing on the people for whom we pray. In order to intercede we need to be detached from persons, to abandon a narrow personal perspective, and to reorientate ourselves so that we see the needs of those for whom we pray in the light of a wider vision. In Gregory of Nyssa's words, we need to learn to see with the eyes of the Dove, to look at reality with the eyes of God.

Much intercession suffers precisely because it is not God-centred. A good deal of prayer for others and for ourselves is not Christian prayer and is not motivated by co-operation, but by selfish individualism. What then becomes of free will? It would seem that God *does* answer such selfish prayers and sends the consequences. The Psalms certainly suggest this.

> Lust came upon them in the wilderness: and they tempted God in the desert.
> And he gave them their desire: and sent leanness withal into their soul. (Ps. 106.14–15)

Our prayer therefore needs purification. Intercession is very close to contemplation, and is in fact a byproduct of the adoration of God. It is vital that we come to this way of praying, not with a clear idea of the way ahead and of our role in it, but with a desire to see and understand. So we open ourselves to the future, bringing the needs of others with us, as part of our receptiveness to God.

We come in our intercession as limbs and organs of a living body. And the realization of the common life of that body is painful. What can it mean to us that we are one with our Christian brothers and sisters in the Third World whose poverty is the direct result of our abundance? What are the social consequences of saying 'Our Father' in terms of fair shares in the family of mankind? To take that prayer seriously will mean suffering. To some it is unbearable, and praying becomes an evasion, an anti-social activity: they prefer the involvement of human contact and human relationships. But in fact to pray at all is to accept our interdependence upon, and solidarity with, the rest of humanity. Julian of Norwich emphasized that 'If I look to myself as a single person I am right naught, but if I look to the whole then I am, in hope, in onehead of love with all my even Christians.'

Jesus tells us little about 'family life', and what he does say consists chiefly of warnings about the danger of families breaking up through the harsh demands of the Gospel. 'Kith and kin' and 'Charity begins at home' are not ideas which belong to the Christian Gospel. On the contrary, the hero of Jesus' best-known parable was a Samaritan, the most hated enemy of Israel. Jesus saw the whole of mankind as his brother, sister, and mother, and the test of discipleship is our response to his presence in the hungry, the naked, and the prisoner. In our prayer then we are being confronted with the disturbing demands of the Gospel.

Again, we are one in prayer also with our brothers and sisters of the great spiritual tradition which spreads across the centuries, and we learn from them and pray with them. Tradition is not a dead thing but a living thing. We are part of the same community of faith as St Augustine, St Benedict, St Francis, St John of the Cross, and the thousands of spiritual guides and gurus. The tradition is vital because we need guidance and spiritual intelligence in order to tell the true from the false, the profound from the superficial, in the confusing world of the spirit. The soil of the spirit needs careful cultivation, for fertility alone may lead to swamp or jungle. The spiritual world is not universally benign, and it is possible to lose one's path and flounder. Hence the importance of solidarity with those who have trodden the path before us. In our individualistic western society, we tend to ignore the reality of *corporate knowledge*, that is, the knowledge which comes from participation in a way of life, and in which we are sharers with others, past and present. We ignore this solidarity in the tradition at our peril, for it is essential if we are to be saved from a slavery to the present and its passing trends.

From the tradition too we will learn to pray as we can and not as we cannot, to pray in the way which is right for us. The Christian spiritual tradition includes the widest possible variety of human beings of differing personality and emotional and intellectual make-up. There are extroverts with a strong artistic sense and a need for ritual, whose prayer life will value material objects such as crucifixes and rosaries, and who will derive great strength from corporate worship. There are thoughtful introverts for whom the way forward is through inner absorption of doctrine, as it becomes integrated into prayer and reflection. There is no one standard, or correct, way to pray. But prayer should aid the maturing of the personality, the union of conscious and unconscious in a process of transcendence, a discovery of the true self which is wholeness.

Christian prayer is the manifestation of Christian Baptism, and it is in the liturgy of Baptism that we see the life of prayer in microcosm. Baptism is a once-for-all event: *ephapax* (Rom. 6.10) is the New Testament word. Yet there is a sense in which we live a Baptismal life, a life of daily renunciation, of daily drowning, of daily dying and rising. The Baptismal liturgy embodies the spiritual life in miniature. In the early church *baptisma* means far more than the term 'Baptism' now signifies. It described the entire rite of Christian initiation, incorporating a series of elements and culminating in the first Holy Communion.

First, there is the renunciation. The candidate strips off his clothes, symbolizing the stripping off of the old nature with its deeds. As St Cyril describes Baptism at Jerusalem at the end of the fourth century, the candidate faces west in the darkness, repudiates Satan and all his works, and then turns round to the light of the baptistery. He is then anointed with the oil of exorcism. So, set free from the tyranny of evil, he approaches the waters.

So, secondly, comes the drowning, the going through the waters, the symbol of Christ's dying and rising (Rom. 6.4; Col. 2.12). The Fathers are full of the symbolism of drowning. The dragon Behemoth lived in the waters, says St Cyril of Jerusalem, and Jesus, by his descent, destroyed the dragon's power. So with the new Christian: 'You go down into the waters bearing your sins . . . you come out brought to life in justice.' The waters of Baptism are seen as both tomb and mother. 'We only live by remaining in the waters', says Tertullian (160–220), while St Gregory of Nazianzus (329–89) tells us that 'Jesus comes out of the water . . . raising with him . . . the submerged world'. Many of the early Fathers speak of the drowning of the demons in the waters. So in Baptism Christians put behind them the seas of eternal death and destruction. But the most powerful expression of the death and resurrection symbolism of water comes in the Holy Saturday liturgy of the Blessing of the Font. The Paschal Candle is plunged into the font as a sign of fertilization, while the celebrant, in the old rite, breathed over the waters, a clear reference to creation as well as to Christ's rising, linking them both in the baptismal process of renewal. The font, wrote Theodore of Mopsuestia (350–428) is 'the womb of the sacramental birth'.

Then, thirdly, the candidate is clothed in the baptismal robe. He puts on Christ (Gal. 3.27). 'Instead of fig leaves', wrote St Ephrem in the fourth century, 'God has clothed men with glory in the baptismal water.'

Fourthly, the newly baptized is signed with the Cross, for it is in Christ crucified that we find 'the Spirit and power' (1 Cor. 1.4). The Fathers speak of the signing as the *sphragis*, a term used originally of the wax seal which was used to indicate possession of cattle. The Christian is thus sealed with the sign of Christ, he bears on his body the marks of Christ (cf. Gal. 6.17).

The fifth act is the baptismal anointing. The symbolic oil of Chrism stresses our participation in Christ. We are *Christ-ened*. The earliest account of Christian Baptism, that of Justin Martyr (100–65), says that 'we come up from the washing and are anointed with the blessed unction'. In 215 the Apostolic Tradition of Hippolytus refers to the anointing with consecrated oil, while St Cyril of Jerusalem (315–86) says, 'Having become worthy of the holy chrism, you are called Christians.' The newly baptised, according to St Cyprian, the Bishop of Carthage (died 258), are to be made perfect by the seal of the Lord. St Ambrose (339–97) tells us that 'after the font, the fulfilment is still to be accomplished', and he links together the 'water bath in the Spirit' and the 'seal of the Spirit', calling the whole process 'Illumination'.

Sixthly, the candidate is given a candle, the sign of Christ's resurrection light, and, the rite of initiation completed, he is received into the fellowship of the Eucharist and receives Holy Communion. The baptismal process reaches its climax in communion. There is a progression from darkness to nakedness, from confession of the creed to drowning, from dying with Christ to the putting on of the new man and receiving of the Spirit, and finally to union. The classic 'Three Ways' of the life of prayer are thus present in microcosm in the baptismal rite. First the Way of Purgation (renunciation, confession, and drowning). Secondly, the Way of Illumination (clothing and anointing—baptism is actually called 'Illumination' by some of the Fathers). Thirdly, the Way of Union (communion). The baptismal sacrifice, like the eucharistic sacrifice, is complete and yet also goes on. For our lives are lived within the baptismal mystery.

The dying and rising in Christ which is dramatically enacted in the liturgy of Baptism has to be renewed and experienced in prayer. All Christian prayer is baptismal. So in all prayer there is renunciation of false paths, confession of sin, and turning to the light. There is the need for deliverance from evil. Again, in prayer there is a daily drowning, a renewal of the experience of the font.

We die daily (1 Cor. 15.31). As the fourteenth-century *Book of the Poor in Spirit* expresses it, 'A man must die inwardly in the ground of the soul.'

In prayer too there is a clothing with Christ, a putting on of the Christ-nature. The Letter to the Colossians brings this out very strongly. In Christ dwells the fulness of God (1.19; 2.9): in Christians dwells Christ, the hope of glory, and every man is to become mature in Christ (1.27–8), coming to fulness of life in him (2.10) and having put off the body of flesh (2.11). In Christ the Christian has died to the old order (2.20) and his life is hid with Christ in God (3.3). He has put on the new nature (3.10).

Again, in prayer, as in Baptism, we bear upon us and within us the Name of Jesus. Thus St Gregory of Sinai, writing in the fourteenth century, says:

> The gift which we have received from Jesus Christ in Holy Baptism is not destroyed but is only buried as treasure in the ground. And both common sense and gratitude demand that we should take good care to unearth the treasure and bring it to light. This can be done in two ways. The gift of Baptism is revealed first of all by a painstaking fulfilment of the commandments; the more we carry these out the more clearly the gift shines upon us in its true splendour and brilliance. Secondly, it comes to light and is revealed through the continual invocation of the Lord Jesus, or by unceasing remembrance of God which is one and the same thing. The first method is powerful, but the second more so; so much so that even fidelity to the commandments receives its full strength from prayer.

All Prayer is a carrying within us of the power of the Name of Jesus.

Prayer too is an anointing of the Spirit. God, says St Paul, has anointed us and put the Spirit in our hearts (2 Cor. 1.21), a verse which St John Chrysostom connects with the baptismal anointing. St John also connects anointing with spiritual insight: 'You have an anointing (*Chrisma*) from the Holy One, and you know all things' (1 John 2.20).

The giving of the lighted candle, an addition to, rather than an integral part of, the baptismal liturgy, also reminds us that all prayer is a standing in the light of the Christ. Christ, and through

Christ's indwelling, all Christians, are to be the light of the world (John 8.12; Matt. 5.14). We are to wear the spiritual armour of light (Rom. 13.12), to be children of light (Eph. 5.8; 1 Thess. 5.5), to walk in the light (1 John 1.7) which comes from God who is light (1.5).

Finally, all prayer is communion with God. The aim of Christian prayer is communion with God in Christ, a union as close as that of Christ with the Father (John 17.21ff).

Baptism and prayer, however, are more than personal experiences. As the Orthodox eastern church has always seen, they are part of the process of cleansing and renewal of the creation. So in the Orthodox liturgy for Epiphany we read:

> Today the nature of the waters is sanctified.
> Christ has appeared in the Jordan to sanctify the waters ...
> At thine appearing in the body
> The earth was sanctified,
> The waters blessed,
> The heavens enlightened,
> And mankind was set loose from the bitter tyranny of the enemy ...
> The earth has been sanctified, O Word, by thy holy birth,
> And the heavens with the stars declared thy glory:
> And now the nature of the waters is blessed
> By thy Baptism in the flesh,
> And mankind has been restored once more to its former nobility ...
> Christ is baptised:
> He comes up out of the waters,
> And with him he carries the universe.

The same theme is expressed in a modern form in the baptismal rite of the Free Church of Berkeley (1971).

> It is right that we should praise you, O Energy of creation, because by your wisdom humankind was born from the womb of the waters, and each passes back into them; but still, at every threat to our continuance, new communities of hope have emerged from a passage through the great seas. And so, may all who, trusting in you, pass through these waters be washed

clean from their brothers' blood and embrace him in peace; may they strip off complicity for guilt and put on the white clothing of justice; may the old man of aloofness be drowned and a new man of solidarity be raised up. By your life-giving Spirit, O God, which at the beginning hovered over the deep, bless these waters as the means of our union with Jesus our Brother, the vanguard of your new creation.

2
Prayer and holiness

Holy be your Name. (Matt. 6.9)

'What interests me is to know how one can become a saint!'
'But you don't believe in God.'
'Exactly. Is it possible to become a saint apart from God? That is the only concrete problem that interests me today.'

ALBERT CAMUS, *La Peste*

Holy
Holy
Holy Lord,
God of power and might.

In the Bible, God is the Holy One of Israel. Holiness and Divinity coincide. The word for 'holy' in the Old Testament is *qadosh*. It stresses that God is essentially different. So in Hosea, God says, 'I am God and not man: the Holy One in the midst of you' (11.9). Isaiah in particular stresses God's holiness, and uses the word *strange* about his work. Some have said that the entire Old Testament religion is a religion of holiness, and certainly the theme of the Holy God, holy and different, is very central. The earliest reference to the Holy God sees him as the God of the Ark (1 Sam. 6.20): the Ark is the throne of the invisible God, and is often equated with God himself (1 Sam. 4.6). Holiness is not merely an impressive power which resides within a sacred object: it is essentially *personal*. God is holy and terrible, he is a God of war, and so soldiers are consecrated persons. To be consecrated is to be set apart for the service of God.

The meaning of holiness in the Old Testament comes out clearly in Isaiah 6, the description of the prophet's vision. The angels sing the thrice-holy hymn 'Holy, Holy, Holy', still an integral part of the Christian liturgy. They cover their faces so that they cannot see God, for holiness involves unapproachableness. And yet they continue their song: 'The whole earth is full of his glory' (6.3). God's glory (*kabod*) means the radiant power of his being, the manifestation of his holy nature, and it is spread over all the earth. So holiness contains both a saving and destructive aspect. God's holiness involves the idea of 'to be terrible' and 'to shine brightly'. God is 'glorious in holiness, fearful in praises, doing wonders' (Exod. 15.11). When God's consuming fire burst out on the sons of Aaron, he says, 'I will reveal myself in holiness in them that come near me, so that I may be glorified before all the people' (Lev. 10.1–3). Isaiah's response to God's holiness is horror: 'Woe is me! I am lost!' Elsewhere in Isaiah, the holy God is a manifestation of judgement, 'The light of Israel shall become a fire, and his holy one a flame, consuming and devouring his thorns and his briers in one day' (Isa. 10.17).

For the holiness of God demands a corresponding responsive holiness in men and women. 'You shall be holy, because the Lord your God is holy' (Lev. 19.1–2). Psalms 15 and 24 bring out the same demand for purity and justice in those who would ascend the holy mountain, while Psalm 77 notes that the way of God is holiness (Ps. 77.13. Cf. Ps. 68.24). In the later prophets, such as Habakkuk and Ezekiel, holiness is linked with moral goodness. In Hosea particularly, God's holiness includes love and compassion (11.8–9). Holiness therefore belongs essentially to God. Things only become holy through him. Thus the ground must be holy because of its nearness to God and use by him (Exod. 3.5; Josh. 5.15). So also the ark (2 Chron. 35.3), the Sabbath (Exod. 20.8, 11), and so on.

However, such holiness is not compatible with the demands of ordinary life. Ordinary people may share it for a time and then discard it. In Old Testament thinking, holiness had little to do with morality (though there are exceptions, such as Leviticus 19.2). Human life was divided between the holy and the common. So Aaron was told to 'distinguish between the holy and the common' (Lev. 10.10), and Ezekiel, when he measures the Temple, is instructed to 'make a separation between the holy and the common' (Ezek. 42.20).

Holiness is equally a concern of the New Testament writers. Jesus is the holy Servant (Acts 4.27,30) who sanctifies himself so that his followers may be sanctified (John 17.19. Cf. Heb. 10.10;

13.12). The word 'holy' (*hagios*) is used in the New Testament about the Scriptures (Rom. 1.2), the Christian vocation (2 Tim. 1.9), the faith (Jude 20), sacrifice (Rom. 12.1), the prophets (Luke 1.70), John the Baptist (Mark 6.20), the pre-Christian saints (Matt. 27.52), the Christian brethren (Heb. 3.1), the children of Christians (1 Cor. 7.14), Christ himself (Acts 4.27,30) and the angels (Mark 8.38), as well as about God (John 17.11). Christians are often described as 'saints' in the Acts and epistles. The meaning of this expression is that Christians are called to offer themselves as a living sacrifice, holy to God (Rom. 12.1), but only because Christ has already offered himself for the church 'that he might sanctify and cleanse it' (Eph. 5.26f). Sanctification has already been accomplished in Baptism. 'You are washed, you are sanctified' (1 Cor. 6.11). It is the work of the Spirit (2 Thess. 2.13). *Hagios* is used 227 times in the New Testament, and 93 of them are references to the Holy Spirit, while 61 of them are references to Christians themselves. All Christians are called to be saints, and are spoken of as saints, but their holiness needs to achieve perfection in each individual (2 Cor. 7.1). This calls for purgation (1 Tim. 2.21) and devotion to the cause of justice (Rom. 6.19).

However, in the New Testament, we do not simply see the continuity of the concern for holiness: we see a radical change in the understanding of the holy. Nothing is unclean or common: not only foods and animals but also people are declared clean (Acts 10.28). 'What God has cleansed, you must not call common' (Acts 10.15). 'Profane' (literally *pro-fano*, outside the temple) is not a Christian word at all. The union of holy and common is foreshadowed in the Old Testament. It is said that God's glory will fill the whole earth (Num. 14.21), and Zechariah says that even the household pots will be holy (Zech. 14.20). So in the New Testament, to be holy is not to be separate but to be close. And the holy and the common are one.

Christians then are called to holiness of life. But holiness is not the same as perfection, and there is certainly progress in holiness. Clement of Alexandria (150–215) was one of the first Christian writers to make it clear that, while Baptism implies perfection, yet there are steps towards the attainment of perfection, and he called the steps *pistis* (faith), *gnosis* (knowledge) and *agape* (love). Later spiritual writers have spoken of the 'Three Ways' in the life of the

Spirit: Purgation, Illumination, and Union. The point is that holiness is not a static condition but a movement. It is not a matter of obedience to rules or observance of a moral code. Holiness flows from the relationship with Christ, built up and nourished by the Word of God and the sacraments. To recognize holiness is to recognize the activity of God in people. More than that, holiness manifests the character, the nature of God. It witnesses to God's transcendent glory, and to the Incarnation—to the immensity and the intimacy of God. That is the meaning of *orthodoxy*, literally 'right glory'. Holiness never points to itself but always beyond itself to God. The saint is essentially someone who communicates and radiates the character of God, his love, his joy, his peace. This sense comes over powerfully in Motovilov's account of the transfiguration of St Seraphim of Sarov. The saint's face glows like the sun.

> 'What do you feel?' asked Father Seraphim.
>
> 'An immeasurable well-being', I replied.
>
> 'But what sort of well-being? What exactly?'
>
> 'I feel', I replied, 'such calm, such peace in my soul, that I can find no words to express it.'
>
> 'My friend, it is the peace Our Lord spoke of when he said to his disciples: "My peace I give unto you", "the peace which the world cannot give", "the peace which passes understanding". What else do you feel?'
>
> 'Infinite joy in my heart.'
>
> Father Seraphim continued: 'When the Spirit of God descends on a man, and envelops him in the fulness of his presence, the soul overflows with unspeakable joy, for the Holy Spirit fills everything he touches with joy ...'

So sanctity communicates itself, radiates peace and love around, infecting its environment with joy and hope. And the world needs saints, Simone Weil wrote, just as a plague-stricken city needs doctors.

To pray is to open oneself to the possibility of sainthood, to the possibility of becoming set on fire by the Spirit. In one of the sayings of the Desert Fathers, a disciple asks Abbot Joseph what more could be done than the keeping of a 'modest rule'. The old man rose, lifting his hands against the sky, and his fingers became like ten flaming torches. He cried, 'If thou wilt, thou shalt be made wholly flame.' The symbol of the holy fire is one with deep roots in spiritual history. In the covenant with Abraham, a smoking fire pot and flaming torch were the signs (Gen. 15). In the account of the sin of Nadab and Abihu, fire came out from the Lord to destroy them (Lev. 10). Similarly in Elijah's contest, the fire of the Lord fell both on the altar of Baal (1 Kings 18) and on the messengers of King Ahaziah (2 Kings 1). Elijah is supremely the prophet of fire who comes before the Day of the Lord. The fire is one of the earliest symbols of divine activity and of the divine presence. The angel of the Lord appeared to Moses in a flame of fire (Exod. 3). The Lord descended on Sinai in fire (Exod. 19), and the mountain had to be consecrated 'lest he break out against them' (19.23–4). The appearance of the glory of the Lord was like devouring fire (Exod. 24). Moses' face shone with glory (Exod. 34). Again in Ezekiel, fire is the symbol of the glory of the Lord (Ezek. 1). Later the fire becomes a symbol of the End and of judgement: in the Synoptic Gospels, *pur* (fire) occurs twenty-two times, fourteen of which are references to the final judgement. Fire too is a symbol of the Holy Spirit (Matt. 3.11; Acts 2.)

It is this latter use, fire as the symbol of the Spirit's presence and power, which occurs most frequently in the mystical writers. To pray is to be open to the divine fire. So St Macarius in the fifth century writes:

> The immaterial and divine fire illuminates the soul and puts it to the test. This fire descended on the apostles in the form of tongues of flame. This fire shone before Paul, it spoke to him, it illuminated his mind, and at the same time blinded his eye, for the flesh cannot endure the brightness of this light. Moses saw the fire in the burning bush. This same fire lifted Elijah from the ground in the form of a flaming chariot ... Angels and spirits in the service of God participate in the brightness of this fire ... This is the fire which pursues demons and exterminates sins. It is the power of resurrection, the reality of eternal life, the illumination of holy souls, the stability of celestial powers.

This flame is at the same time a living flame of love, manifested towards the human race. Thus St Isaac the Syrian in the seventh century speaks of the heart of the sanctified Christian as an intensely loving heart.

> It is a heart which is burning with charity for men, for birds, for beasts, for demons—for every creature ... Such a heart which is softened can no longer bear to see, or hear, from another of any suffering, even of the smallest part, being inflicted on any creature ... He will pray even for the reptiles, moved by an infinite pity which reigns in the hearts of those who love God.

> It was said several centuries earlier of Symeon the Pious that he was not ashamed of the limbs or members of any man, neither was he afraid of seeing men naked, nor to be seen without clothes himself. For he possessed Christ wholly and was himself wholly Christ: and he always contemplated his own limbs or members and those of any other human being as Christ's.

It is this fire of love which is communicated to us through the Spirit in the sacraments. So St Ephrem the Syrian (306–73) addresses Christ:

> See, Fire and Spirit in the womb that bore you.
> See, Fire and Spirit in the river where you were baptised.
> Fire and Spirit in our Baptism,
> in the Bread and the Cup, Fire and Holy Spirit.

Later mystical writers associate this fire with the Passion. So the fourteenth century *Book of the Poor in Spirit*:

> The divine fatherly wisdom flows continually through the Passion of our Lord into panting thirsting hearts which are burned up by the divine fire of love. The fire so dries and burns them that they are seized with an excessive thirst, and in this thirst they run with a flaming desire to the streams and to the wounds of our Lord from which all grace flows. To these they hold their mouths and drink.

The Byzantine mystic St Symeon the New Theologian (949–1022) speaks in a similar way:

> Rejoicing at once and trembling,
> I who am straw receive the Fire
> And, strange wonder!

I am ineffably refreshed,
As the bush of old
Which burned yet was not consumed.

So through the centuries the mystics describe the cleansing and sanctifying power of God as fire. Mechtild of Magdeburg (1210–80) and later Dante (1265–1321) saw God as a river of fire which filled the universe, and within this fire the deified souls of the saints were blazing sparks. In fact, most mystical writers—Ruysbroeck, John of the Cross, Boehme, to name only three—used this fire symbolism. None has expressed it more powerfully and beautifully than Richard of Saint-Victor (died 1173):

> When the soul is plunged in the fire of divine love, like iron, it first loses its blackness, and then growing to white heat, it becomes like unto the fire itself. And lastly it grows liquid, and, losing its nature, is transmuted into an utterly different quality of being ... As the difference between iron that is cold, and iron that is hot, so is the difference between ... the tepid soul, and the soul made incandescent by divine love.

So the life of prayer cannot be separated from this growth in holiness and in this intense, blazing love which comes from the Spirit. The Bible clearly teaches that there is growth in grace. In the parables the growth of the Christian is compared to that of plants (Matt. 13.18ff; John 15.2). The epistles stress growth and movement towards maturity, towards the fullness of Christ (Eph. 3.16–19; 4.13). But growth involves pain and anguish of spirit. The path of self-knowledge and self-scrutiny calls for a willingness to endure deprivation and inner suffering. It is not an easy path, it is the way of the Cross. It involves a confrontation with self, a stripping away of the false self, a purifying of the personality. True religion helps us to grow, but pseudo-religion hinders growth, for it creates and maintains obstacles and barriers. Thus it is that much religion merely censors experience and does not liberate it, stifles human potential and does not allow it to blossom. Much religion is superficial and does not help the journey inwards which is so necessary for spiritual health. There has to be a movement towards the still centre, the depths of our being, where, according to the mystics, we find the presence of God.

The writers of the eastern Christian tradition call this centre of the personality the *heart*, and they therefore call deep inner prayer *the prayer of the heart*. They do not mean, by this expression, to suggest that all prayer is accompanied by the experience of warmth and light. Often the prayer of the heart is marked by numbness and coldness. But the heart, in their terms, is the centre of man, the seat of his conflicts and his joys, the place of the Spirit as well as the centre of feeling and passion. So prayer is concerned with the unifying and integrating of the personality. This is the meaning of the eastern Chrisians' directive to 'put the mind in the heart'. The nineteenth-century Bishop Theophan the Recluse, one of the greatest Orthodox teachers of prayer, described the aim of Christian prayer thus: 'The principal thing is to stand before God with the mind in the heart, and to go on standing before him unceasingly day and night until the end of life.' In the stress on the heart, these teachers are faithful to Scriptural doctrine, which sees the heart as the principle of life. The heart is in fact the spirit (*pneuma*) of a man, it is the innermost centre of his affections.

We come to God then with our whole personalities, not with minds split off from bodies. We come with our bodies, and so a vital prelude to prayer is the attainment of control of the body. It is very important, for example, to find a physical posture which helps, and does not hinder, our practice of prayer. In the west we tend to neglect the question of posture, and our prayers suffer accordingly. There is no one position which is always right for prayer. Sitting on a hard chair, kneeling, perhaps with the help of a prayer stool, standing—all these can be valuable. It is important that we find the posture which helps us. The use of the hands needs some attention, for the hands can be a major source of distraction. They can be occupied by holding them together, by holding them open with palms upwards on the knees, by raising them to the skies. Breathing also matters, and the use of breathing in prayer is an important aspect, again much neglected in the west.

So we come to God with empty hands and empty hearts, in a spirit of poverty and openness. A famous hymn expresses our attitude:

> Nothing in my hands I bring.
> Simply to thy Cross I cling.

This self-emptying is a necessary element in spiritual progress. We need to be set free from false images of our own importance, self-centredness and pride which often stand in the way of sanctification. This is beautifully illustrated in a Zen story.

> The Master Nan-in had a visitor who came to inquire about Zen, but instead of listening the visitor kept talking about his own ideas. After a while Nan-in served tea. He poured tea into his visitor's cup until it was full. Then he kept on pouring. Finally the visitor could not restrain himself. 'Don't you see it's full?' he said. 'You cannot get any more in.' 'Just so', replied Nan-in, stopping at last. 'And like this cup you are filled with your own ideas. How can you expect me to give you Zen unless you offer an empty cup?'

In the eastern church the term used for the liberation of the individual from slavery to passion is *apatheia*. It does not mean 'apathy' but rather freedom from all that would agitate the spirit. So St Nilus in the fifth century says of prayer: 'The condition of prayer is passionless habit, which by means of the utmost love, seizes the spiritual and wisdom-loving mind, and uplifts it to the heights of the spirit.' St Gregory of Nyssa adds that the two essential marks of the struggle against our fallen nature are *apatheia* (detachment) and *parrhesia* (childlike confidence in God).

By detachment the spiritual writers mean the process of stripping away the facade so that we can penetrate beyond it to our true inner nature. In the words of *The Book of the Poor in Spirit*: 'The man who wishes to attain to true peace should detach himself from the senses and penetrate the centre of his soul where there is stability: only there will he find peace and quiet.' In the practice of a life of prayer, a great deal of time has to be spent simply in seeking to attain a state of stability and peace, and of detachment from feelings and thoughts. It is essential, in this quest, that such distractions are recognized and not fought. To fight them is to waste time and energy, and to undermine the work of prayer. To recognize them is part of the discipline of realism. But having recognized them, how should they be dealt with? *The Cloud of Unknowing* in the fourteenth century recommended two methods of dealing with distractions of thought. The first is to 'look over their shoulders' to God. The second 'spiritual dodge' is:

> When you feel that you are completely powerless to put these thoughts away, cower down before them like some cringing captive overcome in battle, and reckon that it is ridiculous to fight against them any longer. In this way you surrender yourself to God while you are in the hands of your enemies, and feeling that you have been overcome for ever. Please pay special heed to this suggestion, for I think that if you try it out it will dissolve every opposition.

St Peter of Alcantara (1499–1562) recognized that one of the most harmful effects of hostile thoughts is to instil in us a sense of shame and fear. So he advises:

> The remedy therefore is to take no account of these temptations, because the sin is not in the feeling but in the consent to it, and in the pleasure therefrom: and seeing there is no such pleasure in this condition but rather the contrary, we may consider it to be a chastening rather than a fault ... Wherefore the remedy ... is not in fearing but in disregarding them: for when they are feared overmuch, the very fear will awaken and stir them up.

But while head-on conflict is an exhausting and ineffective way of coping with distractions, it is essential that they be recognized. For prayer releases tensions and repressed emotions which might otherwise have their discharge in sleep. (Prayer and sleep are actually quite closely related!) To recognize their presence can make distractions into a healing process, and not simply a hindrance to prayer.

The two commonest types of painful distraction are probably feelings of anger and resentment against people, and sexual fantasies. Both often occur at times of great significance such as the moment of communion. People who experience strong sexual feelings, lusts and fantasies of various kinds during communion, or at other times of prayer, are often very worried by this, feeling that they must be guilty of some great sin, and often worry themselves sick with guilt feelings, and may stop going to communion altogether as a result. It is often a relief to know that such feelings are extremely common, and not at all abnormal, and it is important to accept this part of oneself as God-given and redeemable.

The need for inner scrutiny and self-knowledge is emphasized throughout the writings of the great spiritual guides. So Evagrius in the fourth century writes of the need to look deep into the hidden origins of passion: 'Those memories coloured by passion that we find in ourselves come from former experiences we underwent while subject to some passion'. Sixteen hundred years later Freud was to make the same point! Evagrius goes on to point to the conplex range of thoughts and influences.

> We must take care to recognise the different types of demons and note the special times of their activity ... so that when these various evil thoughts set their own proper forces to work, we are in a position to address effective words against them, that is to say, those words which correctly characterise the one present ... In this manner we ... shall pack them off, chafing with chagrin at our perspicacity ... If there is any monk who wishes to take the measure of some of the more fierce demons so as to gain experience in his monastic art, then let him keep careful watch over his thoughts. Let him observe their intensity, their periods of decline, and follow them as they rise and fall, let him note well the complexity of his thoughts, their periodicity, the demons which cause them, with the order of their succession and the nature of their associations. Then let him ask from Christ the explanations of these data he has observed.

To know oneself is a vital element in prayer. For all prayer begins with questioning, with quest for meaning and identity, with hunger. St Bernard calls self-knowledge 'the highest knowledge, the best, the one that brings us nearer to God, the knowledge of ourselves'. Or in the words of Johann Tauler (1300–61):

> I will tell you the shortest way, the most direct: enter your own depths, find out what it is that most hinders your own progress, and keeps you back. Retire within yourselves, for the Kingdom of God is within you ... Go back into yourself, enter into yourself, with the knowledge of what you are.

Self-knowledge and a proper self-esteem go together. We must know ourselves in order to love ourselves, yet love itself precedes knowledge and makes it possible. Self-contempt and self-negation will prevent self-knowledge. You do not want to know someone whom you despise, even if, especially if, that someone is yourself. So we are advised in Scripture, 'Keep your self-respect and value yourself at your true worth' (Eccles. 10.27). Not to respect oneself is to sin, and it is to jeopardize love of neighbour, for we are to love our neighbour *as ourselves* (Mark 12.31). True self-love means not trying to escape from ourselves, but listening to the voices within us. These voices are the human sources of prayer. The human struggle goes on deep down us, and we need to stay with it, and attend to it, entering into its pain and its richness. This involves the acceptance of our fundamental aloneness, not seeking to reduce it, not hoping that friendship, marriage, community, or group will take it away. That aloneness is an integral part of being human, and an essential element in love. It is out of that aloneness that it becomes possible to *respond* rather than merely react to people and needs. Response has to grow and emerge out of the depths of myself: it is *my* response, born out of my inner struggle and inner self-knowledge, out of my spirit, my deepest core. That is what spirituality is about.

So spiritual and psychological progress are very close, though they are not to be identified. The Spirit of God uses the raw material of the human body and soul, emotional, psychological life, self-awareness, care of the body, a healthy relationship to the unconscious—these are as essential to spiritual as to psychological growth. Of course, the Gospel cannot be reduced to psychology, or described adequately in psychological categories, but that does not mean that there is not a great deal of overlap. Perfect love casts out fear: but fear is a psychological condition, and love involves the emotions. Fearing and loving are not merely 'spiritual'. So psychology can illuminate the process of salvation and the path of prayer. For example, in self-examination, it is so easy to repress our anxiety and anger beneath an outward calm, while a timid, anxious man may arouse great irritation in us. I recognize in him my own hidden anxiety. Often it is faults seen in others which point us to something wrong in ourselves.

The mystics however teach that the journey inwards is not simply a path of self-disclosure, but that it brings us to the discovery of God. For God is within, at the deepest centre of our being. So Julian of Norwich can say in her *Revelations of Divine Love* (Chapter 56):

> It came about that I was able to see with absolute certainty that it was easier for us to get to know God than to know our own soul ... God is nearer to us than our own soul, for he is the Ground in which it stands ... So if we want to know our own soul, and enjoy its fellowship, as it were, it is necessary to seek it in our Lord God in which it is enclosed.

The Book of the Poor in Spirit also advises us: 'He who truly desires to find God should enter into himself, and seek God within.' Eckhart, also in the fourteenth century, speaks of a Divine Spark within all people, the Apex, the Ground.

> God is nearer to me than I am to my own self.
> When the soul enters into her Ground, into the innermost recesses of her being, divine power suddenly pours into her.
> When I saw into myself, I saw God in me.
> Where God is, there is the soul, and where the soul is, there is God.
> To gauge the soul we must gauge her with God, for the Ground of God and the Ground of the soul are one nature.

Similarly Ruysbroeck speaks of the 'spark of the soul'.

> It is the inward and natural tendency of the soul towards its source. And here we receive the Holy Spirit, the charity of God. By this inward tendency we are like the Holy Spirit: but in the act of receiving we become one spirit of love with God.

Or again Johann Tauler:

> The Inward Word is so unutterably near to us inwardly in the very principle of our being that not even man himself, not even his own thought, is so nigh, or is planted so deep within him, as the Eternal Word in man.

In order to enable this journey inward to proceed we need to pray for deliverance from falsehood. In the words of T. S. Eliot in 'Ash Wednesday':

> Suffer us not to mock ourselves with falsehood.
> Teach us to care and not to care.
> Teach us to sit still.

The great spiritual tradition refers to the movement inwards as the Illuminative Way. It is a way of experiencing light through darkness, for the light of God strikes the human soul as darkness. But it is a creative, positive darkness, a darkness within which we can move. Darkness achieves what years of study cannot. It is essential therefore not to try to avoid or escape the darkness of spirit, for it is an important part of our growth towards spiritual maturity. (See Chapter 6.) St Gregory of Nyssa expresses it thus in his *Commentary on the Song of Songs*:

> Next comes a closer awareness of hidden things, and by this the soul is guided through sense phenomena to the world of the invisible. And this awareness is a kind of cloud, which overshadows all appearances, and slowly guides and accustoms the soul to look towards what is hidden.

St John of the Cross (1542–91) in *The Dark Night of the Soul* speaks thus of the beginnings of the Illuminative Way:

> This house of sensuality being now set at rest, that is, mortified, its passions extinguished, and its desires set at rest and put to sleep by means of this most fortunate night of sensible purgation, the soul went forth upon the road and way of the Spirit which is that of progressives and proficients, otherwise called the Illuminative Way or the way of infused contemplation.

The reason that the Illuminative Way is described in terms of darkness is simply that the clearer the light shines, the more it blinds and darkens the eye of the soul. It is a deepening of life in faith, and faith is essentially trust in the unseen power of God. This experience of trust is fundamental to life in Christ and to true prayer.

In practical terms, the beginning of contemplative prayer will mean that it becomes progressively more difficult and perhaps impossible to think about God or to use many of the traditional methods of 'saying prayers'. The mind wanders constantly to such an extent that many people mistake the change for a total collapse of their prayer life. In fact, what is happening is that the attention to God is moving from the mind to the will. The best way to pray at this time is by way of short one-word prayers and by the repetition of monotonous phrases—Kyrie Eleison, the Jesus Prayer, litanies, short sentences of Scripture. Thus *The Cloud of Unknowing* gives sound advice:

> A naked intention directed to God and himself alone is wholly sufficient. If you want this intention summed up in a word, to retain it more easily, take a short word, preferably of one syllable, to do so. The shorter the word the better, being more like the working of the Spirit. A word like 'GOD' or 'LOVE'. Choose which you like or perhaps some other, so long as it is of one syllable. And fix this word fast to your heart so that it is always there come what may. It will be your shield and spear in peace and war alike. With this word you will hammer the cloud and the darkness above you. With this word you will suppress all thought under the cloud of forgetting. So much so that if you are ever tempted to think what it is that you are seeking this one word will be sufficient answer. And if you would go on to think learnedly about the significance and analysis of that same word, tell yourself that you will have it whole, and not in bits and parts.

On the other hand, because the mind has become inactive *in* prayer, it needs to be more consistently nourished *outside* prayer. So Bible study, reading which nourishes and feeds the mind, and discussion with other Christians of issues of belief can all help to build up the contemplative outlook. The mind is not abandoned: but in the actual work of prayer it is not central.

The aim of contemplative prayer is union with God. When the Christian mystics speak of union with God, they mean a union of wills. They are not referring to a dissolving of the human personality into the Godhead, in which the human ceases to exist. However, the experience of transformation and union is so wonderful that the descriptive language used is often very extravagant. So St John of the Cross says:

> This bond of love both joins them and transforms them, and makes them one by love, so that although they are different in substance, in glory and in appearance the soul seems to be God and God seems to be the soul.

St John uses the fire symbol to express the intensity of union.

> It must be understood that the fire of love which later is united with the soul and glorifies it is the same fire which earlier beats upon it in order to purify it. In the same way that fire which

> enters the log is that which at first attacked it and wounded it with its flame, drying it and stripping it of its ugly outward appearance, until by its heat it made it fit to enter and transform into itself.

Earlier Ruysbroeck had spoken of the Divine love 'drenching' the soul.

> Their bare understanding is drenched through by the Eternal Brightness even as the air is drenched through by the sunshine. And the bare uplifted will is transformed and drenched through by abysmal love even as iron is by fire.

So in Christian prayer and in the Christian life as a whole, there are stages and there is development, however uneven it may be, and however much individual paths may vary. Aelred of Rievaulx (1109–67), an English Cistercian monk, drew an analogy, in his Second Sermon for Pentecost, with the three stages of the life of Christ.

> Contemplate in Christ three stages, as it were, planned by his wonderful kindness, not for his benefit but for ours. First, he was baptised, then he was transfigured, finally he was glorified. He was baptised in the Jordan, transfigured on the mountain, and glorified at length in heaven. At Christ's baptism the Holy Spirit was shown as a dove, at his transfiguration as a cloud, but after his glorification as fire. Take these three stages to represent three stages in the soul's progress: purification, probation, and rewarding. Christ's baptism represents our purification, his transfiguration our probation, and his glorification our rewarding. We are purified by confession, we are proved by temptation, and we are rewarded by the fulness of charity.

Aelred's division corresponds closely to the classic threefold division of the life of prayer into the Ways of Purgation, Illumination, and Union.

In this way of progress in the life of prayer, a personal guide is an important and much neglected element. The need for a guide has been emphasized in many spiritual traditions—in Yoga, Buddhism, Sufism, as well as in classical philosophy. The *guru* in

Hinduism is perhaps closest to the Christian spiritual guides. The guru is not a teacher or leader: he is a light, one who illumines. The meeting with the guru is seen as the decisive turning point in life, and the guru comes when the individual is ready for his coming. Or there is the Zen master whose acted parables and sayings are reminiscent of the Desert Fathers and of the Old Testament prophets. For in the Old Testament the seer is essentially a man of insight, one who sees clearly ('the Word ... which he *saw*'), and prophecy is a byproduct of such vision and illumination.

In the Christian church, spiritual direction emerged clearly with the Desert Fathers of the fourth century. Here we meet the term *pneumatikos pater*, spiritual father. In the Russian church the term used for the spiritual guide was *staretz*. But the guide in the Christian tradition was less important than in Hinduism, for the Holy Spirit is the true Guide. In the west, spiritual guidance tended, in the Roman and Anglican traditions, to be closely linked with the hearing of confessions, while in much modern Protestantism the whole idea of personal guidance has declined. Richard Baxter, the seventeenth-century Puritan, saw the 'building up of the converted' to be of the greatest importance, and he particularly emphasized the care of the strong Christian, which is so often neglected.

The true Director then is the Holy Spirit: he is the one Master, the one Guru. In him is fulfilled the prophetic hope that 'no longer shall each man teach his neighbour and each his brother, saying "Know the Lord", for they shall all know me ...' (Jer. 31.34). Spiritual guidance therefore is not something added to the life in the Spirit which is given to us in Baptism: it is simply a way of helping us to achieve the full potential, the realization, of the spiritual gifts. It is a way marked by openness and honesty.

So we open ourselves to the heart of a fellow-Christian. The famous German pastor Dietrich Bonhoeffer, who died as a martyr to the Nazi regime, wrote of the importance of this ministry. He pointed out that

> many people are looking for an ear that will listen. They do not find it among Christians, because these Christians are talking where they should be listening. He who can no longer listen to his brother will soon be no longer listening to God either; he will

> be doing nothing but prattle in the presence of God too. This is the beginning of the death of the spiritual life, and in the end there is nothing left.

The greatest spiritual guides have been men and women of prayer and quiet, people possessed by an inner stillness of soul, people who are able to guide others because of their own closeness to God. In the Celtic tradition, the guide was referred to as an *anmchara*, or 'soul friend', and St Brigit is alleged to have said that 'anyone without a soul friend is a body without a head'.

There is nothing autocratic or repressive about spiritual direction. The purpose of seeking a personal guide or director is to find one's own way, one's own direction. So the Benedictine Augustine Baker (1575–1641) stresses that 'the director is not to teach his own way ... but to instruct his disciples how they may themselves find out the way proper for them'. The aim of direction is the achievement of spiritual freedom. This is not incompatible with a concern for method and discipline, and spiritual guidance may centre around a specific way of prayer as, for example, the direction given at Mount Sinai in the seventh century focused on the Jesus Prayer, and from the tenth century this prayer was established on Mount Athos. From the fifteenth century onwards it has been the mainstream of spiritual direction within Eastern Orthodoxy. In the west, St Ignatius Loyola (1491–1556), the founder of the Jesuits, was one who laid great stress on methodology in prayer. The spiritual director for him is essentially one who 'gives exercises'. The director, he says, stands in the middle like a balance and watches for spiritual movements in the individual. He is to be kind, gentle, encouraging and strengthening, preparing the person for times of desolation and aridity, watching for signs of overstrain, and guiding him on his spiritual journey. St Ignatius classifies the qualities of the good director and lays special emphasis on method, technique and intensive spiritual training.

A spiritual guide need not be a priest. Many lay men and women have performed, and continue to perform, this important task. St Symeon, the Orthodox mystic of the tenth century, said that the task of the spiritual father was to be a mediator. He went on to advise his disciples: 'Do not seek to be mediators on behalf of others before you have been filled with the Holy Spirit.' He argued that one who lacks such conscious awareness of the indwelling presence of the Holy Spirit, even if he is a bishop or patriarch, is not entitled to absolve. On the other hand, a lay person who is endowed with personal knowledge of the Spirit may absolve, and he cites the example of his own spiritual father Symeon the Pious. The point he is making is that a spiritual guide is one whose own absorption in God overflows in love for others. Technique and expertise, without prayerfulness and love, is not only useless but positively harmful.

So we can see a number of features in good spiritual guides. First, they are people of *experience.* St Isaac the Syrian in the sixth century advised his readers:

> Confide your thoughts to a man who, though he lacks learning, has studied the work in practice ... Therefore follow the advice of a man who has himself experienced all, and knows how to judge patiently what needs discrimination in your case and can point out what is truly useful to you.

Other eastern writers speak in a similar way. Thus St Symeon the New Theologian (949–1022) tells people to seek 'an experienced teacher with knowledge of the passions', and Macarius, a nineteenth-century Russian guide, tells his readers to seek 'a wise man experienced in the fight'.

Secondly, spiritual guides are people of *holiness.* The guide is valued for his holiness of life more than for his function. He or she is someone with an ability to love others and share their sufferings. The Russian term for a spiritual guide is *staretz*, and Dostoevsky (in *The Brothers Karamazov*) describes a *staretz* as 'one who takes your soul and your will into his soul and his will'. The holiness of the spiritual guide is brought out very powerfully in the story of St Seraphim of Sarov. The saint addresses his disciple:

> We are both together, son, in the Spirit of God. Why do you not look at me?
>
> *Disciple* I cannot look, father, because lightning flashes from your eyes. Your face is brighter than the sun and my eyes ache with pain.
>
> *Seraphim* Fear not, my son. You too have become as bright as I.

> You too are now in the fulness of God's Spirit. Otherwise you would not be able to look at me as I am.

Thirdly, spiritual guides are marked by *discernment*. Throughout the whole tradition the key word is *discernment* (*diakrisis*). Many Christians, according to the teaching of the Desert Fathers, become casualties through excess and through wrong paths. To travel the spiritual way without a guide is dangerous and can lead to madness. Christians who are serious about their faith ought to take very seriously the question of seeking personal spiritual guidance.

Christian life and life in prayer call for discipline and guidance. In particular the life of prayer involves the discipline of attention, for prayer is the direction of all the attention of which one is capable towards God. No amount of warmth or of passion can make up for lack of attention. But such attention calls for the cultivation of an atmosphere in which it becomes possible. The creation of such an atmosphere is one of the purposes of a rule of life. In the external world, ecology is in fashion: environmental issues are a priority. But the creation of a healthy ecology of the spirit is equally important, for prayer needs an environment in which it can grow and flourish. So we need to take seriously such details as the kind of place in which we can most easily be still, the time of day, our physical posture, and so on. Jesus not only went to the desert to pray, but he also instructed his followers to go to a room and close the door when they prayed. The environment matters, in prayer as in the rest of life.

So the point of a rule of life is not to systematize and regimentalize our prayer life but to give it a framework which will help it to be free and to blossom. A rule would include such areas as: celebration of the Eucharist with other Christians; the use of some form of Office (morning and evening prayer) and Bible study; personal and corporate prayer times; occasional retreat periods or quiet days as times of concentrated prayer and recollection; and some form of personal spiritual guidance or confession. It is valuable to work out such a rule in co-operation with a guide or some other committed and reliable Christian friend. Without some kind of rule the spiritual life is likely to become shapeless and sloppy. We need to try to keep a balance between the various ways of praying, and between various kinds of activity, such as intellectual and manual work, sleep, leisure time, and so on. From very early times it was realized that not all prayer is of the same type or at the same level. Evagrius wrote in the fourth century:

> There are five works that help us find favour with God: the first is pure prayer; the second chanting the Psalms; the third reading the Scriptures; the fourth the remembrance with sorrow of heart of our sins, death and the last judgment; the fifth manual labour.

These are precisely the areas which should be incorporated in a rule of life: it should find time for personal prayer, for some form of Office, for Bible study, for penitence and confession, and for manual work.

The creation of a framework, an atmosphere, a structure, is not prayer, but it is a necessary preliminary to prayer. It is within the atmosphere of inner discipline and simplicity that prayer can begin to grow. The eastern church, in its teaching on prayer, focuses on the constant use of the Name of Jesus. The first recorded teaching about the invocation of the Name of Jesus comes in the mid-fifth century writer Diadochus. He recommended the use of the prayer 'Lord Jesus Christ have mercy on me' as a way of cleansing the mind of its sickness, and he recommended this to beginners. The Prayer of Jesus was to be used inwardly and secretly at all times—when dropping off to sleep, when waking, when eating or drinking, while talking. It is seen as a prayer which both *binds* the mind and *unifies* the personality. Thus Philotheus of Sinai in the tenth century says: 'By the memory of Jesus Christ gather together your mind that is scattered abroad. Through the Fall this disintegration has happened, but memory of God restores primal wholeness.'

One of the essential aspects of the use of the Name of Jesus then is the 'binding of the mind'. This is an expression used by the nineteenth-century eastern spiritual teacher Theophan the Recluse. He advises his disciples to 'bind the mind with one thought—or the thought of One only'. It is this process of binding which is the purpose of meditation. What is meant by meditation? In Christian spirituality, the term 'meditation' has generally been used to describe a way of disciplined thinking, an ascetical exercise marked by discipline and sobriety. It involves pursuing one line of thought and renouncing all others. It is therefore a method of reducing the range of activity of the mind, allowing it to centre on one point, to focus. Patanjali in the Yoga Sutras calls meditation 'a current of unified thought'. St Francis de Sales (1567–1622) said, 'When we think about the things of God, not to learn but to kindle our love, that is called meditating.' Through the centuries many schemes and methods of meditating have been devised to help people to achieve this straight thinking under God's guidance. It is not strictly prayer, but rather a preparation for prayer. One simple way to begin to meditate is to take a series of short sayings, from Scripture and elsewhere, and read them slowly so that they become part of us. This 'brooding on the Scriptures' is immensely valuable, and provides us with material for recollection and prayer. 'Brooding' is the key word—not jumping about from one idea to another, but focusing, gently but firmly, on one word or one phrase. St John Climacus (570–649), in teaching people the rudiments of prayer, recommended the careful pronunciation of the words. If thoughts then wandered, he suggested restarting on the word which was last pronounced. He advised slow and monotonous attention to the actual words as the best way to achieve inner concentration.

The stress on the words is important, for *meditari*, from which the word 'meditation' comes, has a very concrete and precise meaning. It means to learn the Scriptures by uttering them in a low voice, murmuring them. For the early Fathers, to meditate literally meant to read a passage and learn it by heart, with one's whole being, using the body as well as memory, intelligence and will. So in the Psalms we are told that 'the *mouth* of the righteous is exercised in wisdom' (Ps. 37.31), a possible reference to this activity. The Carmelites were very realistic in their recommendation that reading has an important place in prayer. To rely on someone else's words to rekindle our own love for God is far more sensible than simply kneeling in grim determination, trying to rekindle it by sheer effort.

However, the Fathers stress that the *quality*, not the quantity, of the words is what matters. So Evagrius says: 'Do not take a delight in the multiplicity of psalms. It casts a veil on my heart. Better a single word spoken from a heart of love than a thousand from a heart of indifference.' Similarly St Symeon advises: 'A single trisagion [i.e. the hymn 'Holy, Holy, Holy'] said with devotion and recollection before going to sleep is worth more than a four hour vigil of empty phrases.'

In the sixteenth century, the Spanish Franciscan St Peter of Alcantara (1499–1562) in his *Golden Treatise of Mental Prayer* gave some very practical guidance on meditation and on the movement from meditation to prayer. His teaching can be summarized under eight heads.

1. If you need to move on to another subject, do so.
2. Avoid too much intellectualism, using more the affections and the will.
3. Do not be too violent or emotional, but practise rather a 'simple subdued gaze'.
4. Avoid the two extremes of fatigue and slackness.
5. Be patient. If prayer does not come, 'change, for the time, prayer into study'.
6. Do not spend too short a time, but allow adequate time for prayer to develop.
7. If you are 'visited by God' and prayer is aroused, stay in prayer, and do not then revert to books.
8. Try to 'unite meditation with contemplation'.

The purpose of such disciplined meditation is to enable us to move within ourselves to the centre of our souls where dwells the Image of God. There we rest and remain in the presence of God, no longer thinking but loving. St Peter, in common with all the great teachers, advises the avoidance of too much mental activity: 'We should strive to avoid in this exercise any excessive intellectual speculation, and should endeavour to treat the matter more with the affections and feelings of the will than with the discursive speculations of understanding.'

Many ways and methods of meditation have been developed throughout Christian history. Some of them, such as those in *The Spiritual Exercises* of St Ignatius Loyola, are complex, though it should be remembered that the Exercises are meant to take thirty days. (The thirty-day retreat was seen as an important thorough preparation also for those training to direct others in prayer.) In the Ignatian meditations, there is a preparatory prayer, followed by two preludes. The first of these is spent in imagining the place where the particular Bible incident happened, while in the second we are meant to tell God what we want from the meditation. Then Ignatius instructs us to use the three faculties of memory, understanding, and will, and these form the body of the meditation. Finally there is a 'colloquy' or friendly conversation with God. Although the method seems complicated, continued use of these meditations will lead to a greater simplicity with more time devoted to a quiet resting in and dialogue with God.

A simpler method of meditating is the so-called 'Sulpician Method', developed by L. Tronson (1676–1700), Superior-General of the Society of Saint-Sulpice in Paris. This method simply involved the consideration of three themes in each passage used: Jesus before the Eyes—Adoration; Jesus in the Heart—Communion; Jesus in the Hands—Co-operation.

Another, more recent, plan of meditative prayer is that suggested by the Jesuit William Johnston in his book *The Still Point* (1971). This involves nine phases:

1 *Relaxation*: sit down, relax, slow down, be still,
2 *Awareness* of God's presence: realize that God is there.
3 *Surrender* to God.
4 *Acceptance*—accept God's will.
5 *Repentance and Forgiveness*—confess sin.
6 *Contemplation*—look at God.
7 *Receiving*—receive the Spirit.
8 *Intercession*—pray for others.
9 *Praise*—praise God.

The aim of meditation is to enable the mind and heart to attain a state of attention. However, one major reason for the lack of attention in prayer is a general lack of attention and lack of mental discipline in daily life. If we allow our minds to wander and to be disordered most of the time, we are unlikely suddenly to find them still and ordered in prayer. So Brother Lawrence, the seventeenth-century Carmelite, gives some sound advice in his *Eighth Letter*:

> One way to recollect the mind easily in the time of prayer and preserve it more in tranquillity is not to let it wander too far at other times; you should keep it strictly in the presence of God; and being accustomed to think of him often, you will find it easy to keep your mind calm at the time of prayer or at least to recall it from its wanderings.

This discipline of the mind involves such things as the avoidance of gossip and trivial conversation, and the building up of inner resources of stillness. Archbishop Anthony Bloom recommended one woman to 'sit and knit in the presence of God' as a way of deepening her growth towards a prayerful spirit. The disturbances which come from the disordered mind are far more serious obstacles to prayer than external noise. So in preparing to pray we need to slow down, and to reduce the range of images in our minds to manageable proportions. The eastern teachers, as we saw above, speak of 'binding the mind'. Mental overcrowding needs to be avoided at all cost.

Because of the importance of preparation it is useful to set aside, where we can, a period of at least an hour for prayer. For St Peter of Alcantara warns us that 'if the time is too short, it is passed in unloading the imagination, and in bringing the heart under control: just at the moment when we are ready and ought to be beginning the exercise, we stop it'. The key to whatever type of meditation we use lies in watching and letting go. One good maxim is to watch your breath and let go of all else.

Above all then, a prayerful spirit is marked by simplicity. To be simple is not the same as to be silly, any more than to be child-like is to be childish. True simplicity is the unifying of the personality, a vision and a life which can cut through the paraphernalia and complications and 'see into the heart of things'. Such a simplicity of spirit is a major product of contemplative prayer. As the Shaker song put it:

> 'Tis the gift to be simple,
> 'Tis the gift to be free,
> 'Tis the gift to come down
> Where we ought to be.

In the process of simplifying the personality, there is a crucial place for silence. Silence in itself can be a destructive force. It need not lead to God. In British prisons there is a rule called Rule 43 under which certain types of offender, mainly sex offenders and 'subversives', are kept in solitude for twenty-three hours out of twenty-four. There is a silence which crushes people, a silence of hatred, a silence filled with fear and terror. There is the silence of the unknown. There is the silence which results from nervousness and embarrassment, which we try to avoid by filling the gaps with noise and chatter. The most powerful enemy of the spirit is the inner silence which comes from the emptiness of one's being. In Ingmar Bergman's film *The Silence* (1962) silence represents the death of God. In Paul Simon's song 'Sound of Silence', silence is a cancer. Yet it is the emptiness of the spirit which is also the place of divine encounter. Out of the deep we call to the Lord.

Creative silence is a necessary part of prayer. Pascal once commented that 'most of man's troubles come from his not being able to sit quietly in his chamber'. St Isaac of Nineveh, who wrote in Syriac towards the end of the seventh century, spoke of the place of silence in prayer:

> Many are avidly seeking, but they alone find who remain in continual silence ... Every man who delights in a multitude of words, even though he says admirable things, is empty within. If you love truth, be a lover of silence. Silence, like the sunlight, will illuminate you in God, and will deliver you from the phantoms of ignorance. Silence will unite you to God himself ...
>
> More than all things love silence: it brings you a fruit that tongue cannot describe. In the beginning we have to force ourselves to be silent. But then there is born something that draws us to silence. May God give you an expression of this 'something' that is born of silence. If only you practise this, untold light will dawn on you in consequence ... after a while a certain sweetness is born in the heart of this exercise, and the body is drawn almost by force to remain in silence.

In silence we first come to listen. Bodily composure and meditation will help in this work. But the essential element in silence is the turning inwards towards 'the still point of the turning world'.

> Descend lower, descend only
> Into the world of perpetual solitude
>
> (T. S. ELIOT)

Through deepening our experience of inner silence, there grows within us a stillness in the midst of turmoil, an emptiness and poverty of spirit. Eckhart calls this positive emptiness 'the central silence, the pure peace and abode of the heavenly birth'. The point at which silence becomes prayer is the point at which God fills the emptiness with himself. In Eckhart's words, 'Here he meets God without intermediary. And from out the Divine Unity there shines into him a simple light: and this light shows him Darkness and Nakedness and Nothingness.'

So we have come to the point at which, through discipline and silent waiting, prayer *happens*. We do not create prayer, but merely prepare the ground and clear away obstacles. Prayer is always a gift, a grace, the flame which ignites the wood; the Holy Spirit gives prayer. The human response is one of adoring love. It is this posture of adoration which is the central posture of worship. 'Religion is adoration' wrote Von Hugel. As in meditation, adoring prayer calls for a concentration. But it is not a fierce mental concentration so much as a focusing of our love, an outpouring of wonder towards God. In meditation there was a simplifying of thought so that we came to think deeply around a single word or phrase or theme until thought gave way to prayer. Similarly in the prayer of adoration we focus ourselves. The mind becomes less active, and we allow ourselves, body and spirit, to rest in an attitude of outpoured offering to God.

Adoration calls for a concentration of our spirits through our bodies. 'Let your soul be in your eyes' was the advice of the great spiritual teacher Evelyn Underhill. In the early stages of prayer, it is useful to focus one's attention on an object—a simple object such as a leaf, a nut, a candle, a picture, or some other focal point for the eyes. Look at this object, and, gently but firmly, allow the distractions and demands from elsewhere to drop into the background. Focus simply and wholly on this object. Do not think. Simply pour out your whole being towards it. Through such a simple focusing of the eyes and heart, we discover a deepening quietude and stillness. But the initial focusing of the eyes is of the greatest importance. Again, in adoration as in meditation, the position of the body calls for attention. We can kneel, focusing our eyes, heart, and attention upon God. Or we can prostrate ourselves full length on the ground. Or we can stand, perhaps bowing profoundly from the waist, slowly and rhythmically, as is the eastern orthodox custom.

One major obstacle to adoration is the fact that we carry over into our prayer the utilitarian and functional notions which govern our work-based society. Our social order is dominated by the concepts of efficiency and production: not only things but people are valued for their results, for what they produce. But worship is not functional. It is freedom from the dominion of work. It is *otium*, rest, peace, leisure, the Sabbath of the blessed. In the Middle Ages, the monastic life was called *otium* because monks, it was said, rejected the life of *negotium*, secular business with its work ethic, and indeed St Bernard described monasticism as *negotissimum otium*, a very very busy leisure time! *Otium* does not mean the absence of labour, but it does mean the absence of alienated labour, wage labour. *Laborare est orare*: to work is to pray, to pray is to work. It is the rejection of justification by works. In adoration we reject that false doctrine. The Kingdom of God is an order in which God is adored for himself. So St Augustine writes in *The City of God* (Book 22):

> All our activity will be Amen and Alleluia.
> There we shall rest and we shall see.
>   We shall see and we shall love.
>   We shall love and we shall praise.
> Behold what shall be in the end, and shall not end.

In our prayer and adoration we anticipate the End of human life—'to glorify God and to enjoy him for ever'.

The prayer of adoration needs to have a special and central place in our personal prayer. In the modern Christian movement called the Charles of Jesus Secular Fraternity—named after Charles de Foucauld (1858–1916)—the prayer of adoration is the central element. Members pray as much as they can before the Holy Sacrament, a quarter of an hour a day, and a whole hour once a week where possible. Through this adoration of Jesus in the Eucharist they are led to a deeper sense of his presence in all human beings. So all our prayer needs to have a solid core of adoration, and nothing is more certain to aid this than periods of silent prayer before the reserved Sacrament. (See Chaper 4.)

We have said that all prayer is the work of the Spirit. The New Testament assumes that the Christian will be aware of the work of the Holy Spirit and of the spiritual gifts in his own life. The great saints too assumed a personal experience of the Spirit. Take, for example, the words of St Bernard of Clairvaux (1090–1153):

> We who have passed from death to life by the Spirit who quickens know by a certain and daily experience—he himself by his enlightening gives us proof—that our vows and groanings do come from him and do go to God, and there find mercy in his sight.

So the New Testament speaks of *charismata*, the gifts which build up the Christian community (Rom. 12.6; 1 Cor. 12), and of *pneumatika*, spiritual gifts (1 Cor. 12.1; 14.1). There are, Paul says, different *charismata* within the Body of Christ, and each of us has a gift. But there are also spiritual gifts (*pneumatika*) which we should 'desire' (1 Cor. 14.1). There is no Christian life without the manifestation of the Spirit, for Christian life means life in the Spirit. The Spirit is life. It is the Spirit who introduces us to the 'depths of God' (1 Cor. 2.10). But the gifts of the Spirit are not sensational or dramatic: Paul includes teaching and service among them.

In the renewal movement which we now term 'charismatic renewal' or 'neo-Pentecostalism' there has been a rediscovery of the need for spiritual experience by many Christians. Many Christians now speak of being 'baptized in the Holy Spirit' as if this were something different from Christian Baptism. The theology of 'baptism in the Spirit', which dominates much Pentecostal thought, is actually the shakiest and least biblical aspect of Pentecostalism. But the essential point which the charismatic renewal has grasped and communicated is the *fact* of spiritual change. A valuable and widely used aid in this context has been the *Life in the Spirit Seminars Team Manual*, and it summarizes some of the differences brought about by the fuller sense of experience of the Holy Spirit. Prayer life changes because there is a greater sense of the reality of God. Scripture comes alive. We are led to tell others about Christ more naturally and easily. There is a deeper experience of sharing of life within the local Christian community. Spiritual gifts manifest themselves. Yet even to speak of the 'charismatic experience' as if it were a different, additional thing to *Christian* experience can be dangerously misleading. All Christian prayer is essentially charismatic for it is *graced* by the Holy Spirit.

One of the words which is often applied to charismatic movements is the word 'ecstasy'. It is a much misused and misunderstood word. Its root meaning is disturbance, loss of balance, upheaval. In this broad sense all Christian experience is disturbing. Yet our culture is largely based on the deliberate exclusion of such disturbing experiences. It is based, in Theodore Roszak's words, on 'a diminished mode of consciousness', or what William Blake called 'single vision', and from which he prayed to be delivered. There has been a decay of symbols, those powerful mysteries which swallow us whole, and through which we gain new insights beyond words. There is a loss of wonder. So much in our society is artificial. There is even a centre in the United States where non-holiday-makers can have their photographs taken outside reconstructions of overseas places of interest which they haven't visited! The effect of the cult of the artificial in spiritual life is seen in the fact that all too often there is a kind of lifelessness and immobility about 'religious' people, a failure to be quite alive. Why? Because the concept of God, which was originally rooted in a vital experience, has become mere lifeless jargon which corresponds with nothing in their experience.

It is this vital experience of God which the early Christians saw as the work of the Holy Spirit, and they described it in a number of ways. First, the experience is one of *power* (*dunamis*). The Spirit is seen in terms of wind and fire, symbols of violent action, and the effect of his coming as a kind of intoxication. Those on whom the Spirit falls are often thought to be drunk, as were the apostles at Pentecost, or mad, as were many of the prophets. For the coming of the Spirit in power changes hesitant, fearful people into people of energy and confidence.

Secondly, the Spirit is seen as the bringer of *freedom*, of liberation. This liberation is often seen today as a kind of 'resurrection of the body', a release from inhibition, a freedom to worship God with the whole of ourselves. For the Spirit is not the opposite of the body, but rather its life. According to orthodox theology it is only God who can inspire us from within without detracting from our freedom. So one sign of divine activity is the sense of greater freedom and peace.

Thirdly, the Spirit gives the power to *pray*. Romans 8 is the key passage for this idea. The Spirit, Paul says, prays within us in thoughts which are unutterable. Fourthly, the Spirit brings about an *ethical transformation*. The fruits of the Spirit, according to

Galatians, are love, joy, peace, and so on. The test of true spirituality is therefore practical and is manifested in changed life-styles. Fifthly, the Spirit is the bringer of *truth.* The Spirit of truth will guide us into all truth. So a vital gift of the Spirit is that of insight and vision. Sixthly, the coming of the Spirit is *ineffable*, for it transcends speech. Finally, Paul insists (1 Cor. 13), the greatest gift is *love.* St Thomas Aquinas agrees: 'Although prophecy is a gift of the Spirit, nevertheless it is not with the gift of prophecy that the Holy Spirit is given but the gift of Charity.'

Traditionally the church has spoken of the 'seven-fold' gifts of the Holy Spirit. Thus the ancient hymn *Veni Creator* prays:

> Come, Holy Ghost, our souls inspire,
> And lighten with celestial fire.
> Thou the anointing Spirit art
> Who dost thy seven-fold gifts impart.

The biblical basis for this is Isaiah 11.2 which says that the Spirit of the Lord will rest on the coming Messiah:

> the Spirit of wisdom and understanding,
> the Spirit of counsel and fortitude,
> the Spirit of knowledge and piety,
> the Spirit of fear of the Lord.

In 1 Corinthians 12.4–11 is another list of 'gifts of the Spirit'. They are: the word of wisdom (*sophia*); the word of knowledge (*gnosis*); faith; powers of healing; power to work miracles; prophecy; discernment of spirits (*diakrisis pneumatōn*); the gift of tongues; and the interpretation of tongues. Some of these gifts are well documented throughout the New Testament as marks of the Christian life. For example, wisdom and knowledge are linked together in New Testament teaching (Eph. 1.17; Col. 1.9). It is the Spirit of wisdom who is the source of knowledge. The First Letter of John tells Christians that 'you have an anointing (*chrisma*) from the Holy One, and you *know* all things' (2.20). The gift of wisdom is seen as one of the greatest spiritual gifts, and in the Old Testament a whole literature, the Wisdom literature, grew up around it. Solomon was seen as the archetypal wise man, while the Psalms frequently stress the necessity of wisdom in the spiritual person. Whilst knowledge without wisdom, faith and love is seen as dangerous, yet *to know* remains a central word in Christian understanding. The gnostics were those who exalted a secret knowledge above all other gifts, but *gnosis* as such is not condemned by Scripture or the Fathers, Faith, however, remains vital, and it is important that we do not seek to replace faith by knowledge, walking by sight and not by faith.

Healing is an important aspect of the life of prayer and a spiritual gift. Not all possess the gift of healing in the specific sense, although it needs to be remembered that in Christian use *therapeuein*, to heal, means far more than the removal of symptoms: it means wholeness of life, harmony, fulfilment. All prayer is therapeutic, all sacraments are healing ministries, and all Christians are involved in healing work. However, it is clear that some human beings, Christian and non-Christian, possess gifts on the psycho-physical level which enable them to convey psychical and physical healing to others. There is nothing intrinsically spiritual about healing gifts, and they can, and do, coexist with a good deal of sin, lust for power, and spiritual exploitation. Prayer and healing are very close. As all prayer is Kingdom-centred, so healing is an element in the proclamation of the Kingdom (Luke 9.1–2). Similarly, the coming of the Kingdom is a process, and healing prayer is a process, not a series of cries at crisis points. Prayer needs to be continuous, and most healing requires time and patience. Again, in healing prayer in Christ's ministry, *touch* was a central part (Mark 5.18–30; 14.35–6, etc.). So Christian people often incorporate the laying on of hands into healing prayer. Closely linked with healing, Paul includes miracles. It is not clear why he distinguishes the two, but he was probably thinking of situations where a new creation seems to take place, rather than a quickening of already existing powers.

The gift of prophecy is closely linked with prayer. Prophecy is concerned with seeing and interpreting the signs of God's activity. Among the early prophets were the ecstatic *nebiim* and the seers at the shrines. There were many false seers and false prophets. The true prophets pointed to the working out of God's will in history and they interpreted events in relation to God's will and plan. Prayer has an essentially prophetic dimension in so far as it involves perception and insight into the workings of God. All prophecy is a byproduct of such insight: contemplation precedes prophecy. Paul rates prophecy high among the spiritual gifts, urging his readers to strive for the things of the Spirit, especially prophecy (1 Cor. 14.1).

Discernment is one of the key ideas in spirituality. It is often given to those who have purified their hearts and in whom the Spirit has taken possession to see more deeply into the hearts of others. This gift of *diakrisis* is the supreme mark of the spiritual guide. It was said of the great Russian staretz Amvrosy:

> He lives at one with you, he is nearer to you than you are to yourself. You feel that his eyes see all that is bad and all that is good in you. And you rejoice that it is so, and that nothing can be hidden from him which exists in you.

Discernment is often associated with clairvoyance. St Anthony in the desert was said to be able to see what was happening in the cities and roads of Egypt. Discernment essentially is an extreme sensitivity which results from close listening to the voice of God. Through this contemplative listening, we come to listen to the voices of the world and of individuals, to see beyond the superficial into the heart and its secrets.

Yet knowledge and discernment must be held together by love. Knowledge without love is very harmful. The Epistle to the Philippians prays that our love may grow with knowledge (*epignosis*) and discernment (*aisthesis*) (Phil. 1.9.). Love needs knowledge and discernment. Paul is critical of those whose zeal for God is not enlightened (Rom. 10.2). In Ephesians and Colossians knowledge is linked with wisdom (*sophia*) (Eph. 1.17; Col. 1.9), while Ephesians 1.18 speaks of 'having the eyes of your heart enlightened'. In these passages, the emphasis is on the need for a Christian to combine knowledge with clear insight and awareness within a life which is shaped by love.

Finally, Paul speaks of tongues and interpretation of tongues. Speaking in tongues is probably the most controversial of the gifts of the Spirit. The phenomenon has never been wholly absent from Christian movements, but it has recently become widespread in the the west through the charismatic renewal. Yet the New Testament places speaking in tongues very low among the manifestations of the Spirit. Tongues first appeared at the initiation of the Gentiles (Acts 10 and 11). Nowhere in the New Testament is tongue-speaking seen as occurring in one individual. On the contrary, the only three occasions in Acts where tongues occur are when they come to an entire community as part of the experience of conversion. In modern Pentecostalism we find the expression 'baptism in the Holy Spirit' associated with tongues. This expression does not occur in Scripture. Where the term 'baptised *with* the Holy Spirit' occurs, it refers to the crisis initiations of Jews and Gentiles. Tongues are never asked for in the New Testament: neither in Acts 2 nor in Acts 8, 10 or 19 are tongues sought. There is certainly no question of every Christian speaking in tongues (1 Cor. 12.30). While Paul does say 'I want you all to speak in tongues' (ibid. 14.5) he has earlier made it clear that his wish does not correspond with fact. Prophecy is preferred, although there is no question of the suppression of tongues (ibid. 14.39) and it is clear from the writings of Irenaeus that tongue-speaking was still common in the church in his day. Yet when Paul speaks of the spiritual gifts in Romans, he never mentions tongues—presumably because he did not to wish to suggest the practice to a church which was innocent of it (Rom. 12.6–8).

It seems then from Paul that tongue-speaking is seen as a manifestation of the Spirit, but not a very important one, and one open to serious abuse. It is at the bottom of the list of gifts in 1 Corinthians 12.8–10 and also in verses 28 and 29. It is possible, Paul says, to speak with the tongues of men and of angels and yet miss the greatest gift of the Spirit which is love (13.1). He sees tongues as a temporary phenomenon in contrast to love: 'as for tongues, they shall cease' (13.8). At the same time, tongues are a way of speaking to God: 'he who speaks in tongues speaks to God, not men ... he speaks mysteries by his spirit' (14.2). It is a gift for private prayer for 'the man who speaks in tongues builds himself up' (14.4). Mark 16.17 uses the term 'new tongues' which may suggest that those who are living the new life in Christ and are part of the new creation (2 Cor. 5.17) speak a new language.

It is important not to overrate tongues, but they should not be despised. Essentially the revival of tongue-speaking is one facet in the recovery of the non-rational aspects of prayer and of the place of the organs of the body, in this case the mouth, in worship. Yet in the New Testament the test of the spiritual gifts is the social test: that is charismatic which is *pros ton sumpheron* (for the common good: 1 Cor. 12.7), which builds up the community (14.1). Special spiritual experience which sets people apart can, like the *gnosis* referred to in 1 Cor. 8.1; simply 'puff up' in contrast to love which 'builds up'. So the test of spiritual growth is practical: how does it work out in real life, in love of neighbour, in service of the brethren? In addition, we need to apply certain criteria to the manifestations which occur in group prayer. One of the earliest diagnostic tests of Christian spirituality is that given in 1 John 4: whoever denies that Jesus Christ has come in the flesh is not of God. The Spirit who is revealed in the prayer group must be the Spirit of Jesus. It must be consonant with Scripture and with the teaching of the church and its sacramental life. If these tests are not applied, there is a real danger of false paths. *Diakrisis*, discernment, is concerned with the acquiring of balance. As Julian of Norwich said:

> By three things a man standeth in this life, by which God is worshipped, and we are sped, kept and saved. The first is use of man's kindly reason, the second is the common teaching of Holy Church, the third is the inward gracious working of the Holy Ghost, and these three are all of one God.

However the New Testament does not teach that the coming of the Holy Spirit will set Christians free from all suffering and all conflict. Rather does the Spirit enable us to share in the sufferings of Christ, and also in his glory. When we cry 'Abba, Father', Paul tells us, it is the Spirit who bears witness within us 'provided we suffer with him in order that we may also be glorified with him' (Rom. 8.15–17). Finally, the New Testament and the Christian tradition do not encourage any great interest in the acquisition of special experiences. The mystics hold rather that it is all too easy for the devil to fabricate them, and that, whatever their source, they can lead to pride and spiritual elitism. Experiences should be accepted but grasped. But the real growth in the life of the Spirit comes in the darkness of faith and in the living of a life of Christian love.

3

Prayer and politics

> Your Kingdom come. (Matt. 6.10)
>
> To clasp the hands in prayer is the beginning of an uprising against the disorder of the world.
>
> KARL BARTH

Christian prayer is inseparable from resistance and struggle. Complacency and the absence of inner struggle is the deadly enemy of prayer. Yet so often we mistake the signs of prayer for signs of an inability to pray. Such marks as searching in darkness, aching for fulfilment, yearning for God in the midst of confusion and perplexity, are signs of living prayer. For prayer is directed towards the vision of the Kingdom of God. According to St Gregory of Nyssa, there is an ancient version of the Lord's Prayer in which the phrase 'Your Kingdom come' is replaced by 'May your Holy Spirit come upon us and purify us'. Elsewhere Gregory describes the Spirit as 'the Kingdom of the Father and the Anointing of the Son'. For the Spirit stands for newness, the new age, a new level of human progress. He is the Spirit of the Age to Come, the initiator of a new order where young men shall see visions and old men shall dream dreams. Prayer which lacks this future orientation is bound to become settled and at ease, a victim of that false peace against which the prophets constantly warn us.

False peace in fact is a kind of paralysis, and of all illnesses of the body paralysis is perhaps the most destructive. It spreads through whole sections of the body politic and the body spiritual as it does through the physical body. And, significantly, in the New Testament, deliverance from paralysis is one of the signs of the presence of the Kingdom of God. But paralysis is only one sign of lack of co-ordination in the body. Loss of control can also lead to inability to effect actions and produce results. Intoxication with chemicals and mental illness can reduce or impair human functioning. Again, in the New Testament, the coming of the Kingdom of God is associated with the casting out of demons, the handling of snakes, and the raising of the dead. The dead are the truly paralysed.

So in the spiritual life we are not only concerned with personal freedom, but also with freedom in social structures, and with deliverance from social paralysis. Social paralysis manifests itself supremely by a sense of inevitability combined with the individual's ineffectiveness to change anything. Such paralysis is not without its attractions. Commitment to change and the vision of a new order demand willingness to face suffering and frustration. It is tempting to fly from this prospect to a religion of resignation in face of the divine force, a theological determinism.

> Sit down O men of God,
> His Kingdom he will bring
> Whenever it may please his grace!
> You cannot do a thing.

There is also a paralysis of the spirit. Many Christians, in the life of prayer, have opted to abandon the use of certain functions of their personalities. Hence Kierkegaard's famous saying that Christianity demands the crucifixion of the intellect. For many, religion seems to involve intellectual dishonesty, or the clogging up of the channels of experience; it is a censoring of reality rather than a liberation. So 'religious' people can be notoriously narrow, trivial and rigid, suffering from a kind of partial paralysis. More than this, for many, many people, the symptoms of spiritual distress are more like a state of reduced activity. Perhaps the church is suffering not from a total paralysis but from a spiritual stroke.

In the New Testament the Kingdom is essentially to do with increased awareness and with power; and the coming of the Kingdom is seen in the context of the healing of the paralysed and the giving of sight to the blind. The immediate indication of the presence of the Kingdom is movement: the lifeless stirs, the blind see, the dead are raised. The Kingdom is the symbol of new life.

Jesus was not unique in proclaiming the Kingdom of God. The imminence of that Kingdom was also a major preoccupation of the Zealot movement, the political revolutionary movement of his day. And it is clear that there are certain common features between

Jesus and the Zealots—the announcement of the Kingdom, the opposition to Herod (Luke 13.32) and to kings (22.25), and so on. Simon the Zealot, Simon Barjona and Judas Iscariot were all included among the disciples, while the cleansing of the Temple, and the condemnation of Jesus by the Romans in a political trial all bring Jesus and the Zealots close together. On the other hand, the non-violent sayings and the teaching of Jesus on loving one's enemies set him very much apart from and in contrast to them. What is important, however, is to realize that the view of Jesus as a 'purely spiritual' figure, preaching a 'purely spiritual' kingdom, is quite false. Jesus was not punished for blasphemy, a religious crime, the penalty for which was stoning (as in the death of Stephen): he was crucified by the Roman occupying power. Crucifixion was the punishment for escaped slaves and for rebels against the state. The title 'Jesus of Nazareth, King of the Jews' was seen as a flagrant attack on the Imperium Romanum. The cross was a political act, the climax of a life of proclamation of the Kingdom of God.

It is not possible to make any sense of Jesus apart from this central and dominating theme of the Kingdom. The entire message of Jesus centres around the Kingdom of God, and this is especially true of the parables. The origins of the symbol of the Kingdom of God go back into ancient Near Eastern myths of God as King. In the Old Testament God is seen as victorious in the conflict with the monsters of chaos in creation, and with the demonic forces of political power in Egypt and Babylon. *Malkuth shamayim* refers to the concrete activity of God, ruling in the history of the world. So after the Exodus, Moses and the people of Israel sang 'The Lord will reign for ever and ever' (Exod. 15.18). But the theme of a *future* Kingdom of God to be established on earth derives from the prophets (see Mic. 2.12; 4.1–7; Isa. 24.21–3; 33.22; 52.7–10; Zeph. 3.14–20; Obad. 21, etc). It was from the prophetic movement that there arose the theme of the kingdom of God as the climax of the age, and the inauguration of a new age. The clearest evidence of Jewish hope in the time of Jesus is the Kaddish prayer of the Synagogue, possibly the basis of the Kingdom clause in the Lord's Prayer:

Magnified and sanctified be his great name in the world which

> he has created according to his will. May he establish his Kingdom in your lifetime, and in your days, and in the lifetime of all the house of Israel even speedily and at a near time.

In the Lord's Prayer, however, we pray 'Your Kingdom *come*'. The use of the word 'come' in reference to the Kingdom seems to be unique to Jesus. Normally in Jewish usage, the Kingdom of God is *established* or *appears:* what *comes* is the New Age. Jesus, in his preaching and prayer, unites the theme of the catastrophic Kingdom of God with that of the New Age of God's justice.

It is important to stress that the Kingdom, in the biblical understanding, is not an interior 'spiritual' presence, nor is it a hope for a wholly different order. It is to transform the face of the earth and of human history. The hope of the prophets was for the coming of a corporate society on earth in which men would beat their swords into ploughshares and their spears into pruning-hooks (Isa. 2.4), a society characterized by peace and non-violence (11.5–9), by feasting (25.6–8), and by an awareness of God's glory (40.3–5). The prophetic hope is for the proclaiming of the Year of Jubilee in which the land and its people are to enjoy freedom (Lev. 25; Isa. 61), and it is this hope which Jesus adopts as the basis of his ministry (Luke 4).

In the ministry of Jesus, it is claimed, the Kingdom has come. So what are the signs of its coming? First, the forces of evil have been overcome. Jesus says plainly 'If I by the Spirit [or 'finger' in Luke] of God cast out devils, then the Kingdom of God has come upon you' (Matt. 12.28; Luke 11.20). The conflict with Satan is fundamental in the account of the wilderness temptations, as well as in the subsequent casting out of devils. In Jesus' ministry Satan falls like lightning from heaven (Luke 10.18–19). Secondly, the miracles of Jesus manifest the presence of the Kingdom. It is in relation to the miracles that Jesus states that 'the Kingdom of Heaven has been taken by force' (Matt. 11.12), and proclaims 'Blessed are your eyes, for they see, and your ears, for they hear' (Matt. 13.16; Luke 10.23). Jesus' miracles are signs of the Kingdom, signs of *dunamis.* Thirdly, the preaching of the Gospel. Among the signs of the Kingdom listed in Jesus' reply to John the Baptist's inquiry is the fact that 'the poor have the Gospel preached to them' (Matt. 11.5). The law and the prophets were until John:

since that time the good news of the Kingdom of God has been preached (Luke 16.16). Fourthly, the Kingdom is present through the gift of salvation. The Kingdom is itself a gift (Luke 12.32) and is to be received as by a little child (Mark 10.15). And the enjoyment of the Kingdom is not reserved for the future. 'Blessed are the poor in spirit, for theirs *is* the Kingdom of heaven' (Matt. 5.3). Jesus says to Zacchaeus, '*Today* is salvation come to this house' (Luke 19.9). Finally, the most certain sign of the Kingdom is Jesus himself, the Messiah and Son of Man.

'Blessed are the poor.' 'The poor have the Gospel preached to them.' The theme of good news for the poor, the *anawim*, the little people, is crucial to Christianity. The history of the Jewish people is the history of God's choice of the little ones, the despised and rejected of the earth. So God chooses a small and insignificant tribe of slaves to be his chosen ones, and from this tribe, he chooses the least and lowliest of the sons of Jesse to be David the King. The God of Israel is emphatically on the side of the poor, against the mighty and strong ones of the world. So in the Law of Moses and in the prophets, it is the response to the poor—the alien, the orphan, the widow—which is the test of one's fidelity to God. And this too is the test of authentic prayer. The test comes out most clearly in Isaiah. God is not impressed, the prophet says, with the worship of Israel, with the 'vain offerings' and the incense, the 'calling of assemblies': 'When you spread forth your hands, I will hide my eyes from you: even though you make many prayers, I will not listen: your hands are full of blood' (Isa. 1.15). How then will this situation be changed so that God will hear the prayer? By ceasing to do evil and learning to do good: 'Seek justice, correct oppression; defend the fatherless, plead for the widow' (1.17). So the test of spirituality is a practical test, and particularly the test of attitude to the poor.

> It is you who have devoured the vineyard, the spoil of the poor is in your houses.
> What do you mean by crushing my people, by grinding the face of the poor? (3.14–15)

> Woe to those who decree iniquitous decrees, and the writers who keep writing oppression,
> to turn aside the needy from justice and to rob the poor of my

> people of their right, that widows may be their spoil, and that they may make the fatherless their prey! (10.1–2)

And this test is repeated throughout the prophets.

Christian spirituality is the spirituality of the Poor Man of Nazareth who took upon himself the form of a Servant. To know God is to do justice and plead the cause of the oppressed: to know God in Christ is to share in his work of establishing justice in the earth, and to share in his poverty and oppression. For in Christ, God becomes a little poor man, a member of an oppressed race, an exploited class, a colonized nation. God in Christ becomes poor and oppressed, making himself one with all the poor and oppressed peoples of the earth. And Christ in his ministry identifies himself with the prophetic mission, to 'set free those who are downtrodden' (Luke 4.19). To follow the way of the Kingdom is therefore to follow him who fed the hungry, healed the sick, befriended the outcast, and blessed the peacemakers.

That is why Matthew 25 is so crucial a passage for Christian spiritual life. In the judgement, Jesus tells us, the important question is going to be about whether one recognized Christ in the hungry, the naked, and the prisoner.

> Then the King will say to those at his right hand, 'Come, O blessed of my Father, inherit the Kingdom prepared for you from the foundation of the world; for I was hungry and you gave me food, I was thirsty and you gave me drink, I was a stranger and you welcomed me, I was naked and you clothed me, I was sick and you visited me, I was in prison and you came to me.' Then the righteous will answer him, 'Lord, when did we see thee hungry and feed thee, or thirsty and give thee drink? And when did we see thee a stranger and welcome thee, or naked and clothe thee? And when did we see thee sick or in prison and visit thee?' And the King will answer them, 'Truly, I say to you, as you did it to one of the least of these my brethren, you did it to me.' (Matt. 25. 34–40)

The Gospel demand is a practical demand. It is useless to worship the God who is present everywhere, and ignore his presence somewhere. To fail to recognize Christ in the hungry and thirsty, in the stranger and the naked, in the sick and the prisoner, is to deny the Incarnation. Equally prayer which does not have this direct human and social application is not Christian prayer.

The Kingdom calls us to service of Christ's little ones. But it also calls us to a new way of life, a new inner quality, a spirituality of gentleness and non-violence. To pray 'Your Kingdom come' is to pray that the life of the disciple who seeks that Kingdom may be transformed. The New Testament is clear that the way of the Kingdom is the way of non-violence, the way of suffering and the rejection of war, the way of the Cross. So the way of war and violence is superseded. Not that violence is evaded in Christ: there is still the wrath and the fury. But the Passion is the taking of this wrath into the person of the Sufferer. Christ treads the wine press of the wrath of God (Isa. 63.3) but it is his own blood which is shed, as he reconciles all things to himself. The Cross stands for the overthrow of evil through suffering love, through goodness. Gandhi saw that non-violence cannot work in those who do not have a living faith in the God of love. In fact, he would only allow a non-violent action which was proportionate with the degree of peace that the mind had achieved. Hence his remark to Nehru, 'If you have a sword in your heart, it is better to bring it out and use it.' When a Christian missionary asked Gandhi, 'Are your fasts a form of blackmail?', he answered, 'Yes, the same kind of blackmail that Jesus exerts upon you from the Cross.'

So when we pray that the Kingdom will come on earth, we are praying for a renewed world order, a new age of peace and justice. Paul stressed that entry into the Kingdom lay through much suffering (Acts 14.22), not the suffering of passive acquiescence but that of struggle within a fallen world. His hope was for the renewal of the whole creation and its deliverance from oppression and bondage (Rom. 8.19f). In the Letter to the Hebrews, Christ is seen as the high priest of 'the good things to come' (9.11) who has appeared 'at the end of the ages' (9.26). His Kingdom is one which cannot be shaken (12.28); unlike the present city which will not last, we seek the City which is to come (13.14). Again, in Revelation, the City of God is to come to earth and transform it. The redeemed will reign on earth (5.9–10). The New Jerusalem comes down from heaven to earth (21.1ff). The early Fathers insisted strongly against the heretics that the Kingdom of God included this earth and was not 'purely spiritual'. Irenaeus, for example, strongly attacks those who deny the coming of the Kingdom on earth.

> Inasmuch therefore as the opinions of certain persons are deceived by heretical discourses, they are both ignorant of God's dispensations, and of the mystery of the resurrection of the just, and of the earthly kingdom which is the beginning of incorruption, by means of which kingdom those who shall be worthy are accustomed gradually to partake of the divine nature; and it is necessary to tell them respecting those things, that it behoves the righteous first to receive the promise of the inheritance which God promised to the Fathers, and to reign in it, when they rise again to behold God in this creation which is renovated, and that the judgment should take place afterwards. For it is just that in the very creation in which they toiled or were afflicted, being proved in every way by suffering, they should receive the reward of their suffering, and that in the creation in which they were slain because of their love to God, in that they should be revived again; and that in the creation in which they endured servitude, in that they should reign.

Irenaeus goes on to say that the Kingdom will involve the renewal of the creation: it will be 'restored to its primeval condition' and 'the creation, having been renovated and set free, shall fructify with an abundance of all kinds of food, from the dew of heaven, and from the fertility of the earth'. (*Against Heresies*, 5.32–3)

The theme of the Kingdom of God as the renewal of the material order is closely linked with the Christian doctrine of Incarnation. For it is matter and flesh which is to be saved. The Incarnation of Christ witnesses to the sanctifying of flesh, to the fact that God, in the words of St Gregory Palamas, has 'made the flesh an inexhaustible source of sanctification'. Christian spirituality is flesh-based spirituality. So the Incarnation is not merely a doctrine; it is a principle of life, and it is the root of Christian prayer. All our prayer is centred upon and operates within the redeemed humanity of the Word made flesh. And in the Christian understanding of Incarnation, we can isolate four key elements.

The first is the insistence that God took flesh. The First Letter of John is most emphatic about the flesh of Christ as the only true basis of spirituality. John speaks of the divine *sperma* (seed: 1 John 3.9). He speaks of the Word which we have handled (1.1) and says that 'every spirit which confesses that Jesus Christ has come in the flesh (*en sarki*) is of God, and every spirit which does not confess Jesus is not of God' (4.2–3). The flesh is crucial. In the words of Tertullian (160–220), 'It is on the flesh that salvation hinges (*caro salutis est cardo*).' 'If Christ's being flesh is found to be a lie,' he says, 'then everything that was done in it was done falsely . . . God's entire work is subverted.' Irenaeus (130–200) put it in this way:

> If the flesh is not saved, then the Lord did not redeem us with his blood, the chalice of the Eucharist is not a share in his blood, and the bread which we break is not a share in his body. For the blood cannot exist apart from veins and flesh and the rest of the human substance which the Word of God truly became in order to redeem us.

This insistence on the reality of the flesh of Christ, and on the sacredness of human flesh, is an essential part of Christian belief. The flesh is to be saved. In the words of the fourteenth-century eastern writer St Gregory Palamas, 'The flesh also is transformed. Together with the soul, it is raised on high, and enjoys divine communion, becoming the domain and dwelling place of God.'

Secondly, Christians claim that he who took flesh is true God. For if this had not been so, salvation could not have occurred. So St Athanasius wrote:

> Man could not be deified if joined to a creature, or unless the Son were true God. Nor could man be brought into the Father's presence unless it had been his natural and true Word which had been put on the body.

Thirdly, the purpose of the Incarnation is the taking of manhood into God. We are to become, in the words of a late New Testament writer, sharers in the divine nature (2 Pet. 1.4). God became what we are to make us what he is. We have seen how central is the idea of *theōsis* (deification) in Catholic mysticism. But it all depends upon the Incarnation.

Finally, Christians insist that Christ is not some lesser divine being, a demi-god, but that he is equal to the Father. Within the Godhead there is equality. 'In this Trinity', says the Athanasian

Creed, 'none is afore or after another, none is greater or less than another.'

So the Christian view of Incarnation makes certain basic assumptions. It assumes that the flesh and matter are sacred, that they are not hostile, alien forces, opposed to God and godliness. It assumes that God is capable of relationship with matter, for if he is not capable, the Incarnation cannot have happened. It follows then that God and humanity cannot be wholly separate, and that the doctrine of God must be relevant to human life. For the true image of God is humanity. Against this orthodox teaching, however, the early heresies presented a series of alternative views of the relationship between God, matter, and humanity, all of which undermine Christian spirituality. The 'Monophysites' taught that there was only *one* nature in Christ, the divine: the purpose of worship therefore is to enable Christians to move *away* from the human to the divine. According to Canon Liddon, the nineteenth-century Anglican divine, Catholic worship is meant to 'enable the soul to mount to the unseen and the supersensuous'. So, on this view, there is an absolute disjunction between human and divine. Again, the Gnostics taught a doctrine of salvation through knowledge (*gnosis*), saw the world as divided into those who possessed the knowledge, the *illuminati*, the initiates, and those who did not, and saw matter as the source of evil. The Arian movement, which for a time became the official religion of the Roman Empire and has affected much of modern pseudo-Christianity, held that the essence of God could not be communicated. In this it raised all the central issues of Christian theology and spirituality, for it denied the possibility of relationships within the Godhead, between God and man, and between man and man.

The doctrine of the Incarnation therefore is of the greatest importance for Christian prayer. It is the basis both of Christian mysticism and of Christian social action. Through the Incarnation we experience God as very close to us. In the words of the carol:

> The Word in the bliss of the Godhead remains,
> Yet in flesh comes to suffer the keenest of pains.
> He is that he was and for ever shall be,
> But becomes that he was not for you and for me.

Julian of Norwich in the fourteenth century described God as *courteous* and *homely*, a unique merging of two concepts which, in medieval thought, would be seen as mutually incompatible. Courtesy, the quality proclaimed in *Sir Gawain and the Green Knight* and the literature of the knightly tradition, was the keynote of chivalry and implied a high social status. Homeliness, on the other hand, means intimacy, closeness, tenderness. Yet God, claims Julian, is both courteous *and* homely, the high and lofty one who becomes small and lowly. Through the Incarnation, God has become close to us, and this closeness is not simply 'spiritual'. Julian lays great stress on the presence of God in our physical nature too.

> For I saw with absolute certainty that our substance is in God, and moreover that he is in our sensuality too. The moment the soul was made sensual, at that moment was it destined from all eternity to be the City of God. And he shall come to that City and never quit it ... Our substance and sensuality together are rightly named our soul, because they are united by God. That wonderful city, the seat of our Lord Jesus, is the sensuality in which he is enclosed, just as the substance of our nature is enclosed in him, as with his blessed soul he sits at rest in the Godhead. (*Revelations of Divine Love*, Chapters 55 and 56)

So the human and the divine are not so rigidly separated as some Christians imagine. The human spirit and the Holy Spirit are not totally distinct. The Christian tradition speaks rather of the human spirit being taken up into God. So our limbs, according to St John Chrysostom, become the limbs and organs of the Holy Spirit, while St John of the Cross says that we breathe forth ourselves the Holy Spirit in this world. The human and the divine are all mixed up together, as the leaven of the Kingdom is mixed with the lump of human dough (Luke 13.20). Grace has only the raw material of our imperfect nature to work with.

The Christian therefore is essentially a materialist, and spirituality has a materialistic basis. Our spiritual life arises from our human life, for it is whole human persons who are made in God's image. And it is the whole of human nature which God has taken to himself. It is totally wrong then to see spirituality as a way of opting out of the human struggle. Worship and the respect for the material order are inseparable. During the iconoclastic controversy of the eighth century, St John of Damascus asserted the central place of matter in the Christian understanding.

> I do not worship matter, but I worship the Creator of matter, who for my sake became material, and accepted to dwell in matter, who through matter effected my salvation. I will not cease from reverencing matter, for it was through matter that my salvation came to pass.

So our prayer is based upon a relationship with God who took to himself human flesh. It is through the flesh that salvation comes.

Today meditation and 'spirituality' are being offered as commodities, as products of the social order, *but* as leisure-time activities which have no effect upon society. Spirituality has become 'privatised', banished to the private sector of life. Yet the future of our society is inextricably bound up with the future of the human spirit. The beginnings of our modern society were marked by the subversive contemplative spirit of St Thomas More. More's *Utopia* (1516) is still extraordinarily topical, and, already in the sixteenth century, he is critical of the new order for its monopolies, its rising prices, and its increased unemployment. The new economic order which emerged involved the dissolution of the monasteries and the rejection of monasticism as a perversion of human nature.

True spirituality is not a leisure-time activity, a diversion from life. It is essentially subversive, and the test of its genuineness is practical. Discipleship involves a real transformation of character. What are the fruits? The prophets saw the closest link between spirituality and ethics. So Ezekiel describes 'the man who is righteous and does what is just and right'.

> He oppresses no man, he returns the debtor's pledge, he never robs. He gives bread to the hungry, and clothes to those who have none. He never lends either at discount or at interest. He shuns injustice and deals fairly between man and man. (Ezek. 18.16–17)

It is, in fact, in the process of dispensing justice to the poor and needy that the knowledge of God is found. 'He judged the cause of the poor and needy: then it was well with him. Was not this to know me? says the Lord' (Jer. 22.16). And this link between the knowledge of God and social justice recurs throughout the prophetic writings. So Amos writes that God condemns those who sell the righteous for silver and the needy for a pair of shoes, and who turn aside the way of the meek (2.6–7). Without social justice, the worship of the people is condemned as vain.

> Even though you offer me your burnt offerings and cereal offerings, I will not accept them, and the peace offerings of your fatted beasts I will not look upon. Take away from me the noise of your songs; to the melody of your harps I will not listen. But let justice roll down like waters, and righteousness like an everflowing stream. (5.22–4)

As a result of the injustice and infidelity of Israel, Amos announces that there will be a famine in the land.

> 'Behold, the days are coming', says the Lord, 'when I will send a famine on the land; not a famine of bread, nor a thirst for water, but of hearing the words of the Lord. They shall wander from sea to sea, and from north to east; they shall run to and fro, to seek the word of the Lord, but they shall not find it.' (8.11–12)

Similarly, in Hosea, the prophet complains that there is a lack of faithfulness and kindness and knowledge of God in the land, and this is linked with the prevalence of stealing, murder, and so on (4.1–2). The people are being destroyed through lack of knowledge (4.6). The evil of worship without justice is again emphasized by the prophet Micah.

> With what shall I come before the Lord, and bow myself before God on high? Shall I come before him with burnt offerings, with calves a year old? Will the Lord be pleased with thousands of rams, with ten thousands of rivers of oil? Shall I give my first-born for my transgression, the fruit of my body for the sin of my soul? He has showed you, O man, what is good; and what does the Lord require of you but to do justice, and to love kindness, and to walk humbly with your God? (Micah 6.6–8)

But it is Isaiah who most vehemently denounces worship which is blind to social evil.

When you come to appear before me, who requires of you this trampling of my courts? Bring no more vain offerings; incense is an abomination to me. New moon and sabbath and the calling of assemblies—I cannot endure iniquity and solemn assembly. Your new moons and your appointed feasts my soul hates; they have become a burden to me, I am weary of bearing them. When you spread forth your hands, I will hide my eyes from you; even though you make many prayers, I will not listen; your hands are full of blood. Wash yourselves; make yourselves clean; remove the evil of your doings from before my eyes; cease to do evil, learn to do good; seek justice, correct oppression; defend the fatherless, plead for the widow. (Isa. 1.12–17)

Similarly, the New Testament teaches that love of the brethren is the way to the love of God, for it is impossible for us to love God whom we have not seen if we do not love the brother whom we have seen. The knowledge of God is a human knowledge. The Jews realized that we do not know God in himself but only in the process of obedience. When God revealed himself as Yahweh, the *Living* God, he revealed that it was in the process of *living*, and in that process alone, that he could be known. And in the Incarnation, God becomes a living Man. It is in the midst of human life that we grow in the life of prayer.

However, it is also true that the pursuit of a prayerful life of simple love and discipleship sets us in isolation from and opposition to the mainstream, mammon-directed culture in which we live. We become deserters from technocracy, disaffiliating ourselves from its power, rejecting its false values. To pray is to drop out in the most profound and positive sense. In the early centuries of the church, men and women of prayer lived their daily lives as part of one Christian community in contact with the pagan world. When Christianity became 'established' and 'respectable' (the Constantinian era), the movement to the desert began, not out of fear, but out of a desire to maintain the purity and revolutionary vision of the Gospel within a compromised church. Today, as the Constantinian era comes to its close, it is striking that the contemplatives are returning from the deserts to the cities, and are playing their part in the renewal of the church's life.

One of the greatest contemplatives of our time was Thomas

Merton, the Trappist monk from the Abbey of Gethsemani in Kentucky, who died on 10 December 1968, and in Merton's writing there is a good deal that will help to illuminate the connection between contemplative prayer and social criticism. Merton held that America, and the west generally, had become alienated from spiritual values by technology and the pursuit of power and wealth, and that only a renewal of contemplation could heal its sickness. When, several years after Merton's death, Daniel Berrigan made his famous statement that 'the time will shortly be upon us, if it is not already here, when the pursuit of contemplation becomes a strictly subversive activity', he was very close to Merton's thinking. But both Merton and Berrigan recognized that much contemporary spirituality was harmful and escapist. A spiritual quest which is concerned only with the private world of the individual, with the attainment of his own 'enlightenment', can simply become another resource of the culture, a commodity. To divide contemplation from prophecy is to damage and maybe destroy both.

Merton held that solitude and interior prayer were closely linked with the awakening of the social conscience. Like an earlier contemplative, Father Alfred Delp, a Jesuit who was imprisoned in Nazi Germany, he believed that liberation always begins on the plot of earth on which one stands. Delp had written in his prison meditations:

> Great issues affecting mankind have to be decided in the wilderness, in uninterrupted isolation and unbroken silence. They hold a meaning and a blessing, these great, silent, empty spaces that bring a man face to face with reality.

It is in solitude, in the depths of a person's own aloneness, that there lie the resources for resistance to injustice. On the other hand, a resistance which has not been wrought out of inner spiritual struggle must remain superficial or degenerate into fanaticism.

Merton saw that the spiritual life was the life of the whole person, and he rejected the smug self-assurance of the pious, who knew all the answers in advance, knew all the clichés of the inner life, and could defend themselves against all the demands of being fully human. He knew only too well the dangers of 'bogus interiority', the distortion of the inner life by which concentration on oneself becomes an evasion of risk and struggle. Bogus forms of contemplation, as manifested in the large number of meditation schools of dubious nature, are concerned with avoiding conflict and reducing tension. Merton however emphasized that Christian faith was a principle of struggle and questioning before it became one of certitude and peace. And this emphasis was most marked in his understanding of the desert as a place of struggle and purification (see Chapter 7). By 'the desert' Merton, along with Charles de Foucauld and the Little Brothers of Jesus, did not mean simply the literal physical desert, but the stripping down of the spiritual life to basics, to bare essentials, to nakedness of spirit. Merton once defined contemplation as 'the preference for the desert'. For the desert experience was an experience of solitude in which God appeared to be absent. It was the presence of conflict and struggle which distinguished true silence from false, for true silence is 'a repeated bending over the abyss'. Merton held that solitude and silence were essential to the common good, for it was in solitude that a man became fully awake. It is this wakefulness, this insight and enlightenment, which preserves religion from fanaticism, and Merton saw fanaticism as the greatest temptation of the modern age.

So for Merton the understanding of prayer is crucial to the understanding of social change. There is no split between spirituality and social responsibility. He sees prayer as 'a consciousness of man's union with God' and 'an awareness of one's inner self'. Self-knowledge, as all the mystics insist, is the beginning of sanctity, but it is only the beginning. There must be a movement beyond the self to God, a real transformation of consciousness. Spiritual progress therefore involves a recognition of this false consciousness and of the false self, and Merton links this with individualism which has dominated western theology and politics for several hundred years. This individualism, he claims, is primarily an economic concept with a pseudo-spiritual and moral facade, and is in fact sheer irresponsibility. In confronting this false consciousness, we begin the process of recovery of the divine image in man.

Merton's theology of prayer and his concern with social change both derived from his understanding of the nature of salvation as the taking of manhood into God, and his realization that the Incarnation was the basis of all true Christian mysticism and social action. Ironically, he died on the same day as Karl Barth to whom mysticism was highly suspect, though Barth, like Merton, saw that resistance to injustice derived from Christology. The monastic life, in Merton's view, was not a way of evading the Incarnation and the common life of humanity, but a specific way of sharing in that life. Monastic prayer was a deep confrontation with the alienation of modern man, and was thus particularly vital to the undermining of illusion and falsehood. Merton held that the unmasking of illusion belonged to the essence of the contemplative life. The monk, he claimed in a paper given at Bangkok on the day of his death, 'is essentially someone who takes up a critical attitude towards the contemporary world and its structures'.

It is not only in the monastic life, however, that one should expect to see the growth of a spirit of resistance. The development of contemplative prayer itself includes the development of doubt. Doubt is not the enemy of faith but its colleague. A heightened awareness and perception will bring with it an intensified level of doubt and distrust of conventional wisdoms and solutions, a radical questioning of established approaches. But to do this is to become a marginal person. Merton saw this very clearly. In 1968, describing the place of monks in the modern world, he said, 'In speaking for monks, I am really speaking for a very strange kind of person, a marginal person.' Monastic life is both affirmation and protest: its aim is liberation. Merton believed that if one penetrates, by detachment and purity of heart, to the inner secret of the ground of one's ordinary experience, one attains to a liberty which nobody can touch. Yet it was only the person who had fully attained his own spiritual identity who could live such a life of true freedom. In one of his instructions on prayer, Merton referred to the relationship of faith and doubt.

> The best way to pray is:stop. Let prayer pray within you, whether you know it or not. This means a deep awareness of our true inner identity. It implies a life of faith, but also of doubt. You can't have faith without doubt. Give up the business of suppressing doubt. Doubt and faith are two sides of the same thing. Faith will grow out of doubt, the real doubt. We don't pray right because we evade doubt. And we evade it by regularity and by activism. It is in these two ways that we create a false

identity, and these are also the two ways by which we justify the self-perpetuation of our institutions.

So the contemplative life, whether in the monastery or in the world, is concerned with the unmasking of illusion and false identity.

Solitude and solidarity are therefore inseparably linked. Solitude is essential, for it is in solitude that one attains a deepening of awareness of the world's needs. In solitude too one attains an identification with the sufferings of Christ in the world. This compassion comes out clearly in the Epilogue to Merton's *The Seven Storey Mountain* (1948). Here Christ addresses Merton in his solitude.

> Everything that touches you shall burn you.
> Do not ask when it will be,
> or where it will be,
> or how it will be.
> On a mountain or in a prison,
> or in a desert or in a concentration camp,
> or in a hospital or at Gethsemani.
> It does not matter.
> So do not ask me, because I am not going to tell you.
> You will not know, until you are in it.
> But you shall taste the true solitude of My anguish and of My Poverty.
> I shall lead you into high places of My joy and you shall die in Me.
> And find all things in My Mercy, which has created you for this end . . .
> that you may become the brother of God,
> and learn to know the Christ of the burnt men.

It is wrong to stress the virtues of compassion, love and sensitivity to people in Christ, and to ignore the New Testament's frequent warnings against blindness and lack of perception. It is more important to see clearly than to behave well, for action arises from vision. The contemplative who can stand back from a situation and see it for what it is is more threatening to an unjust social system than the frenzied activist who is so involved in the situation that he cannot see clearly at all.

But prayer is not merely subversive, though it is at least that: prayer is also political because it is involved with the process of changing the world. The Gospel and the Liturgy are concerned with the renewal of the material world, with the transformation of matter, with New Creation. This is not a new idea, the product of 'liberalizing' tendencies in the post-war period, as some would have us think. It is a very old idea, rooted in the Old Testament, in the Law and the Prophets, where the created order is the good creation of God and the sphere of God's activity.

But we need to clarify what we mean when we speak of 'the world'. Does not the Christian renounce 'the world' at Baptism? Is the Christian not called to be 'otherworldly', and doesn't St John say that 'the world is in the power of the evil one'? Is prayer not concerned with what Dr Edward Norman, the 1978 Reith Lecturer, called 'the ethereal qualities of immortality' rather than with the transformation of this world?

The tension between 'this-worldly' and 'otherworldly' concerns has been said to be the central paradox of Christianity, and part of this paradox arises from the fact that in the Bible the word 'world' is used in different senses. World, *kosmos*, can simply mean the universe (Matt. 13.35) or the organized human community (Matt. 5.14) or, as in the writings of St John, the fallen world order under the dominion of sin. Thus we read, 'My kingship is not of this world; if my kingship were of this world, my servants would fight, that I might not be handed over to the Jews; but my kingship is not from the world' (John 18.36). Or 'The reason why the world does not know us is that it did not know him' (1 John 3.1) and 'Do not wonder, brethren, that the world hates you' (3.13). It is in this sense that Baptism into Christ involves the renouncing of the world, because 'the world is very evil'. And yet the world is also seen as the good creation of God, the object of his love and continued concern, and the sphere of his redemptive work.

Thus in the Mosaic Law there is strong emphasis on the importance of the material world. The land belongs to God, and he is its only Landlord. (Gen. 1.1; Ps. 95.5; Deut. 10.14). It is from this basic assumption that all the complexities of land legislation derive —the teaching about the landmark, the condemnation of usury, and the symbols of the Year of Release and the Year of Jubilee (Lev. 25; Deut. 15). 'The profit of the earth is for all' (Eccles.

5.9), and it is in the midst of the earth that God works salvation (Ps. 74.12–14). It was against the overthrow of the Law with its concern for social justice and a right care of the earth that the prophetic protest was directed. The prophets are concerned more with the transformation than the preservation of the world. So in Second Isaiah, for example, the final salvation is seen as a second creation, and the drying up of the waters as the prelude to a cosmic redemption (Isa. 51.9–10). Earlier, Isaiah of Jerusalem had referred to the setting up of the mountain of the Lord within the earth. 'They shall not hurt or destroy in all my holy mountain; for the earth shall be full of the knowledge of the Lord as the waters cover the sea' (Isa. 11.9). Ezekiel speaks of the transforming of the desolate land into Eden (Ezek. 36.35). So the hope of the prophets is a hope for a renewed, resurrected world. The creation itself is seen in the context of the End. Unlike the pagan myths in which the creative cycle was ritually re-enacted each year, the Eden myth in the Old Testament was firmly rooted in history, and the new creation too was set within history, although going beyond it.

It is against this background of the prophetic hope for a new age that the teaching of Jesus about the Kingdom of God and the 'new commandment' of mutual love must be understood. In the opening chapters of Luke's Gospel, Mary, the mother of Jesus, proclaims her Magnificat in which she celebrates the fact that God has put down the mighty from their seats and has exalted the lowly, has filled the hungry with good things and sent the rich away empty (1.52–3). Jesus' own ministry begins with a proclamation of good news to the poor, the captives, the blind, and the oppressed (4.18–19). His teaching is strongly against the accumulation of possessions (12.15) and he urges his disciples to sell their possessions in order to win heavenly treasure (12.32–4). They cannot serve God and Mammon, he tells them (16.13). Against the idolatry of wealth Jesus points to a new social order based on service and humility. He is opposed to domination, and describes himself as one who has come to serve, not to be served.

Mutual service and mutual love: these were the hallmarks of the early Christian community, expressed in the two Greek words *diakonia* (service) and *koinonia* (common life). The believers had all things common (*koina*, Acts 2.44; 4.32) and they continued steadfastly in the apostles' doctrine and *koinonia* (2.42. 'Fellowship' is a very weak word to translate this term: it represents a concrete, visible communism. So Tertullian (165 A.D.) contrasted the 'fraternal stability of our community of goods' with the 'Roman system of individualism' which leads to disintegration. The early fathers are filled with descriptions of the apostolic communism. The *Didache*, one of the earliest Christian liturgical books, instructs believers to share everything with their brothers, 'for if you are sharers in the imperishable, how much more in the things that perish'. Similarly the Epistle of Barnabas says: 'You shall communicate in all things with your neighbour, you shall not call things your own; but if you are partakers in common of things which are incorruptible, how much more should you be of things which are corruptible.' The Epistle to Diognetus speaks of Christians as having 'a common table but not a common bed', while Justin Martyr says, 'Now we bring what we have into a common stock and communicate to everyone in need'.

There are many other examples of such testimony to the fact that the common life was a spiritual reality expressed in material terms. In the fourth century, St John Chrysostom looks back to the apostolic age as one of pentecostal sharing.

> It is not for lack of miracles that the Church is staid, it is because we have forsaken the angelic life of Pentecost, and fallen back on private property. If we lived as they did, with all things common, we should soon convert the whole world without any need of miracles at all. (Homily 25 on Acts)

For the essential pentecostal experience was seen as one of common life in the Spirit of the risen Lord. The new life of the Resurrection meant the dissolution of private property, the end of the old realm of death and selfishness, and the emergence of a new humanity. The early fathers look forward to a new age in which all wealth is shared wealth. So St Augustine says, 'You give bread to whoever is hungry, but it would be better if nobody was hungry and you gave to nobody.' His teacher, St Ambrose, had made the same point when he wrote:

> It was in common and for all, rich and poor, that the earth was created. Why then, O rich, do you take to yourselves the monopoly of owning land? Nature does not know the rich; it

> brings forth only the poor. It is not with your wealth that you give alms to the poor, but with a fraction of their own which you give back; for you are usurping for yourself something meant for the common good of all. The earth is for every one, not only for the rich.'

Or St Basil in similar vein said, 'Community of goods is a way of life more adequate than possession of private property, and it alone is in conformity with nature.'

The early fathers are full of this kind of language, testifying to the essentially social nature of their spirituality. It is often said that the early church was merely looking for the return of Christ and therefore showed no interest in social change. This is a serious over-simplification. What is abundantly clear both from the New Testament and from the writings of the early fathers is the fact that the early Christians saw themselves as part of a new creation, the 'age to come', whose powers were already at work. They were shaping a new pattern for the human community, a pattern of love and sharing, the pattern of the social life of God himself. 'Your Kingdom come, your will be done, *on earth as in heaven*' meant, literally, that the life-style of the Godhead was to be manifested within the human community. A contemporary Indian Christian, Samuel Rayan, has expressed it thus: 'New Testament spirituality is the spirituality of broken bread (our earth) and shared wine (a life of friendship).'

The Christian community thus witnesses to the life of the Kingdom, the life of God, not only in its preaching, but in its life. But this involves suffering, for *koinonia* in Christ is a sharing in his cross (Phil. 3.8–10). Our prayer can never therefore be purely individualistic. All prayer is Kingdom-centred because it is oriented towards the coming of the 'age to come', on earth as in heaven. All prayer is social, because it is rooted in *koinonia*, sharing, in the life of God. And all prayer is therefore political, because it is an essential element in the transformation of the world.

So Christian prayer is, in the deepest sense, political: in the deepest sense, not the superficial sense. Political depth and spirituality meet at the point where the inner revolution and the outer revolution are seen as one and indivisible. The fate of the soul is the fate of the social order. Worship celebrates the redeeming, liberating work of

God in Christ, and participates in that work. Worship becomes political in the superficial sense when it loses that rootedness in the work of God, and becomes a ritual celebration of the prevailing social and political values of the day. It becomes a ritual enactment of the status quo. In that sense political religion is dangerous and anti-Christian, and its most notorious recent manifestation was in Nazism. God is invoked to sanctify and justify the dominant political ideology. At the personal level, prayer becomes a way of reinforcing one's own status, needs and values. Thus the prayer of John Ward, sometime Member of Parliament for Weymouth.

> Oh Lord, thou knowest that I have lately purchased an estate in fee simple in Essex. I beseech thee to preserve the two counties of Middlesex and Essex from fire and earthquake; and as I have also a mortgage at Hertfordshire, I beg of thee also to have an eye of compassion on that county, and for the rest of the counties, thou mayest deal with them as thou art pleased. Oh Lord, enable the bank to answer all their bills and make all my debtors good men, give a prosperous voyage and safe return to the Mermaid sloop, because I have not insured it, and because thou hast said, 'The days of the wicked are but short', I trust in thee that thou wilt not forget thy promise, as I have an estate in reversion which will be mine on the day of the death of the profligate young man Sir J. L . . . g. Keep my friends from sinking, preserve me from thieves and housebreakers, and make all my servants so honest and faithful that they may always attend to my interest and never cheat me out of my property night or day.

Ward's prayer strikes us as funny and eccentric, but he is doing no more than personalizing the 'preservative' character of much political religion, expressed in liturgical forms and ceremonial functions.

It is not in this sense that we call prayer political. On the contrary, the worship of the crucified Jesus by the early Christians was both an alignment with one killed for sedition, and also an act of rebellion against the Roman power. The impact of the Christian Gospel on the politics of the Roman Empire was to subvert them, as the early heretic Celsus realized very well. He wrote:

> Since demons rule in the world, anyone who wishes to live there

> must show them veneration and submit to their ordinances. And therefore one must also submit to rulers, even if they demand that one takes the oath in their name. Through this belief Rome grew great, and it is not right to reject their gods and accept a god who is not even able to give his followers a patch of earth or a home, so that they have to slink about secretly in constant fear.

Celsus accused the early Christians of *stasis*, rebellion, for, through their irreligiousness, they were introducing revolt into the heavenly realm amongst the gods, *and therefore* into the religio-political world on earth whose stability and order corresponded to that of the heavens. Their worship was subversive of the stable order.

Christian action arises from, and is sustained by, Christian worship and prayer. In the Church of England, there is a long tradition in which the Eucharistic worship of the church has been seen as the basis of social action and social criticism. So Father Adderley, writing of his friend Stewart Headlam, said that for Headlam 'the Mass was the weekly meeting of rebels, a society of rebels against a Mammon-worshipping world-order'. Headlam, the rebellious curate of Bethnal Green in the 1870s, is in fact a good example of someone who saw the closest link between the sacraments and social change. He described the Eucharist as 'the feast of National Emancipation', 'the Great Emancipator's Supper', 'the service which tells of brotherhood, solidarity, co-operation'. Headlam also saw a close link between the sanctifying of bread and wine in the Christian Liturgy, and the sanctifying of human work and pleasure in the world. So he wrote:

> I hold it as an eternal truth that the Incarnation and Real Presence of Jesus Christ sanctifies all human things, not excluding human passion, mirth and beauty, and in this firm conviction I am constantly strengthened by the fact that so many regular and devout communicants both here and elsewhere enjoy heartily the drama, music and dancing.

Headlam's colleague, Charles Marson, whose book on the church is significantly called *God's Co-operative Society*, wrote similar words:

> Sacramentalism in the doctrine of the Lord's Supper definitely implies that the fellowship of the altar becomes null and void

unless that principle of sharing is carried away from the altar into the human fellowship of the world in which that altar is placed.

But it was Conrad Noel (1869–1942) and the Catholic Crusade which formed around him at Thaxted in Essex who most vividly expressed in action and in vigorous polemic the politically revolutionary character of Christian worship and prayer. In 1919 Noel wrote a small pamphlet entitled *Uplifting the Son of Man as the God of Justice in our Midst, Being notes on the spiritual and legal bearings of Processions of the Host*. He wrote:

> In Thaxted the little community which worships at the Parish Church has made some attempt to recover that personal devotion and revolutionary zeal which are equally necessary to the reality and wholeness of the Faith. In Processions of the Host . . . one may find a living illustration of this union of ideas, and a demonstration of the fact that wherever our Lord is present to do battle with the powers of the world, he meets with the same furious opposition which darkened his path in Galilee. Hearing that there was to be just such an opposition to our Procession—arising not from simple Evangelicals, but from rowdies of a neighbouring town backed by four or five residents from whom our movement had already received more violent opposition in the matter of Social Justice—we were the more determined to lift up our Lord in the public ways as the God of Justice and Comradeship. In face of the threat of our opponents that the Blessed Sacrament should never return to the church again, we remembered that as our Lord met without fear or shame the scoffs and threats of his enemies in Palestine, so now he would have his followers bear him aloft amidst the Hosannas of his friends and the curses of his foes, for 'I, if I be lifted up, will draw all men unto me'.

To Noel, worship and struggle went hand in hand, for they were part of the process of bringing in the new world. To one Anglo-Catholic priest who felt that worship and polemics did not go well together, Noel wrote:

> Our Lady who exults in the Holy War in which the mighty are dragged down from their seats will, I doubt not, accept our reparations . . . You people are so refined and gentlemanly: there

> is no fire and no challenge about you . . . You would have been unhappy amid the 'vulgar' theological fights (sometimes with fists) of the early Christians, or in the blood and thunder period of the Blessed Martyr of Canterbury.

All our prayer, all our worship, is within the struggle of the Suffering Lamb of God, faced with the destructive forces of the old world. We pray with our vision of the coming Kingdom of justice, love and peace before us. It is this Kingdom which is anticipated in the Christian Eucharist, the Breaking of the Bread, to which we shall now turn.

4

Prayer and communion

> Give us today our daily Bread. (Matt. 6.11)
>
> We ask then that our bread, which is Christ, be given to us daily, so that we who abide and live in Christ may not cut ourselves off from his grace and his body.
>
> ST CYPRIAN

> Blessed are you, Lord God of all creation. Through your goodness we have this bread to offer.

So begin the offertory prayers of the Roman Mass. The Christian Eucharist or Mass depends upon the doctrine of Creation. It is because the created world is *sacramental* that we can have sacraments in the Christian Church. What does that mean? It means that God reveals himself and communicates himself through the created world, through matter. The divine glory is seen through the material creation. The seventeenth-century Anglican writer Thomas Traherne said:

> You never enjoy the world aright till the sea itself floweth in your veins, till you are clothed with the heavens and crowned with the stars, and perceive yourself to be the sole heir of the whole world, and more than so, because others are in it who are everyone sole heirs, as well as you.

According to the nineteenth-century liberal thinker Harnack, the early Christians understood a sacrament to mean 'anything sensuous whereby something holy might be thought or enjoyed'. The word came to mean 'an outward and visible sign of an inward and spiritual grace'. But the sign does more than represent, it actually *effects* what it signifies. A cup symbolizes drinking. A red flag symbolizes danger. But a facial expression or a warm hug is more than a symbol: it is a sacrament, for it expresses and conveys the personality behind it. The specifically Christian sacraments are not freak interruptions of the natural order. All reality is sacramental. As the eastern Orthodox spiritual writers say, the world is a sacrament.

The poets and visionaries, Christian and non-Christian, have seen the world and natural things as sacramental. So Wordsworth spoke of flowers which suggested thoughts that lie too deep for tears; Tennyson spoke of the flower in the crannied wall as microcosm of God and man; Roden Noel of God's holy sacrament of spring, and Kingsley of the wayside sacraments of our hedgerows. All sacraments, whether of nature or of grace, derive from the one great sacrament of Creation, for the universe is the form in which the beauty of God's mind manifests itself. The sacraments of sun, moon, sea and earth, bird and beast, are completed by the sacrament of man, the climax of the creative process, the image of God himself. The sacramental principle, the conveying of spirit through matter, runs through the entire universe. So Teilhard de Chardin, in his profoundly moving book *Hymn of the Universe* speaks of 'the whole earth my altar'.

It is within this created, sacramental, God-revealing world that the church is placed. The New Testament speaks of the church as the *pleroma* (fullness) of Christ. Christ is the great High Priest who, by offering his blood, has redeemed us, and the church shares in his priesthood. There in Christ is the perfect sacrament of God: he is the perfect Man who perfectly images God. So if Creation is the first fundamental sacrament, the second is the Incarnate Lord, and the third is the church, derived from Christ, the extension of the Incarnation, or, as Irenaeus calls the church, the Son of God. He writes:

> The church is the fountain of the living water that flows to us from the heart of Christ. Where the church is, there is the Spirit of God, and where the Spirit of God is, there is the church and all grace.

All our prayer takes place within the context of the church and of its *catholicity*. The word 'catholic' tends nowadays to be used to mean 'universal' as if it were a geographical or statistical notion. But it comes from the Greek *kath' holou* which denotes inner wholeness and fullness. The church is a symbol of the recreated world.

As the church is placed within the created universe, so the

Eucharist, the Breaking of the Bread, the Mass, is placed within the church, and is the centre of its life and common prayer. The Christian Eucharist is the culminating point both of the action by which God sanctifies the world in Christ, and of the worship which the human family offers to God through Christ. From its earliest days the church has linked the Eucharist with creation. St Irenaeus speaks of it as 'the first fruits of his own creation'. Bread, 'an element of creation', and wine, 'which is of the same creation as ourselves', are offered 'as the first fruits of his own gifts under the new covenant' (*Against Heresies*, 4.17).

To understand the Christian Eucharist we need to look back to the worship of Israel. The life and spirituality of Israel centred around the great liberating event of the Exodus from Egypt, and this great event was annually celebrated and re-enacted in the Passover. The day of Passover was to be celebrated from generation to generation as a *memorial*, a 'feast to the Lord' (Exod. 12.14). It was a sacrificial meal, a solemn recalling of the mighty act of God in the deliverance of his people, but also a reliving of the Exodus experience. The Hebrew word translated 'memorial' is *zikkaron* and means far more than 'remembrance'. It means rather a liturgical celebration in which the great saving acts of the past are relived as present reality.

> And you shall tell your son on that day, 'It is because of what the Lord did for me when I came out of Egypt.' And it shall be to you as a sign on your hand, and as a memorial between your eyes, that the law of the Lord may be in your mouth; for with a strong hand the Lord has brought you out of Egypt. (Exod. 13.8–9)

As the Jews celebrated the Passover ritual, these words were used:

> Blessed art thou, O Lord, our God, King of the earth, who hast given to thy people Israel this season of festivity for joy and for a memorial (zikkaron).

As the food was eaten, the Jews relived the experience of deliverance from Egypt; they were one with their forefathers in a sacramental mystery. A lamb was to be taken, a lamb unblemished. On the fourteenth day of the month it was to be killed and roasted.

> They shall eat the flesh that night, roasted; with unleavened bread and bitter herbs they shall eat it ... In this manner you shall eat it: your loins girded, your sandals on your feet, and your staff in your hand; and you shall eat it in haste. It is the Lord's Passover. (Exod. 12.8,11)

This experience of Exodus and Passover is the essential background to the Christian understanding of Cross and Eucharist. Christ our Passover, says St Paul, is sacrificed for us (1 Cor. 5.7). Christ is seen in the New Testament as the fulfilment of the sacrifices of Israel. What does this mean?

To see how the Christian church used the theme of sacrifice as a way of both talking about and celebrating the great act of salvation wrought by God in Christ, we need to look at the way in which Christ is actually described. The language used is sacrificial language. First, Jesus is seen as the Paschal Lamb (1 Cor. 5.7; 1 Pet. 1.19), the unblemished lamb offered at the Passover. Secondly, he is seen as a sin offering. On the Day of Atonement, once a year, the High Priest entered the Holy of Holies in order to cleanse the community of Israel. The Letter to the Hebrews speaks thus of Christ:

> Nor was it to offer himself repeatedly, as the High Priest enters the Holy Place yearly with blood not his own; for then he would have had to suffer repeatedly since the foundation of the world. But as it is, he has appeared once for all at the end of the age to put away sin by the sacrifice of himself. (Heb. 9.25–6)

In Romans 3.25 St Paul describes Jesus as a *hilastērion*, translated variously as 'expiation' or 'propitiation'. In the Greek version of the Old Testament this word is used of the lid of the Ark or mercy seat which was sprinkled with blood on the Day of Atonement. It was the place where the mercy of God was supremely manifested. So Jesus is explicitly described as the means of removal of sin using the imagery of the Day of Atonement. Thirdly, Jesus is seen as the scapegoat—'he himself bore our sins in his body on the tree' (1 Pet. 1.24). This image comes from Leviticus 16.22 where the scapegoat, loaded with the sin of the people, 'shall bear all their iniquities upon him to a solitary land'. So St Paul says that Jesus 'was made sin' for us (2 Cor. 5.21). Fourthly, Jesus is seen as the sacrifice which brings in the covenant between God and the people. So at the Eucharist he says that he will not drink again of the fruit of the vine until the day when he drinks it in the Kingdom (Mark 14.24). St Peter refers to the sprinkling of his blood (1 Pet. 1.2), again recalling the act of Moses, and this symbol is repeated in Hebrews 9.19.

Finally, Jesus is the Lamb of God who takes away the sin of the world (John 1.29). This is in some ways the most interesting title of all because it does not seem to come straight from any one Old Testament symbol. The Passover lamb, for instance, did not take away sin. In this idea there seems to be a mingling of several themes into one. Probably the main source for it is Isaiah 53.7: 'Like a lamb that is led to the slaughter ... so he opened not his mouth.' For that passage ends: 'Yet he bore the sin of many, and made intercession for the transgressors' (53.12). What seems to be happening here is that the stricken, slaughtered servant of Isaiah 53, compared to a lamb, is being interpreted in the light of the Passover sacrifice.

Much more could be said about the sacrificial way in which the work of Jesus is seen in the New Testament, but the essential point is that his work of salvation, and specifically his death, is seen in terms of the Jewish rituals of sacrifice. He is seen as both the pure spotless offering of the Day of Atonement *and* the scapegoat who takes away sins. He is both pure and clean, the one without sin, and the one who became sin for us, who bore our sins in his own body to the tree. He is both sacrificial lamb and victorious king: dying as the Paschal Lamb at Passover time, yet reigning as King from the tree of glory. And in the Eucharist, the memorial of his body and blood, the new covenant, all this is celebrated and relived by the Christian community: the unleavened bread of the Exodus, the outpoured blood of the covenant, the marriage supper of the Lamb, the anticipation of the Kingdom. Let us then look at the origins of the Eucharist in relation to Jesus' impending death and sacrifice.

The Last Supper took place on the night before Jesus died. He took bread and wine, blessed them, and said: 'Take, eat: this is my body which is given for you ... This is my blood of the new covenant which is shed for you ... Do this in remembrance (*anamnesis*) of me.' This language would have been familiar to the disciples, for it was the same sacrificial language of the Jewish liturgy. 'Do this in remembrance of me' or 'for my memorial' means, not a simple mental remembering, but a recalling, a reliving, as in the Passover experience. Not only the word *anamnesis* but even the Greek word for 'do' has sacrificial connotations, for to do is to offer. But more important, the whole context of the meal, eaten at Passover time, and possibly in the context of the Passover meal itself, was sacrificial. The first three gospels say that the Last Supper took place on 'the first day of unleavened bread' (Matt. 26.17; Mark 14.12; Luke 22.7), while St John puts it a day earlier, 'before the feast of the Passover' (13.1) and says that the trial occurred at 'the preparation of the Passover' (19.14). In John's account then the death of Jesus occurs at the time the Passover lambs were slain. The question of whether the Last Supper was a Passover is an important one which has occupied scholars a good deal, but it is not our concern here. The point is that the whole drama of the Passion and Death occurred within, and was interpreted in the light of, the celebration of Passover: Christ the Paschal Lamb was sacrificed. And the Eucharist was to be the proclamation, the setting forth, of his death until his coming again (1 Cor. 11.26). The Eucharist is the Christian Passover, as the redemption wrought by Christ is seen as a new Exodus.

From the earliest days Christians have seen the work of redemption as an Exodus. Jesus the Messiah is the new deliverer, the new Moses. St Matthew in his arrangement of his Gospel certainly views Jesus as a new Moses, bringing the new Law. In the last book of the New Testament, Revelation, the redeemed sing 'the song of Moses and the Lamb' (15.3). In 1 Corinthians St Paul explains that the Exodus story was written for the present age, for Christians 'upon whom the ends of the world have come' (10.6), and he immediately goes on to speak of the Eucharist. This Exodus theme recurs in many Christian hymns. Thus at Easter we sing:

> The Lamb's high banquet we await
> In snow-white robes of royal state,
> And now, the Red Sea's channel past,
> To Christ our Prince we sing at last.

The Church of Sweden says this in its Collect for Easter Day:

> Almighty and Eternal God, who didst deliver thy people out of Egypt by the hand of thy servant Moses, and didst command

> them to observe the Passover annually and eat the Paschal Lamb: bring us also, O heavenly Father, out of the spiritual Egypt, and make us partakers of the true Paschal Lamb, thy Son, Jesus Christ, our Lord ...

The early church used the language of Passover about Christ and the Eucharist. So Hippolytus of Rome (*c.* 170–236) speaks of 'the cosmic and universal Pasch', while St Cyril of Jerusalem in the fourth century says:

> There we have Moses sent by God into Egypt; here we have Christ sent by the Father into the world. There the task is to free the oppressed people from Egypt; here to rescue men tyrannised in the world by sin. There the blood of the lamb wards off the destroyer; here the Blood of the true Lamb, Jesus Christ, puts the demons to flight.

Hippolytus too links the Passover with the celebration of the Eucharist: 'You will eat in a house: there is one synagogue, there is one house, there is one church, in which the true Body of Christ is consumed.'

At the Passover, unleavened bread (*azymes*) was to be used. (The feast of unleavened bread was originally distinct from Passover: see Exod. 23.15; Lev. 23.6–8, etc). St Paul speaks of unleavened bread in 1 Corinthians 5.7–8 in his interpretation of Christ as the new Passover Lamb, while Hippolytus writes:

> Let the Jews then eat the azymes for seven days, let them strive on during the seven ages of the world. But as for us, Christ our Pasch is sacrificed, and we have received a new paste for his holy mixing.

The Eucharist then is the celebration of, the dramatic reliving of, the great and saving mystery of Christ's work of deliverance.

The Eucharist was central to the life and prayer of the early church. One of the earliest accounts we have of the primitive Eucharist comes from Justin Martyr who died around 165. He writes:

> When we have thus washed a man who has accepted the teaching and has made his profession of faith, we bring him to those who are called brethren, where they are assembled, to offer prayers

> in common for ourselves, for the person thus illuminated, and for all others everywhere, with might and main: that we, who have learnt the truth, may be granted to prove, through our deeds also, good citizens and keepers of the commandments, that we may obtain eternal salvation.
>
> At the end of prayers we embrace each other with a kiss. Then bread and wine is brought to the President of the brethren, and a cup of water and wine: this he takes and offers praise and glory to the Father of all, through the name of his Son and of the Holy Spirit: and he gives thanks at length for our being granted these gifts at his hand. When he has finished the prayers and the thanksgiving, all the people present give their assent, with *Amen*, a Hebrew word signifying 'So be it'. When the President has given thanks, and all the people have assented, those whom we call deacons give a portion of the bread, over which thanksgiving has been offered, and of the wine and water, to each of those who are present, and they carry them away to those who are absent.
>
> This food is called Eucharist with us, and only those are allowed to partake who believe in the truth of our teaching, and have received the washing for the remission of sins and for regeneration: and who live in accordance with the directions of Christ. We do not receive these gifts as ordinary food or ordinary drink. But as Jesus Christ our Saviour was made flesh through the Word of God and took flesh and blood for our salvation: in the same way the food over which thanksgiving has been offered through the Word and prayer which we have from him—the food by which our blood and flesh are nourished through its transformation—is, we are taught, the flesh and blood of Jesus who was made flesh.

There is now a good deal of evidence from the early Christian centuries about how these Christians worshipped. Pliny, writing of Christians in Bithynia around 112, says that they met before dawn for devotion and instruction, and later for a common meal. Irenaeus (130–200) says of the Eucharist:

> Giving directions to his disciples to offer to God the first fruits of his own created things ... he (Jesus) took bread and gave thanks and said, This is my Body. And the cup likewise ... he confessed to be his Blood, and taught the new Oblation of the

> New Covenant; which the church, receiving from the Apostles, offers to God throughout all the world.

He goes on to stress that 'the bread which is produced from the earth, when it receives the Invocation of God, is no longer common bread, but Eucharist, consisting of two realities, the earthly and the heavenly'. For the early Christians then this Eucharist was the focal point of all their life and prayer: and throughout the ages it has remained so. What do we do when we celebrate the Eucharist?

There are four actions, which follow from the actions of Jesus: he took, he blessed, he broke, and he gave. First, he took: the action which we now call the Offertory. Bread and wine are taken and offered, and with them we are offered. In many churches today the bread and wine are carried from the back of the church by the people and placed on the altar. They are the offerings of the people, offerings taken from the earth and from the work of humankind. This bread is not some special religious bread: it is bread which has been through the industrial process, bread which has been manufactured by men. For lack of bread and as a result of maldistribution of bread, people starve and go hungry. It is this bread, bread tainted with human sin and selfishness and greed, which is offered at the Offertory. It brings with it the stain and injustice of the world from which it comes. Similarly this wine is real wine, the same wine which leads to drunkenness, alcoholism and death. It is worth looking a little more closely at this point.

There are many references to wine in the Old Testament, including some one dozen cases of drunkenness. The Wisdom literature in particular warns against the use of wine. Yet Jesus at the Last Supper uses wine as the sacramental foretaste of the life of his Kingdom. In the Jewish ritual, wine was to be drunk on the Sabbath and other festivals, and four cups on Passover eve. Jesus goes further, and links the wine with his covenant of blood: it is 'the blood of the covenant' (Mark 14.24). Wine in Hebrew was called 'the blood of the grape' and Passover wine was always red. Also Jesus links the wine with the coming feast in the Kingdom of God. Now the 'cup of blessing', taken after the meal, was the third of the four Passover eve cups. The fourth cup was traditionally associated with the coming Kingdom, the new age. And it is wine, real wine, not unfermented grape juice, which is used: the church is emphatic that a Eucharist celebrated with something other than alcoholic wine is not valid.

G. K. Chesterton once contrasted the Rubaiyat of Omar Khayyam with the Gospel of Christ. Christ, he says, made wine not a medicine but a sacrament, while Omar made it not a sacrament but a medicine. Omar drinks to drown his sorrow, Christ to celebrate his joy. Omar says, 'Drink, for you know not whence you come, nor why. Drink, for you know not when you go, nor where. Drink, because the stars are cruel and the world as idle as a humming top. Drink, because there is nothing worth trusting, nothing worth fighting for. Drink, because all things are lapsed into a base equality and an evil peace.' Christ, by contrast, says, 'Drink, for the whole world is as red as this wine with the crimson of the love and wrath of God. Drink, for the trumpets are blowing for battle, and this is the stirrup cup. Drink, for this is my Blood of the new Testament that is shed for you. Drink, for I know of whence you come, and why. Drink, for I know of when you go, and where.' The wine is the wine of rejoicing and of pleasure, the sign of exhilaration and of the Spirit. So St Ambrose begins one of his hymns: 'Laeti bibamus sobriam/Ebrietatem spiritus—' 'Let us joyfully drink of the sober drunkenness of the spirit.' So Canon Stanley Evans once described a Christian as 'a controlled drunk, purposively intoxicated with the joy of the life which is perpetually created by God himself'.

So at the Offertory of the Eucharist we offer bread and wine. In bread are contained the elements of earth, air, water, and fire, combined with the art and skill of the sower, reaper, and baker. The wine too is the fruit of the earth and of human work—the vine cut back in the winter so that it can burst forth into fruit, the symbol of sacrifice and joy, the wine of merriment. In offering these substances we offer not only the fruits of earth, for they are not wheat and grapes, but also the results of human work, and with them we offer our lives. As St Augustine said, 'There are you on the paten, there are you in the chalice.'

And yet in a sense the bread and wine offered at the Offertory are not ordinary. Of course, they bring with them their history of production and their involvement in the fallen world. But already, through the action of taking and offering, they are contained within the offering of the humanity of Christ, for they are a gift of the church, the Body of the risen Christ. So the late Frederick Hastings Smyth, a Catholic socialist of great influence in America, wrote of the Offertory in this way: 'The bread and wine at the Offertory set forth structures in history which have been brought out of the fallen world into the first stage of its redemption.' The church, in this act, is being presented by Christ to himself. St Paul expresses it well. Christ, he says, loved the church so much and gave himself for it, that he might sanctify and cleanse it with the washing of water (that is, Baptism) that he might *present it to himself*, a glorious church, not having spot or wrinkle. (Eph. 5.25–7)

Jesus took bread and wine, and so do we, offering with them the whole of human labour and human pleasure. We are offered not just our 'spiritual lives' but our total selves, our intellects, our sexuality, our physical defects, our psychological hang-ups, our spots, our warts, and our madness. What is not assumed cannot be healed. Blessed are you, Lord God of all creation. Through your goodness we have this person to offer, which the womb of woman has given, and human hands have influenced, shaped, and damaged. It will become the Body of Christ.

The second action of the Eucharist is the Great Thanksgiving, the Eucharistic Prayer, the 'Canon of the Mass'. Jesus blessed: and the central act of the Christian liturgy is the blessing invoked upon this bread and wine. The Eucharistic Prayer begins with an act of praise (the Preface) which reaches its climax in the hymn Holy, Holy, Holy, in which we join with the whole company of heaven. As St John Chrysostom says: 'The angels surround the priest. The whole sanctuary and the space around the altar are filled with the heavenly powers to honour him who is present on the altar.' And from the Sanctus we move to the prayer that the Holy Spirit may descend, the prayer which is known as the Epiclesis. Like the Sanctus hymn itself, it is of great antiquity. St Cyril of Jerusalem says: 'After we have sanctified ourselves with the Trisagion, we pray God to send his Holy Spirit down on the offerings so that he may make the bread his Body and the wine his Blood.' Earlier still, the Liturgy of Hippolytus of Rome prays: 'Send down, we pray, Lord, your Holy Spirit on the sacrifice of the community: gather it, unite it, and grant to all the holy people who are its members to be filled with the Holy Spirit.'

In our modern Eucharistic rites the invocation of the Spirit is seen as central to the Eucharistic Prayer. So in the Series Three liturgy of the Church of England we pray: 'Grant that by the power of your Spirit these gifts of bread and wine may be to us his Body and his Blood,' and later we ask God to 'Renew us by your Spirit, inspire us with your love, and unite us in the Body of your Son, Jesus Christ our Lord.' In Eucharistic Prayer 2 of the Roman Mass also we pray: 'Let your Spirit come upon these gifts to make them holy, so that they may become for us the Body and Blood of our Lord Jesus Christ' and 'May we who share in the Body and Blood of Christ be brought together in unity by the Holy Spirit.'

It is the transforming power of the Holy Spirit which brings about the change, changing bread and wine into the Body and Blood of Christ, and changing human beings into his risen Body, sharers in his life. A recent Anglican-Roman Catholic document, the Agreed Statement on the Eucharist (1971), expressed it thus:

> In the eucharistic celebration we anticipate the joys of the age to come. By the transforming action of the Spirit of God, earthly bread and wine become the heavenly manna and the new wine, the eschatological banquet for the new man: elements of the first creation become pledges and first fruits of the new heaven and the new earth.

So bread and wine, and also human persons, are transformed, and in this action the Eucharist sums up and expresses the whole of Christian life and prayer. For in all life, the sanctifying power of the Spirit is fundamental. Unless the Spirit falls in flame, there is no life. All prayer, like all Eucharistic celebrations, is the work of the transforming Spirit. Our part is Offertory: God consecrates and transforms. So the Eucharistic Prayer is, in the words of the Roman Missal, a 'prayer of thanksgiving and sanctification'.

The Eucharistic Prayer is the centre of all Christian prayer, the centre of all liturgy, the centre of our common life together, and it is therefore extremely important that this Great Prayer, as it is sometimes called, should express as fully and completely as possible the beliefs and intentions of the church in this central act of its life. The Eucharist is the centre of the church's worship, and the Eucharistic Prayer is the centre of the Eucharist. In the Eucharist the sacrifice of Christ, his work of redemption, is made present and active. What is this sacrifice, and in what sense can we call the Eucharist a sacrifice?

Sacrificial language has been applied to the Christian Eucharist from the second century onwards, for the sacrifice of Christ and the Eucharistic Memorial have always been seen as going together. They are not two separate sacrifices, nor is the latter a repetition of the former, as so many Protestant writers in the past have thought: they are the same sacrifice. The Eucharist is Christ, present and active now in the fullness of his redeeming work. And that fullness does not simply mean the Cross but the whole work of God in Christ from his Incarnation through the Cross to his Resurrection, Ascension and the pouring out of the Holy Spirit on the church. St John Chrysostom expressed it by saying: 'We do not offer a different sacrifice like the high priest of old, but we ever offer the same. Or rather we offer the *anamnesis* of the sacrifice.'

The early Christian Fathers speak of the Eucharist as the new sacrifice of which the earlier sacrifices were simply types and shadows: the Eucharist however is the sacrifice of the last days. The sacrifice of Christ includes not only his death but all that contributed to it, and culminates in his resurrection and ascension. The New Testament nowhere speaks of the 'sacrifice of the cross' and does not equate sacrifice with death, for the essential priestly work of intercession continues in the heavens. 'He holds his priesthood permanently because he continues for ever. Consequently he is able to save those who draw near to God through him, since he always lives to make intercession for them' (Heb. 7.24–5). Again the same writer says that 'we have an altar whereof they have no right to eat who serve the tabernacle' (13.10). The altar mentioned here cannot mean the cross since it was not there that the blood of sacrifice was offered: crucifixion was in any case a bloodless form of death. Rather Jesus entered once into the Holy Place, taking with him his own blood, and thus securing an eternal redemption (9.12).

The Greek word *thusia* (sacrifice) was applied to the Eucharist as early as the Didache (about 100 A.D.) and by Justin Martyr (about 150 A.D.). St Cyril of Alexandria in the fifth century expressed it in this way:

> We proclaim the death, in the flesh, of the only begotten Son of God, Jesus Christ, and acknowledge his return to life from the

dead and his ascension into heaven, and as we do this we perform the bloodless sacrifice in the churches: thus we approach the consecrated gifts of the sacrament, and are sanctified by partaking of the holy flesh and the precious blood of Christ, the Saviour of all.

The sacrifice of Christ is not simply his death on the cross: if it were, the only way in which we can enter into it is by remembering it or repeating it. But the sacrifice is not simply a past event. It is his total work of redemption—life, death, resurrection and ascension. Charles Wesley's hymn expresses it well:

Victim Divine, thy grace we claim
While thus thy precious death we show;
Once offered up, a spotless Lamb,
In thy great temple here below,
Thou didst for all mankind atone,
And standest now before the throne.

Thou standest in the holiest place,
As now for guilty sinners slain;
The Blood of sprinkling speaks and prays
All-prevalent for helpless man;
Thy Blood is still our ransom found,
And spreads salvation all around.

We need not now go up to heaven
To bring the long-sought Saviour down;
Thou art to all already given,
Thou dost e'en now thy banquet crown:
To every faithful soul appear,
And show thy real presence here.

The third action of the Eucharist is the breaking of the bread, the Fraction. St Ephrem the Syrian, in the fourth century, speaking of the breaking of the bread, wrote: 'At that moment when his sacred body is broken, then we recall his immolation: let all the limbs of the body tremble at the moment of the immolation of the Only Begotten.' After blessing the bread, Jesus broke it. In the Didache or Teaching of the Twelve Apostles, a document from the early church, this prayer is used over the broken bread:

> We give thanks to Thee, our Father, for the life and knowledge which thou didst make known to us through thy Son Jesus. To thee be the glory for ever and ever. As this broken bread was scattered upon the mountains, and being gathered together was made one, so may thy church be gathered together into thy Kingdom from the end of the earth.

So the breaking is associated with division and unifying, it is a sign of peace and fellowship. The 1955 Liturgy of the Reformed Church of France takes up these words in its Eucharistic Prayer.

> Make us to live the Resurrection life: that he may dwell in us and we in him. Send us thy Holy Spirit, that in receiving this bread and this cup he may make us communicate in the Body and Blood of our Lord Jesus Christ. For it is by him that thou dost create, that thou dost sanctify, that thou givest life, that thou dost bless and give us all these good things. As the corn was once scattered in the fields, and as the grapes were once dispersed on the hills, which are now gathered together on this table in the bread and wine, so, Lord, may thy whole Church be gathered together from the ends of the world into thy Kingdom. Come, Lord Jesus. Amen.

We can see the broken bread as a symbol of the Christian body, scattered throughout the world, and yet one. Yet there is another aspect of the breaking, for just as we are offered with the bread and wine at the offertory so at the fraction, it is our lives which are to be broken and poured out in and for Christ. In all Christian life, there is the element of breaking. So Dom John Chapman called the point of transition from mental, word-centred prayer to a deeper and more silent way of praying the ligature', from the Latin ligo, to bind or bandage. Often the breaking point is seen as a breakdown, but breakdown can also be breakthrough. We break the bread in order to share it in unity: we are broken so that our lives can be shared with others in a deeper way.

And so we reach the climax of the Eucharist, the Communion, the sharing in the Body and Blood of Christ. Holy Communion is the climax not simply of the Eucharistic rite but of all Christian prayer. It is truly a communion in the Holy Spirit (2 Cor. 13.13). St Ephrem the Syrian said that Jesus

> called the loaf his living Body and filled it with himself and with the Spirit . . . Take it and eat it in faith, never doubting that it is my Body, and that whoever eats it in faith is eating fire and the Spirit . . . Eat it, all of you, and eat the Spirit in it, for it is truly my Body.

The same writer wrote in one of his poems:

> In the Bread we eat the power that cannot be eaten;
> in the Wine we drink the Fire that cannot be drunk.

So in the Communion we become sharers in the Divine life, in the very communion of God. We receive the Body of Christ which we already are: so we eat what we are, and become what we are. And this communion with God is not simply a personal state of bliss, it is shared with the rest of the Body. It is truly and deeply mystical, the life hidden with Christ in God, and we are caught up into this hidden life as a family, as a common unity.

In the action of the Eucharist we can see the pattern of all spirituality: offering, blessing, breaking, and sharing. Our lives are offered to God within the redemptive offering of his Son. They are laid open to the sanctifying, consecrating power of the Spirit. They are broken and poured out in union with Christ for the life of the world. And they are, through Christ, brought into unity and communion in God with other lives which have been brought into Christ's Body. In this fourfold action we see the work of the Trinity, the creative, redemptive and sanctifying work of God in Christ through the Spirit. So after all the people have received communion the Eastern Church sings:

> We have seen the True Light.
> We have received the Heavenly Spirit.
> We have found True Faith in adoring the Undivided Trinity.
> The Trinity has saved us.

The Eucharist is a sharing in, and continuation of, God's creation of the world. If Baptism is a microcosm of Christian life, so is the Eucharist. Together they symbolize and realize a life of cleansing and nourishing, both themes united in the Pauline symbol of the Body of Christ, the *soma Christou.* The Body which is plunged beneath the water is the Body which hung and suffered and rose, and it is the Body which we eat and are. So the Eucharistic action is the pattern of all Christian action: the offering of materials and human potential to be used only according to redeemed means and ends; the recognition that such offering and commitment to action involves brokenness of body and spirit; the movement towards a life and society which is marked not by competition and egocentricity but by co-operation and self-transcendence.

All our life in the world is meant to be eucharistic. And yet we share the Eucharist in an unsharing world, a world in which bread is not equally distributed in communion. In this non-eucharistic world, it is the top fifteen per cent who use up the marvellous achievements of science and technology in order to indulge in a crude materialistic life-style which prevents communion and ravages the created order. We share this Eucharist in a world of waste. The sacrament is reserved for the sick and needy: the bread of the world is thrown away. But the problem of waste disposal is not only one of enforced hunger: what falls from the rich man's table is not crumbs, but poisons and plastics. And because recycling is unprofitable in a system where profit rules, we foster a throwaway philosophy. We share the Eucharist in a polluted atmosphere, a world which treats the seas and rivers as drains and sewers, as receptacles for poisons, radioactive waste, crude oil, sewage, and accumulated rubbish. It is in this wasteful and waste-producing environment that we gather to celebrate the sacrament of shared resources and outpoured life.

The Eucharist is essentially a social act, and in our world it becomes a subversive act, an act of disaffiliation. It is the sacrament of equality in an unequal world. The connection between communion and equality comes out strongly in Luke's account (22.14–28) where immediately after the institution of the Eucharist, the disciples are squabbling about seniority. And Jesus insists on the serving (diaconal) character of his ministry: 'For which is greater, one who sits at table, or one who serves? Is it not the one who sits at table? But I am among you as one who serves (22.27). Again, in John's account of the same day, it is the element of humble service which is stressed in the story of the feet-washing (John 13.1–15). But the feet-washing becomes a meaningless ritual unless we take seriously the command of Jesus to 'wash one another's feet'. If Christian worship had revolved around feet-washing instead of bread-sharing, it is intriguing and depressing to think that now we would be involved in theological disputes about whether the feet should be sprinkled or totally immersed, whether the right or left feet should come first, who was authorized to wash feet, whether women's feet could be washed, and, even more serious, whether women could wash feet! In theological disputes about the Eucharist, we are in danger of forgetting that the Eucharist is meant to apply outside the church walls, just as the feet-washing is.

So the Eucharistic bread is the symbol of all bread shared. As we saw in the last chapter, the early church stressed that *koinonia*, the common life centred on the breaking of the bread, had social consequences for the world. We share the Eucharist in order to be able to share the world. God feeds us so that we can help to recreate the world. It is the vision of a recreated, transformed world which lies behind—and beyond—the sometimes elaborate ritual which has come to surround the celebration of the Eucharist, in the west and particularly in the east—candles, incense, brightly coloured vestments, bells, and so on. What is the point of all this?

Conrad Noel of Thaxted, whose views on worship and politics were quoted in the last chapter, expressed very well the purpose and point of ritual and ceremonial in church services. He wrote:

> All that appeals to our bodily senses that we use in our worship . . . incense, vestments and lights and music and flowers, is used as an outward sign that God has redeemed the body and its appetites and that God must be worshipped by the body and its appetites. If the body is the temple of God's Holy Ghost, then those who defraud men's bodies of proper nourishment and proper shelter and proper rest are robbing temples, and that is the sin of sacrilege. It is bad to break into a church and steal the crucifix from God's altar. It is worse to underpay God's poor.

Thus Noel immediately passes from ritual and ceremonial to justice, as did the prophets. His central point is that ceremonial represents the offering of the body to God. Through ceremony and rite all the senses are being used. There is the use of sight in observing colour and light and splendour; of voice in the singing of hymns and songs and the chanting of the liturgy; of smell in the beautiful spices which make up incense; of touch in the sign of peace, laying on of hands, sprinkling with holy water, and the gift of communion; and of hearing in the music and the proclamation of the Word of God. For we are not pure spirits, and if our worship is 'purely spiritual' it is incomplete because only part of us is being offered.

But ritual, symbol, and justice cannot be separated. The Old Testament prophets fearlessly condemned worship and prayer which ignored social justice. Take, for example, Amos 5.21ff:

> I hate, I despise your feasts, and I take no delight in your solemn assemblies. Even though you offer me your burnt offerings and cereal offerings I will not accept them and the peace offerings of your fatted beasts I will not look upon. Take away from me the noise of your songs: to the melody of your harps I will not listen. But let justice roll down like waters, and righteousness like an everflowing stream.

Similarly Isaiah attacks the multitude of sacrifices.

> Bring me no more vain offerings: incense is an abomination to me. New moon and sabbath and the calling of assemblies—I cannot endure iniquity and solemn assembly ... When you spread forth your hands, I will hide my eyes from you; even though you make many prayers I will not listen. Your hands are full of blood. (Isa. 1.13,15)

On the other hand the prophets emphasize that worship *will* be acceptable when justice is also achieved (e.g. Isa. 2.2–4; Mic. 4.1–8; Zeph. 3.9–13). Zechariah (5.5–11) and Ezekiel (36.26) envisage the future of the Temple of the Lord to lie in a renewed Israel in which injustice has been banished and there are no more hearts of stone.

In the ritual and ceremonial of Christian worship then we are offering our bodies and our whole personalities to God, but we are also anticipating the age to come. Worship should be as happy, as glorious and as awe-inspiring as it can be, for it is meant to help people to grasp the vision of unspeakable wonder and glory. In the symbolism of the liturgy we are caught up into mysteries beyond the power of words, the mysteries of death and rebirth, of dust and glory, of darkness and light. Symbols speak to us more powerfully than words, because they are beyond explanation and they cannot be understood. They swallow us whole, and we become part of them. This is of the essence of worship, and this is why we should never expect to 'understand' everything that we do, capture it all in our heads. In worship we are entering into the mystery of the universe, the mystery of the infinite and eternal God. If we catch something of that splendour beyond words, we have made some progress.

In the Eucharist we believe that Jesus Christ is present under the forms of bread and wine, and we speak of his 'Real Presence'. That sounds a strange expression, for how can a 'presence' not be 'real'? What the term is trying to communicate is that the Eucharist is not merely the memorial of an absent, past, historic Jesus, but that he is truly present with us, he is in the present not the past. The bread and wine *become* the body and blood of Christ; so they are not merely signs, Christ's body and blood are really present and really given and received. That this was so was never doubted from the early days of the church until the Reformation of the sixteenth century. The early fathers emphasize the presence of Christ in the sacrament with such strength and frequency that it would be impossible in a short space to make more than passing references to some of them. Thus St Ignatius complains that the Docetic heretics 'abstain from the Eucharist because they do not believe that it is the flesh of our Saviour Jesus Christ'. Justin Martyr says that 'we have been taught that the food, over which thanks have been given, is the flesh and blood of that Incarnate Jesus'. St Irenaeus says that in the consecrated Eucharist there are 'two parts, an earthly and a heavenly' and that Christ 'acknowledged the bread as his body, and established the mixed cup as his blood'. St Athanasius says that through the Eucharistic Prayer 'the bread becomes the body and the cup the blood of our Lord' and that 'the Word descends upon the bread and the cup, and his body comes to be'. St Ambrose says that 'by means of the mystery of the holy prayer' the bread and wine 'are transformed so as to be flesh and blood'. The early liturgies are equally explicit. The Liturgy of St James prays that the Holy Spirit 'may make this bread the Holy Body of thy Christ and this cup the Precious Blood', while the Liturgy of St John Chrysostom prays that he would 'make this bread the precious Body and that which is in this cup the precious Blood of thy Christ . . . changing them by the Holy Ghost'.

But in the writings of such fathers as St Gregory of Nyssa and

St John of Damascus we find the beginnings of the view that the bread and wine, through the transforming power of the Spirit, are no longer ordinary bread and wine but are *changed*. So St Gregory:

> I truly believe that the bread sanctified by God's Word is made into the Body of God the Word, for this Body as well was bread, but it was sanctified by the indwelling of the Word. Just as when ordinary bread and wine, received by the Lord for the relief of hunger and thirst, were changed into divine power—his Body and Blood—so today the same thing happens: for as the Grace of the Word sanctified the body consisting of bread, so now bread, according to the saying of the Apostle, is sanctified by the Word of God and prayer [1 Tim. 4.5], becoming the Body of the Word, not by eating and drinking, but by being changed immediately into the Body of the Word, as is stated by the Word itself: 'This is my Body'.

St John of Damascus writes in a similar way:

> Not the ascended body comes down from heaven, but the very bread and wine are made into the Body and Blood of God. As bread and wine and water, by being partaken, are changed naturally into the body and blood of the partaker and become not another body, different from its former body, so bread and wine and water, by the invocation and inspiration of the Holy Spirit, are supernaturally made into Christ's Body and Blood and comprise not two bodies but one and the same.

The point they both make is that at the natural level there is a change: earthly substances are changed into the body of the eater. So in the Eucharist through the power of the Spirit the bread and wine are changed at the supernatural level into the life of Christ himself. It is useless to argue about how the change occurs: it is a spiritual change, not a chemical or scientific change. That does not make it less real unless one rejects the reality of the spiritual. Yet although the change is spiritual in *manner*, it is physical in *consequences*: the bread and wine do in actual material fact become the body and blood of Christ, and because of this they are venerated physically and materially by Christian men and women. That is why we bow the knee (genuflect) when we enter a church in which the Sacrament is reserved in a tabernacle or other vessel: we give to the Presence a physical and material reverence. Like the

Incarnation, the doctrine of the Real Presence of Christ in the Sacrament is an affront to the false spirituality which wishes to keep God away from matter and from smallness. Just as God took to himself a human body and became small, 'weak, helpless and speechless, in measure a span', at Bethlehem, so in the Sacrament he becomes as small as a tiny piece of bread. In both it is the materiality and intimacy of the presence which is so important, and to some so offensive. And here too is the central wonder of the Christian revelation, that God took flesh of Mary and daily renews his presence as God made Man in the Eucharistic Presence. In the words of Betjeman's poem 'Christmas':

> No love that in a family dwells,
> No carolling in frosty air,
> Nor all the steeple-shaking bells
> Can with this single Truth compare—
> That God was Man in Palestine
> And lives today in Bread and Wine.

The Real Presence of Christ in the Sacrament is a fact, yet it is not to be seen in isolation from other forms of his presence. Jesus is not 'the prisoner of the tabernacle', that dreadful phrase of decadent pietism. St John Chrysostom makes a close connection between the presence of Jesus in the sacrament and his presence in the poor and despised, and he speaks of 'the sacrament of the brother'. So in his Homily 50 on St Matthew's Gospel he says:

> What is the use of loading Christ's table with vessels of gold if he himself is dying of hunger? First, satisfy his hunger, then adorn the table with what remains. Tell me, if you saw a man in need of even the most necessary food, and if you should leave him standing there in order to set the table with dishes of gold, would he be thankful to you? Would he not rather be angry? ... But consider well that this is the way you treat Christ when he goes about as a pilgrim, a homeless vagabond, and when instead of taking him in, you embellish the floors and walls and capitals of columns and suspend lamps from silver chains, but refuse even to visit him when he is in chains. I am not saying this to criticise the use of such ornaments. We must attend to both, but to Christ first.

The poor man, says Chrysostom, is a bigger temple than the temple made with hands. 'This altar you can see elevated everywhere in the streets and you can sacrifice upon it at all times.' In similar vein, Clement of Alexandria had quoted an alleged saying of Jesus, 'You have seen your brother, you have seen your God.' Today, Sydney Carter, the modern hymn-writer, in his song 'Jesus and Mary' takes up Chrysostom's and Clement's theme: 'The poor of the world are my body'. It is not possible to worship Jesus in the sacrament and to ignore him in the suffering bodies of his children, or rather it is possible, and it is a blasphemy.

Because Jesus is present in the sacrament we adore him there. From the very early times the Eucharist has been reserved, or set aside in some special place, for the communion of the people. Adoration of the sacrament too was assumed in the early church. 'Approach', says St Cyril of Jerusalem to communicants, 'bending, and saying in the way of adoration and veneration, Amen.' St Ambrose and St Augustine both use a mystical interpretation of 'Worship his footstool' to refer to the Eucharist. St Ambrose speaks of 'the flesh of Christ which to this day we adore in the Mysteries'. 'No one', says St Augustine, 'eats that Flesh unless he has first worshipped . . . We sin in not worshipping.' However, the emphasis here and throughout the early writings is on adoration within the framework of the Eucharist itself. The sacrament was, however, reserved and taken away from the Eucharist. Tertullian and other early writers mention the practice of reserving the consecrated bread in the houses of Christian people to ensure that they were able to receive communion at home on days when the liturgy was not celebrated. Justin Martyr at Rome in the mid-second century says that the deacons at the Eucharist carry the sacrament 'to those not present'. By the third century reservation of the sacrament at home is witnessed to by writers in Africa and Rome. In fact, one writer of an early Christian document *De Spectaculis* (abous 240 A.D.) complains of the behaviour of the lax Christian: 'After the dismissal from the Lord's sacrifice, he hastens to the circus, and still bearing with him as is usual the Eucharist, this unfaithful communicant carries around the holy Body of Christ amidst the vile bodies of harlots.' No clearer testimony could there be to the ancient practice of reserving the sacrament. Evidently most Christians, and not just the very devout, were expected to receive Holy Communion daily, and to take the sacrament home with them for this purpose. There is nothing in Justin or any other ancient writer to suggest that reservation of the sacrament is only, or even mainly, for the sick. Early communion from the sacrament reserved was for all the confirmed: in fact, only one early writer refers to the communion of sick persons from the reserved sacrament—a story told by Denys of Alexandria of the last communion of a dying person around 250 A.D.

So in very early Christian times the place for the reserved sacrament was the homes of Christian people. In the third century, however, Christians started to acquire special buildings for worship, but because of persecution and danger the sacrament was not reserved there. When the persecutions ended in the fourth century there seems to have been little change in the situation, though the Council of Nicea, in Canon 13, laid down that 'concerning the dying, let the ancient and canonical rule still be kept: that none be deprived at the hour of death of the most necessary Viaticum'. (This rule is still binding on Anglicans and is probably a requirement that the sacrament be reserved in each parish.) There is no certain evidence that the altar of a church was used as the place to reserve the sacrament before about 800. The first instance of reservation on the high altar comes from Anglo-Saxon England, in Ethelwold's poem on the monastery at Lindisfarne around 802, and there is some evidence that this was then the normal English custom. Outside England there is no evidence of reservation at the altar anywhere in the west until the late ninth century. A decree from one ninth-century Gallican council orders that 'nothing may be placed upon the altar except the capsa and (i.e. containing) the relics, or perhaps the four Holy Gospels of God, and the pyx containing the Lord's body for the Viaticum of the sick'. By the later Middle Ages, permanent reservation of the sacrament in churches on or near the altar had become the norm, though the locations varied: aumbries in the wall in Italy and Spain, built-in sacrament houses in Germany and Holland, tabernacles in France and the Rhinelands, and the hanging pyx in England and some other places. But in all the Christian literature of the first thousand years there is no definite evidence that any person visited a church in order to pray before the reserved sacrament, and there seem to be no examples of prayers addressed to the blessed sacrament in these early centuries.

It was the northern countries where reflection on the meaning of the sacramental presence of Christ led to an intensifying of reverence and adoration. So the English devotional writer Lydgate in the fourteenth century says: 'When thou comest to the holy place —cast holy water in thy face—Then look to the high altar—and pray to him that hangeth there.' Earlier than this there is evidence of devotions to the blessed sacrament in an organized way at Canterbury Cathedral around 1078. There Archbishop Lanfranc ordered a procession of the Host on Palm Sunday, and instructed the people to bow the knee at the words 'Hosanna to the Son of David'. The introduction of processions of the Host on the Feast of Corpus Christi came later, and in 1404 we read that at Pavia 'the Body of Christ began to be carried about through the city of Pavia, as hath been commonly done since'. But devotion to the sacrament, and adoration arising out of the liturgy, seem to have originated in Northern Europe, and particularly in England.

Of course, the primary purpose of the Eucharist is communion, and the primary purpose of reserving the sacrament also is communion. But the adoration of Christ in his sacramental presence is surely a legitimate and right growth out of belief in that presence. So let us refer to two practices which have become widespread in the west as aids to prayer. The first is the practice of prayer before the reserved sacrament, either by individuals or by groups of people gathered together. This practice is strongly emphasized by the Little Brothers of Charles de Foucauld, that remarkable and important modern Christian movement, and is an essential and central part of their spirituality. In his book *Seeds of the Desert*, first published in 1953, Père René Voillaume says that the two themes of Jesus in the Gospels and Jesus in the Eucharist were the poles around which the life of Charles de Foucauld revolved. He spent years of silence and prayer in the deserts of the Holy Land, and there for hours he would remain on his knees, motionless before the presence of Jesus in his sacrament. Charles's faith in the real presence of Jesus in the sacrament was crucial to his whole life and prayer, and the sacrament reserved was the centre around which everything was to revolve. The presence of Jesus there was to shape the fraternity into a holy family. Voillaume writes:

> Concentrated as it was in this fervent cult of Jesus' presence in the Host, his piety contained in germ a completely Eucharistic life. Meanwhile the beloved presence of Jesus was not only the starting point of his prayer life, it was in this attitude that he always prayed. (*Seeds of the Desert*, 1972 edn, p. 35)

So the presence of Jesus in the sacrament, and the love which he excites in us there, overflows into a presence in the world through his body and through his people, and into a love which reaches out to all. From the experience of Charles de Foucauld in his prayer before the sacrament grew a whole movement of Christian people, the Little Brothers and Little Sisters and those linked with them, which has placed adoration of Jesus in the sacrament at the centre of its life. Père Voillaume stresses the place of exposition of the sacrament, silent adoration at night, and the creation of Adoration Fraternities. It is Jesus' own adoration of God which must flow into us through the Eucharist. For all prayer is not only *to* God but originates with God and in God. To pray before the sacrament is therefore to open oneself up to the possibility of renewal, to open oneself up to the prayerfulness of God. 'Adoration', says Voillaume, 'is admiration of the supreme mystery of the Divinity, hidden in eternity' (ibid., p. 66). We adore in order to love, to absorb into our own beings the being of God.

The second practice associated with the reserved sacrament is called Benediction. This is a simple and deeply moving rite in which the sacrament reserved is exposed on the altar in a vessel called a monstrance, a round container for the host with a design like the rays of the sun. Hymns are sung to the sacrament exposed, there is time for silent worship, and the climax of the rite is the lifting up of the Eucharistic Christ in silent blessing of the people. It is surprising how much controversy has raged in the Church of England over this simple act of blessing. Of course, if one does not believe that Christ is present in the consecrated bread, such an act is blasphemous and idolatrous. But we do believe that Christ is both present and present to bless. To stress our dependence upon God and upon his blessing and empowering of us is very important, and can help to correct the tendency to become centred on ourselves. In our worship and life, when all has been said—and rightly said—about our co-operation with God and each other, about solidarity, fellowship, sharing and so on, there remains a vital element of passivity, of waiting upon God, of simple abiding.

> Nothing in my hands I bring,
> Simply to thy Cross I cling.
> Naked come to thee for dress,
> Helpless, come to thee for grace.
> Foul, I to the Fountain fly.
> Wash me, Saviour, or I die.

It is this state of abandonment to God, waiting for his blessing, which is stressed in Benediction. This is perhaps why Benediction often appeals to the poor, the simple, those on the fringes of the church to whom God in the sacrament reaches out long before they consciously come to receive him, and who can receive his blessing before they are sure of who it is they are adoring. One writer has compared the monstrance at Benediction to the Statue of Liberty which dominates New York harbour with its great torch. At the base of the statue are the words 'Give me your tired, your poor, your huddled masses yearning to be free'. Similarly in Benediction God calls us from our poverty and our tiredness to experience, if only for a few moments, the silence of eternity and the depths of his own being.

The eucharistic life should flow out from the central offering of the church into smaller eucharists and eucharist-based prayer cells and groups. For all prayer is eucharistic in that it flows out from this shared life which the Eucharist both expresses and creates. But the shared prayer group is often a very simple and 'non-liturgical' (that is, not rigidly structured) time in which fellow Christians pray together in word and in silence. Jesus clearly envisaged the small group as playing a vital role in building up the Christian community. 'When two or three are gathered together in my name, there am I in their midst' (Matt. 18.20). In the preceding verse, Jesus tells his disciples that 'whenever two of you on earth agree about anything you pray for, it will be done for you by my Father in heaven' (18.19). In many modern churches we have lost the intimacy and the Gospel purity of the small group. Small group worship and life is not a modern gimmick, a response to economic pressures or declining congregations: it is a return to Gospel Christianity.

So from the central act of sharing in the Eucharist it is of great value in a local Christian community for smaller gatherings of Christians to meet for shared prayer. For many people the prayer group is the context in which personal prayer grows most rapidly. As we support each other, and pray with each other, we ourselves are given voice and strength to pray. Prayer groups are of immense variety in style and structure, and there is now a good number of books about them, particularly those written under the influence of the Charismatic renewal. But there are certain essential features. First, there needs to be a time of quiet recollection in which together we recognize and accept each other as equal members of the Body of Christ, and silently pray for and express our solidarity with each other in Christ. This recollection period might end with some corporate act of commitment to each other—perhaps the Kiss of Peace. There is no reason why a prayer group should not be entirely silent, and it is important to stress this since so many people seem incapable of being silent for long in prayer, and a prayer group in which people seek to grow in silence together can help. But one should not despise the voice which God has given us to praise him. Some shared act of prayer, for example, saying together the hymn 'Come Holy Ghost, our souls inspire', can be used to open up the group to the activity and power of the Holy Spirit. The most important element is that of moving towards God, centring all the thoughts and feelings of the group on God, perhaps using an image (a crucifix, candle, picture, or some central object) or a short verse of Scripture.

In the Charismatic-type prayer group, and in many such groups among more conservative evangelicals, a lot of time is given to reflection on the Scriptures. The Word of God controls the group, and the Word is studied in order to integrate its meaning and message into our lives. This is not a simple study group: the purpose of reflection on the Bible is the deepening of the prayerful spirit. Through absorbing the Word of God into ourselves we come to be shaped and formed by it. In the intimacy and informality of the small group it is possible to brood on Scripture passages in a way which is not possible in the more formal reading of the Word in the liturgy. But the small group arises from the liturgy and flows into it to enrich it. John Gunstone has a lot to say about these Word-centred prayer groups in his book *A People for his Praise* (1978).

Other groups may be more directly eucharistic and Sacrament-centred. In the 1950s the 'house church' movement was pioneered by Ernest Southcott in Leeds. This was a movement based upon the celebration of the Eucharist in people's homes, and the story of it is told in Southcott's *The Parish Comes Alive* (1955). The house church was not, and is not, to be viewed as a short-term strategy nor as an evangelistic operation directed to those on the fringe of the church. It was, as for the New Testament, a theologically necessary part of the life of the Body of Christ. St Paul often sent greetings to the church in people's houses (1 Cor. 16.19; Rom. 16.3,5; Col. 4.15). These house churches were not merely temporary centres where no 'parish' had been established, but rather each colony of the church was filled out with smaller units. The house church is simply a smaller cell, a microcosm of the larger unit. In the 1950s John Robinson claimed that the theological recovery of the idea of 'the church in the house' is one of the most important tasks of our generation, and his words are still true. Using the image of the vine in St John, Robinson suggested that the house church represented the taproot of the vine, the life of the tree which was most closely in touch with the clinging soil of everyday life. So it is the house church, the smallest eucharistic unit, which feeds new life into the parish church as the innumerable taproots nourish the stock of the vine.

So in Word and Sacrament the smallest Christian units are of vital importance if the church is to grow and be nourished. Wherever two or three are gathered together, it is the whole church, the Body of Christ, which reads the Word of God and celebrates the Eucharist. When we pray 'Give us today our daily Bread' we pray as the whole church, shaped and united by the Eucharistic action: offered, consecrated, broken, and shared.

5

Prayer and penitence

> Forgive us our sins as we forgive those who sin against us. (Matt. 6.12)
>
> I will confess therefore what I know of myself, and what I do not know: for what I know of myself, I know through the shining of your light; and what I do not know of myself, I continue not to know until my darkness shall be made as noonday in your countenance.
>
> ST AUGUSTINE

The idea of sin is a *theological* one: it has to do with our relationship with God. To be in a state of sin, in Christian terms, is to be in a state of separation from God: without a belief in a God to whom we can personally and intimately relate, and from whom terrible separation is possible, the idea of sin is meaningless. Morality can, of course, survive and exist without belief in God: ethical norms, however variable, are not dependent on religious belief. But sin is a *religious* notion. Not only that, it is a notion which is rooted in a particular view of God and his relationship to the world. Jesus speaks of God as Father and points out that if human fathers, in their sinful condition, still know how to give good gifts to their children, how much more will 'your Father who is in heaven' give good things to those who ask (Matt. 7.11).

We referred in the first chapter to the uniqueness of Jesus' use of 'Father' as a personal and intimate expression. But the idea of God as the Father of Israel goes deep into the tradition of the Old Testament. Jacob speaks of God as 'the God of my father' (Gen. 31.5), the 'God of my father Abraham . . . God of my father Isaac' (32.9). The Psalms address God as Father (Ps. 89.26) as does Second Isaiah (63.16) and Jeremiah (3.19). But it is Hosea who most dramatically portrays God as husband and father of the people: Israel is his beloved son (Hos. 11.1). But because the relationship with God is intimate and personal, the prophets insist, it can be broken. It is possible for human beings to cut themselves off from God and incur God's *wrath*. The notion of the wrath of God is so unfamiliar and even repulsive to our modern liberal ears that we need to examine it, for it is impossible to do justice to the biblical teaching about sin without it.

Can we really believe in an angry God? Is not the idea of God's wrath a relic of outdated views of a vengeful and terrifying God, a contradiction of the God of love proclaimed by Jesus? In beginning to think about the 'wrath of God' we need to reject any notions of two Gods, one of justice and one of mercy, or any ideas which see God's anger in terms of some moral failing or unresolved tension within God. Yet wrath is a necessary aspect of the nature of God as revealed in Scripture, and one which we ignore or bypass at our peril. And quite clearly we do ignore it, not least in modern liturgies. So in the modern Anglican version of the Venite (Ps. 95), for centuries the heart of the morning office of the church, the crucial concluding words have been lost.

> Harden not your hearts as at Meribah,
> as on that day at Massah in the desert
> when your fathers put me to the test;
> when they tried me, though they saw my work.
> For forty years I was wearied of these people
> and I said, 'Their hearts are astray,
> these people do not know my ways.'
> Then I took an oath in my anger:
> 'Never shall they enter my rest.' (Ps. 95.8–11)

There is a strong tendency today to remove all 'hard sayings', anything which speaks of wrath and vengeance, from the liturgy, and to produce a god who is all gentle and compassionate, a god who fits comfortably into the liberal idealist world. The welfare state god, the god of 'caring and sharing', is very clearly present in modern liturgies, while the God of righteousness and judgement is missing. But Christians hold to belief in a God who is both terrible and tender, gentle and 'consuming fire', a God of judgement and mercy. St Gregory of Nyssa stressed the paradox of God's terrible beauty in his *Life of Moses*.

It would seem that the attractiveness of the divine beauty has

> something terrifying about it, and this is characterised by qualities which seem the exact opposite of bodily beauty. For what makes bodily beauty desirable is that it is pleasant to the sight, soft to the touch, and not at all connected in our minds with fear or sternness. But that divine, incorruptible Beauty is at once something stern and terrifying ... The love of God is made up of a fearsome, imperturbable fortitude ...

God's wrath therefore is not incompatible with his love, they are aspects of the same character. His wrath is the clear shining of his light which of its nature burns up injustice and oppression. The opposite of wrath is not love but neutrality: wrath and love are essentially one. The wrath of God is the Bible's expression for his essential hostility to all evil.

The Bible does not see the love and wrath of God as two conflicting impulses, wrath restraining love from time to time: on the contrary, wrath is tempered with mercy. In the New Testament it is nowhere said directly that God is angry. Two words are used for wrath, *orge* and *thumos*, and when they are used, wrath is seen as something ordained by God but distinct from him, a kind of indirect relationship to God. Nobody in the New Testament speaks of appeasing or 'propitiating' God's wrath, a grotesque idea which has entered into and seriously damaged the Christian doctrine of the atonement. On the other hand, the New Testament does say that we can *escape* the wrath of God. Wrath is as inseparable from love as darkness from light. To reject, and live apart from, the love of God is to enter the world of wrath, of ruin, of disaster. Wrath is not a deranged divine temperament, nor is it justice opposing love: it is the inevitable consequence of a rejection of God's love.

We have spoken of 'the world of wrath' and the New Testament speaks of us as being by nature 'children of wrath' (Eph. 2.3). In order to understand this language, we need to understand the notion that sin is a state of being, that there is a solidarity in sin, and that sin is more than the sum total of individual acts of wrongdoing. The Christian faith stresses the gravity of sin. It cannot simply be forgotten, and it is often hard to forgive ourselves for past sins. Sin of its nature transcends the time process, it is a vast oppressive world. Confronted with the world of sin, the individual sinner feels helpless and alone.

Could my tears for ever flow,
Could my zeal no respite know,
All for sin cannot atone.

An individualistic doctrine of sin will not be adequate if we are to see the depths and seriousness of our predicament. There is a solidarity in sin just as there is in grace. Sin is not a matter of a number of perverted wills which can be readjusted by a little social engineering. Sin is a state, a condition, or, as Julian of Norwich put it, 'sin is a lump'. Only by seeing this can we make sense of the important doctrine of Original Sin which is so often misunderstood.

In the fifth century there occurred the Pelagian controversy, and Pelagianism has been called 'the British heresy' because it had been claimed that Pelagius, like many British people, held that we could save ourselves by hard work. That is not correct, but it is correct to see that the central issue in that controversy had to do with the nature and seriousness of sin. Pelagius saw human beings as separated individuals, capable of either good or evil. Evil was to be found, alongside good, within the individual soul. Against this view, St Augustine stressed the solidarity of humanity in sin. Sin is a condition of separation from God in which the whole of humanity is involved. So in the biblical teaching about the Fall, what is outlined is not an event which happened to a solitary couple in Paradise, but an event which happened to the species *homo sapiens* in its historical development. Sin is social, involving a distortion of the historical process. Individualistic ideas of sin are not only inadequate but actually harmful, for they foster trivial and childish notions of sin and repentance. So individuals become absorbed with individual, mainly sexual, immorality, but have no way of relating their individual acts to the great structures of evil which disfigure and threaten the whole created world.

To be in a state of sin is to be separated—from God, from others, and from oneself. Through sin the face of God is obscured. So the prophets see sin as a lack of knowledge of God or a false image of God, idolatry, and this lack of knowledge is shown in a lack of mercy and compassion in human society. And this sin is all-pervasive, so that the Bible tends to speak of it as somehow objectified and separate from man. So we have such terms as 'the sins of the fathers', 'the powers of darkness', 'Satan', and 'the flesh'. Paul personifies sin: sin, he says, came into the world (Rom. 5.12), sin reigns (5.21; 6.14), sin enslaves (6.6,17,20). And this sin has become a massive disorientation of human society, it is 'the world', the fallen world order which is renounced at Baptism.

Now this social dimension of sin does not mean that human beings are mere robots, helpless, predetermined creatures in a fallen, hopeless, and doomed world. It does mean that we have to recognize that there are structures of evil in the world which are greater and more entrenched than a mere series of personal defects. There will be no understanding of Christian social responsibility which does not face up to the 'principalities and powers' which have twisted and distorted social and political systems. Sin is a lump, and we are part of it. To grasp the immensity of sin is vital to an understanding of the mystery of God's redeeming work in Christ. As Martin Luther wrote:

> Ignorance of sin of necessity brings in its train ignorance of God, of Christ, of the Holy Spirit, and of all things. For let no one think that he will become a theologian or a good reader or hearer of Holy Scripture if he minimises the evil of original sin and does not correctly understand it.

But if sin is social and corporate, how much more so is this true of the work of redemption and reconciliation. All our prayer is part of the mystery of reconciliation and renewal in Christ. In prayer we are taken into the saving work of Christ. Karl Barth, the great German theologian, described reconciliation in this way.

> 'Reconciliation' is the restitution, the resumption of a fellowship which once existed but was then threatened by dissolution. It is the maintaining, restoring and upholding of that fellowship in face of an element which disturbs and disrupts and breaks it.

Prayer is fellowship with God, the healing of a broken relationship, but it can only occur in Christ and in his great atoning work of prayer. There is therefore a close connection between prayer and the Cross.

Christians believe that God has reconciled us to himself in Christ who made peace by the blood of his Cross and united things on earth and things in heaven. The purpose of human life is union with

God, and this is the purpose of Christian prayer: prayer, life, and the work of Christ on the Cross are a unity. Yet the work of Christ, his sacrifice, is both complete and yet daily renewed. Jesus gave his life a ransom for many (Mark 10.46), his life was poured out for the forgiveness of sins (14.24), yet after his Resurrection he gives to his apostles the power to forgive sins. Again Paul insists that God has reconciled us in Christ, but he also insists that the ministry of reconciliation has been given to us (2 Cor. 5.8). In the church we are proclaiming not a dead Christ but a living Christ, and we are his Body, we share his life. So the mystery of Christ is not a past event but an ever-present reality, a living power.

The Christian life is not simply the contemplation of God but also involves discipleship and sharing. And in the Cross we can see three ways in which our life of prayer is deepened. First, through the Cross we share in God's love and in God's nature. We share a common life in the divine light (1 John 1.5–7), the divine seed is in us (3.9). We have put on a new nature, renewed after the image of its Creator. So the old nature of sin is being abolished and a new nature substituted (Col. 3.9). Because of this new nature, the divine nature, we are able to forgive as God forgives (Eph. 4.32; Col. 3.13), and to love indiscriminately as God loves (cf. Luke 6.32–6). Secondly, through the Cross we share in Christ's life. But if we claim to dwell in him we must live as he lived (1 John 2.6). Throughout Romans, Galatians and Colossians it is emphasized that we have died with Christ and now share his risen life. So we are enabled to love as Christ loved, moving beyond the 'Golden Rule' to the New Commandment (John 13.34) and to serve others as Christ serves (John 13.1–17), to accept others as Christ accepted us (Rom. 15.1–7), to live for him and not for ourselves (2 Cor. 5.14). Thirdly, through the Cross we share in Christ's death. We share his sufferings (Phil. 3.10), carry his death with us (2 Cor. 4.10), even 'complete the full tale of Christ's afflictions' (Col. 1.24). We share the divine condescension—'let this mind be in you' (Phil. 2.3–14). We are urged to give our lives as he did and to try to be like him (Eph. 5.1). We are to replace dominion by *diakonia*, service (Mark 10.42–5). We are to accept innocent suffering (1 Pet. 2.20; 3.14). We are to suffer hostility in the world and to carry the Cross (Luke 14.27–33). We are to crucify the flesh (Gal. 5.24), the lower, unredeemed nature.

The New Testament sees the Cross then as both a historical work of God in Christ, and also a way to be followed, the 'Way of the Cross', the imitation of God in Christ. We are called then to a life which is marked by penitence. In a sense all Christian life and all prayer is the recollection and renewal of Baptism, it is a response to Baptism and to the knowledge of acceptance and forgiveness which we have from God. Sometimes this general renewal and constant recommitment is brought home to us vividly by specific acts. Thus on Holy Saturday we renew our baptismal promises and are sprinkled with water from the newly blessed font. Again, when we enter a church we often sign ourselves with holy water as a reminder of our Baptism and a challenge to us to live lives of penitence. Through our Baptism and its constant renewal in sacrament and prayer, we should be able to say, as the early Christians did, that 'we have passed from death into life' (1 John 3.14). And yet our daily lives are marked not only by deepening consciousness of grace, but also by repeated falls into sin. Like St Paul the good that we would we do not, and the evil that we would not we do. So the vision at the centre of our lives comes to be clouded over by sin. And this double consciousness is reflected in the liturgy of the church, the combination of penitence and praise, of dust and glory.

The heart of the Gospel is the fact that God in Christ has forgiven us our sins, has restored us to fellowship, and has brought us into his Kingdom. And this Gospel is proclaimed to sinners, to men and women conscious of their frailty, failure, and helplessness. Yet there is the world of difference between a sense of failure which leads to overpowering guilt and despondency, and a sense of failure which issues in penitence and joy. Penitence is something essentially different from guilt and masochism. It is an inner attitude, a commitment to examine one's own inner motives and intentions, and, bringing them into consciousness as far as we can, to acknowledge them to God. The Christian believes that God freely justifies the person who turns to him through faith in Christ, confessing his sins. Penitence is a constant attitude of turning to God in trust, and of humbly accepting his forgiveness.

Forgiveness, the Christian insists, is a free gift, but repentance is costly. For sin is destructive and needs to be attacked and undermined: a new order of things has to be established which reverses and undoes the work of sin. Paul in Romans 5.15–19 contrasts the enormity of sin with the enormity of redemption. If many died, he says, through one man's trespass, much more have the grace of God and the free gift become abundant for many. So as the judgement following the trespass brought condemnation, so the free gift which follows many trespasses brings justification. Through the trespass, death reigned: through the abundance of grace and the free gift, life reigns. So forgiveness reverses the process of sin. Forgiveness is the public virtue of Christianity, the exact opposite of vengeance (the predictable response). Unlike vengeance which merely perpetuates a process of action and reaction, forgiveness brings about a new chain of relationships by introducing a new and unpredictable factor into the situation.

But how can this Gospel factor of forgiveness become a continuing reality in the life of prayer? Confession and forgiveness need to be central elements in all prayer, corporate, personal, liturgical, free. In the Eucharist, there is usually an act of penitence at the beginning, which culminates in the cry Kyrie Eleison—Lord have mercy. In the Divine Office, there is always a place at some point for a daily self-examination and confession: traditionally in the west this has come at the beginning of the final office of the day, Compline or Night Prayer. In personal prayer too there has to be an element of self-examination and confession. But most of all we need to see a place within our lives of prayer for the practice of confession within the sacramental rite which exists for that purpose, the Sacrament of Reconciliation or Sacrament of Penance. What is this?

To go to confession is an ancient Christian practice. The early church, however, was much more rigorous over the matter of sins committed after Baptism than we are today. The person was admitted into an order of penitents, clothed in a penitential robe, and he joined other penitents in a special part of the church. Period of penance might last from the forty days of Lent to several years, and during this period strict continence, long periods of prayer and almsgiving were obligatory. But one was only admitted to do penance once. If afterwards one then fell into grave sin, it was too bad: there was no further remedy. The practice of repeated acts of confession and absolution did not arise for some centuries, and when it did, it was frowned on by official church spokesmen and regarded as a sign of permissiveness and laxity! Thus the Council of Toledo, a meeting of the Spanish bishops, in 589 issued a stern warning:

> It has come to our notice that certain people in certain parts of Spain are doing penance for their sins in unworthy fashion and not in accordance with the directives of the church: for every time they sin they go to the priest for absolution. For this reason, and to put an end to such a detestable and presumptuous way of behaving, this holy council has decreed as follows: Penance will be administered in accordance with the old official forms: namely, the sinner who repents of his sin must receive the laying on of hands many times as a penitent. He is forbidden to go to communion. Once he has in the estimation of his bishop completed his period of expiation he may be re-admitted to the Eucharist.

Nevertheless the new practice spread. While public penance was still referred to by Thomas Aquinas, the practice of private confession at frequent intervals quickly established itself, and in 1215 the Fourth Lateran Council established the practice of a minimum annual confession and communion at Easter ('the Paschal Precept') as normative in the western church.

What is the point of going to confession? The practice has been condemned as 'priestcraft', as introducing 'a priest between my soul and god', as destroying the free access of sinners to Christ without others as intermediaries, as encouragement to further sin, as 'Popish', and so on. However, the pioneers of the Catholic revival in the Church of England in the nineteenth century were correct to see the revival of sacramental confession as absolutely central to their work. Thus John Keble could say, 'We go on working in the dark, and in the dark it will be, until the rule of systematic confession is revived in our church.' In other words, confession is not a drastic remedy for the desperate or the grave sinner, or an extra devotion for the super-pious or fastidious: it is a necessary element in every Christian growth in prayer and life.

When we make a confession within the framework of the Sacrament of Reconciliation, we are participating in the mystery of Christ's reconciling work. This is the sacrament of reconciliation and peace: here Christ who won for us forgiveness of sins specifically mediates that forgiveness to a specific sinner in a specific place. Christ's forgiveness is here made real to the individual. There is nothing essentially different in the way confession works from the way the other sacraments work. The claim that a priest 'stands between the soul and God' could perfectly well be used as an objection to Baptism, to the Eucharist, to anointing, to any and every sacramental ministration. The priest in confession acts in the same capacity as he does in any other sacrament. Here, as elsewhere, God uses the human relationship to communicate divine grace and power. In this ministry, there is a renewal of Baptism. The grace of the baptismal event is restored to us, and we are again received into the fellowship of Christ's Body. As sin is social, so this essentially social sacrament restores us to communion with the Body.

Confession is a way of making systematic and effective the essential struggle against evil which is so central to the life in Christ. It is not an abnormal, crisis activity, but is part of the day-by-day, domestic ministry of the church. Of course, there are crisis points in our lives when it is urgent and essential that we make our confession, 'make a clean breast of it', and nothing but such open acknowledgement of sin will suffice. And, of course, there are people for whom sacramental confession and the assurance of forgiveness is more necessary than for others. Yet the ministry of reconciliation, communicated to an individual human being by another individual human being within the Body of Christ, is a necessary and normal part of the life of grace. Every priest at his ordination is told 'Whose sins you forgive, they are forgiven; whose sins you retain, they are retained'. The forgiveness of sins is therefore central to the exercise of his priesthood. It is hard to see how that ministry can be exercised in any meaningful way without the practice of self-examination and thorough, personal confession.

For it is to *me* that the gift of forgiveness is given. Penance is the most intimate and most personal of all sacraments. The Gospel demand 'Repent!' comes to me, and only I can decide to respond. This is not a contradiction of the essentially social character of sin. But repentance must begin with me. Its consequences are social, and there is a solidarity in salvation as in sin. But the confrontation with the sin in me, the opening up of myself to the Light—this is only done in the solitude of my own being. I come alone into the Light. There are no general absolutions in the Gospel: every human being comes alone face to face with God. Here Jesus Christ confronts me with the choice between death and life, between selfishness and discipleship. There is no way of reaching the Kingdom by somehow being swept along with a crowd. Similarly there can be no comfortable dodging of the demand to repent by a muffled, embarrassed general confession which evades the self-scrutiny and the confrontation with sin. In the sacrament we are brought face to face with the demand of Gospel repentance. The ministry of reconciliation is delivered to me, for my own sins.

What then does it mean in practice to 'go to confession'? The mechanics are simple. The person wishing to make a confession goes to a priest, either by appointment or at a set time in church, and kneels down or sits facing the priest in the place appointed for this purpose. The priest will welcome the penitent and give him or her a blessing. The penitent then proceeds to confess his sins, mentioning how long it is since his last confession (unless, of course, this is his first confession, in which case he says so). After the confession, the priest may give advice if it has been sought, though it should be emphasized strongly that the giving of advice is not a necessary part of the sacrament, and in many cases is not called for and should not be given. The purpose of the sacrament is forgiveness, and so, after giving a penance, or simple act done out of gratitude (saying a prayer or reading a passage of the Bible, for example), the priest will give the absolution. Then he will bless the penitent who goes back to his place and says his penance before leaving.

That is the basic framework, but there are as many variations in the way in which a confession is made as there are Christian people confessing. The place and position, for example, may vary. In the past, confessions were often made in an anonymous atmosphere in a large structure called a confessional box. The priest was hidden from the penitent by a screen or grille. In many Anglican churches there was, and still is, a modification of this by which a kneeling desk is situated next to a chair, with or without a screen in between them, and so there is not the same degree of anonymity, though there is a formal structure for the relationship. However, since the revision of the rite in the Roman Church since 1974 the old structures have gone in many places. Priest and penitent face each other across a table in a 'reconciliation room'. There is more informality and warmth in both the setting and the way of making the confession. There will be Scripture readings, prayers said together, and an emphasis on the pastoral, rather than the judicial, role of the priest. It is important for each person making a confession to do so in the way which is right for him, and which enables him to confess his sins fully and honestly.

Frequency of confession too varies a good deal from one person to another. Once a month will be right for some people, while for others a quarterly confession is more valuable. It is helpful to discuss this with the priest who is to hear the confession. Choosing a confessor is important. The question of spiritual guidance or direction was referred to in Chapter 2, and is obviously related to the practice of confession. Often the confessor and the spiritual director are the same person, and this is probably the best arrangement. Spiritual direction, however, is not necessarily given in the confessional, and the two activities may be separated in time and place, even though the people are the same. But sometimes there are circumstances which make it right that the confessor and director should be different. For instance, a spiritual director need not be a priest. The question of lay confession and absolution is an important one but cannot be gone into here. But the practice of moving from one priest to another for confession is thoroughly bad, and should only happen for the most extreme of reasons.

Regular confession should be seen as an important aspect of regular prayer. Its purpose is not only the removal of sin but the recovery of the Holy Spirit. St Jerome in the fourth century saw this clearly. Writing of the confessor, he said, 'He imposes his hand on the subject and invokes the return of the Holy Spirit.' In the recent revision of the rite, the stretching out of the hands over the head of the penitent has been restored at the absolution, thus linking absolution with the other sacraments of healing and strengthening, the sacraments of the Holy Spirit. The *Order of Penance* (1974) makes it clear that the absolution 'shows the connection between the reconciliation of the sinner and the paschal mystery of Christ, and the part that the Holy Spirit plays in the forgiveness of sins' (paragraph 19).

A confession, if it is to be full and thorough, needs to be preceded by a rigorous self-examination. The purpose of self-examination is self-knowledge leading to repentance, and we can only repent of what we know. So we try to look beneath and beyond the facades and pretences which we build around us, and to see the reality of our own sin. This involves facing the fact of projection, the process by which we disguise our real condition and our inner conflicts, and cast all the responsibility for our ills onto the behaviour of others. We face our lack of faith, our unwillingness to trust, our defences by which we protect ourselves against the reality of God. Repentance involves both self-acceptance and self-denial, and these two are not contradictory. To accept ourselves is to see ourselves as we really are. To deny ourselves is to renounce the ego or false self which surrounds us with false goals and facades: the stripping away of this false consciousness is a vital first step in repentance and in the process of inner prayer. Self-examination is not morbid introspection or self-condemnation, but the honest, fearless confrontation of the self, and its abandonment to God in trust.

Many old forms of self-examination consisted of 'sin lists', and even today many of the guides seem to be based on Old Testament methods, for example, following the pattern of the Ten Commandments. But a 'Ten Commandments moral theology' is not really adequate for examining oneself in the light of the Gospel. We need to go deeper than simply going through a list of personal violations of rules, looking more closely at the corruption of the will than at the particular external acts committed. Sin does not consist only in transgression of external laws, but in an inner alienation of the personality from God. So we need to find forms of self-examination which will help us to understand our own situation better in the light of God's revelation; and which will also help us to see our sin in its social context. It is unlikely that we shall see a renewal of the Sacrament of Penance unless there is a renewed understanding of the nature of sin and a deepening of Christian conscience.

Self-knowledge, the spiritual writers tell us, is also God-knowledge, and theology is closely related to spirituality. So we are trying to see how the theology, the truth about God, becomes true *for me* and *within me*. In self-examination we face the conflict which is at the heart of our beings, the conflict which we seek to disguise by our bogus sense of assurance, blocking off doubt in the insecurity of pseudo-conviction. Yet deep down we cannot hide from our ambivalence, and within us are the roots of holiness and of blasphemy. Camus said that every blasphemy is a participation in holiness: we can only really love God and other people at the expense of being able to hate them. In the same way, one makes more progress in wrestling with crises and with God than one does in living a life of respectability shielded from adversity. Respectability is usually a form of protection against conflict: it is also a protection against growth. For, as Rilke said once, 'If my devils are to leave me, I am afraid my angels will take flight as well.' One of the greatest enemies of the spiritual life is pseudo-innocence. In self-examination and confession we try to rid ourselves of it.

Our task then is not to eliminate conflict, struggle and doubt but to learn to live in the midst of them through the light of faith. Our aim is not inner security and spiritual ease, putting to death the difficult awkward side of us which persists in disturbing the tranquillity and order of the soul. Christian penitence always has something of the knife-edge about it. We may banish the doubting, troubled side of us to the unconscious, but it is still there and will cause more trouble if it is not recognized, or, as so often, hidden beneath a facade of triumphalist faith and certainty. Repressed doubt can lead to the worst kind of fanaticism: the zealot, the fascist, the spiritual rapist who assaults the souls of others and bombards the world with the noise of his own insecurity. Self-examination means honestly recognizing our own insecurity and the reality of our doubt, without embarrassment, without guilt, trying to see how doubt and struggle are part of the life of faith. The Spanish writer Unamuno wrote: 'Those who believe they believe in God, but without passion in the heart, without anguish of mind, without uncertainty, without doubt and even at times without despair, believe only in the idea of God, not in God himself.' From spiritual smugness and the lifelessness of idols may the fiery troublesome God deliver us.

One way of self-examination which many find helpful is to use the Beatitudes in Matthew 5. The Beatitudes were addressed to the disciples of Jesus who came to him on the mountain away from the crowds (5.1). They are not general hopes addressed hopefully to the world at large, and still less are they utopian idealist sentiments with no demand for the human being now. They are an invitation to the life of the Kingdom of God, a life which brings with it unspeakable joy and ecstasy, but which will entail suffering and struggle.

Blessed are the poor in spirit. How do we practise detachment? Are we seeking simplicity, avoiding waste and the accumulation of unnecessary possessions? What does austerity mean in modern circumstances? How do we rid ourselves of encumbrances, superfluities, things which serve simply for effect, and so on? Do we have a place for silence in our lives? Or are our lives overcrowded with unnecessary words? What about poverty of the mind, the refusal to acquire useless information, preferring instead the *ascesis* of intellect which pursues one end with dedication? Poverty of mind is more necessary than poverty of the body, for the amount of mental baggage we acquire is enormous. In seeking poverty of spirit, we seek to be free of compulsions to acquire and possess, free therefore to receive what life has to give us.

Blessed are the meek. Are we humble? What about arrogance and conceit in our lives? Do we try to understand and therefore respect others? So much of what seems to be religious conviction goes hand in hand with a violent spirit: we defend our positions with arrogance, aggression, violence, and we seek to crush our opponents, to smash them, despising them in the process. Are we seeking to become non-violent and gentle in spirit? How often does our commitment to principle lead to contempt for people? Christian meekness is not weakness or lack of principle. It is a strong virtue and requires great inner spiritual strength. Are we seeking to build these inner resources of meekness?

Blessed are the peacemakers. Are we *making* peace, positively making it? What are we contributing in our district to human unity, to the removal of divisions and barriers? Do we possess inner peace, stillness of soul, serenity? Is there a movement towards peace and harmony (*shalom*) within my personality, in the relationship of body and mind, the integration of the personality? Inner peace is vital in the peacemaker: only the non-violent of spirit, as Gandhi stressed, can live the non-violent life. As he once told Nehru, 'If you have a sword in your heart, it is better that you bring it out and use it.' Peace of soul is intimately bound up with physical stillness and quiet. What about detachment from anxiety, not attempting to suppress or get rid of anxieties, which would be fruitless, but seeking to become detached from them? What about peace of mind, the quest for inner mental calm? We can only make peace if we are on the way to attaining peace.

Blessed are those who hunger and thirst for justice. Justice and peace stand and fall together. Only false peace can abide with injustice. So we need to cultivate that sensitivity which cannot rest while injustice abounds, that holy restlessness which refuses to be at ease while others suffer. Christian concern for justice must go beyond the 'eye for an eye' morality of the Pharisees. In the New Testament love and justice are not opposed: love is the culmination of justice, justice the practical expression of love. How do the demands of justice in society and in political structures enter into our self-examination?

Blessed are the pure in heart. 'Purity of heart is to will one thing' wrote Kierkegaard, perceiving the essential simplicity and directness of this demand. Are we aiming at utter sincerity, seeking to avoid compromise and duplicity? Do we perpetuate deceitfulness, sophisticated and subtle forms of lying which undermine purity? Purity goes beyond the area of sexuality with which it is often identified. It involves a passion for the authentic, the genuine, abandoning the promiscuity of not discriminating between truth and falsehood. Do we try to see through the unreal to the real, to retain our integrity and identity and not allow ourselves to be swallowed up in affairs and causes? Harry Williams defined chastity as 'the capacity so to sift my experience as to be enlarged and enriched by it instead of being diminished or destroyed'. Inner purity is seeking a direction, an orientation, seeing God.

This is only a very brief introduction to how the Beatitudes can form a basis for self-examination. Another approach is to use the traditional Seven Deadly Sins: Pride, Anger, Envy, Lust, Gluttony, Sloth, and Avarice. Many years ago Conrad Noel used them very effectively in his pamphlet *Sins and Their Cure.* Here Noel provided questions based on the Seven Deadly Sins. For example:

> Have I been sluggish and indifferent to wrongs done to God and my neighbour, content that men, women and children should live stunted lives?
>
> Have I been so busy putting the world to rights that I have

neglected my wife or husband or children, my father or mother?

Do I believe that God wills beauty in nature and in man's work? Have I tried to apply this standard to life?

Have I allowed thoughts about the evils of the world to make me depressed or neurotic, instead of stirring me to action against these evils?

Have I through cowardice or false charity failed to make public another's bad deeds when it has been necessary to do so in the public interest?

Have I taken pleasure in telling my neighbour of his bad deeds, or talked about them when it has not been necessary to do so?

Have I been a popularity hunter?

Have I through pride sought unpopularity?

Have I thanked God for his gifts of food and drink by real enjoyment of them—using them in comradeship and appreciation to keep health and gaiety, not dulling my vigour by excess either in eating or drinking?

If I gamble, in what spirit have I done so? As a Christian sport, or in deadly earnest for the sake of gain? Have I gambled to the hurt of my family, or with anyone who cannot afford to lose?

Have I been prudish about God's gift of sex, calling unclean what God has made clean?

The point about the Seven Deadly Sins is that they are normal and common but none the less destructive. A very penetrating examination of them comes in Monica Furlong's little book *Christian Uncertainties* (Hodder 1975), a book which is of great help in self-examination. She reminds us that Hieronymus Bosch in his painting 'The Seven Deadly Sins' shows the envious man being torn apart by dogs, the lustful man being eaten by wild beasts, the slothful man being beaten, the angry man being castrated, and so on. In other words, the greatest harm done by sin is to ourselves, through a death-dealing kind of possessiveness. These sins need a close, prayerful look.

First, *Pride*. Do we cling to our false identity, our image, our purported superiority to others? Gregory the Great put pride at the head of the list of sins, for pride is a form of idolatry, self-adoration, self-love. We become the centre of the universe. But pride, as Reinhold Niebuhr showed, can be a corporate sin, 'collective pride', national self-deification. How does pride affect us? In lust for power and control of others? In making ourselves into little gods? In allowing ourselves to be conned by the pretentious and proud claims of social and political groups?

Secondly, *Anger*. Do we distinguish normal healthy anger from sinful destructive anger? Do we feel that the expression of anger is beneath us, and so allow all our repressed anger to boil up inside, festering, eating away into our personality? Repressed anger is really poisonous. It can turn inwards into depression, or it can appear in twisted forms such as envy, bitterness, cruel sarcasm, and so on. Anger which is so repressed becomes buried very deep within us so that we cease to be able to recognize it and so to confess it. We need to learn from our anger about ourselves, to suspect our capacity for 'righteous indignation' and moral outrage, to question our motives. Jesus related anger to murder (Matt. 5.22), and we need to realize how injurious and harmful is our anger, our rudeness, our contempt for others. The real remedy against anger is to learn how to use our aggression to the glory of God—to imitate the wrath of the Lamb, that burning zeal for righteousness which was purified by gentleness and love.

Thirdly, *Envy*. Are we guilty of the sin of the eyes, the sin of competition which is encouraged and propagated by advertising techniques? Envy begins with the erection of a false image of others, which is then sought after. So we lose respect for ourselves and for the other whom we envy rather than love. How concerned are we with status and position? Do we have a true self-love, the only remedy for false self-love?

Fourthly, *Lust*. Again, it is essential that we distinguish sexual desire from its distortions, or true lust from sinful lust. It is the *sinful* lusts of the flesh that we renounce. Do we despise our sexuality? Are we afraid of our desires? Do we allow our own sexual fears to lead us to fail in compassion and understanding of others? Do we treat others as mere material for the satisfaction of our sexual hunger? Monica Furlong has well defined lust as 'the condition in which love becomes swallowed in hunger'. Yet hunger is not sinful, nor is it wrong to satisfy that hunger. Lust is sexual hunger which is out of control, hunger which dominates the person. Opposed to such uncontrolled lust is the virtue of chastity. Are we seeking chastity and so seeking to escape the slavery of a lustful, self-destructive way of life?

Fifthly, *Gluttony*, a sin closely linked to lust. Just as a true assessment of the seriousness of lust depends upon a high view of sexuality, so in order to appreciate the evil of gluttony we need to hold food and the body in high regard. Gluttony arises when we seek to use food and drink not as sources of pleasure but as drugs, anaesthetics, ways of escape from reality. Compulsive greed is the enemy of real pleasure. Do we really appreciate food and drink, seeing all food and all drink as sacramental? Are we sensitive to the needs of the hungry and the poor as we eat and drink, and do we take this into account in our practice of fasting? Do we treat our bodies as machines into which we can pump any number of noxious substances?

Sixthly, *Sloth*, the sin of *acedia*, which is much more than laziness. It describes the inability to act when one knows that it is necessary and right. Sloth is not merely time-wasting or inactivity. In fact, overactivity and obsession with time is one of the greatest threats to our inner lives, and a degree of sanctified laziness is something we need to learn. Sloth is not simply inactivity, but more the inability to rouse oneself from the midst of death, from compulsions, from the tyranny of habit; it is a paralysis of the spirit. Are we slothful in this sense, paralysed in our situation, refusing to act when justice demands? Are we indifferent to wrong and suffering, more concerned for peace and quiet? Sloth is the ultimate sin of omission, the state of doing nothing which allows evil to triumph. So we are right to confess that we have sinned 'in the good we have not done'.

Finally, *Avarice*, the sin of greed. The New Testament word is *pleonexia* and it means excess, the state of wanting more and more, 'ruthless greed' (Mark 7.22, New English Bible). Against this vice, the New Testament places the virtue of *epieikes*, translated as moderation. But this has nothing to do with the political vice which masquerades under the name of 'moderate' as opposed to 'extremist': in fact, moderation is an extreme demand for simplicity of life and for justice, *against* avarice and oppression. So St Paul defended his ministry by saying that he had injured no one, spoiled no one, and taken no more than his fair share (2 Cor. 7.2). In our society, avarice is often disguised under other names, as in *Pilgrim's Progress* where the covetous man was called Mr Prudent-Thrifty: so today we are likely to be addressed by 'enlightened self-interest' or 'private enterprise' or 'the virtue of competition'. Are we allowing ourselves to be seduced by the spirit of the age under its various names—through advertising, through the prevailing secular morality of accumulation of goods, through the false view of man which values him for what he has rather than what he is? Are we worshippers of Mammon rather than Christ? Bertrand Russell once said that 'it is preoccupation with possession more than anything else that prevents men from living freely and nobly'. Are we seeking to create a more equal and less broken society, or are we content to acquiesce in the midst of wealth and squalor—sloth living upon accumulated avarice?

Again, these questions are not exhaustive, of course, but are merely suggestions for beginning self-examination through the Seven Deadly Sins. In no way are they out of date: indeed the American psychiatrist Karl Menninger has suggested some new ones to add to the list. There are many other approaches which can be used. New Testament passages such as 1 Corinthians 13 or Galatians 5 can be used effectively. So can the much-despised lists of sins provided one does not become obsessed with minutiae or confuse sinfulness with quantity of acts committed. The purpose of self-examination is the identification of the trouble at the root of our beings, the stripping bare of the spirit, and the tackling of falsehood. It therefore involves wrestling and conflict, not a mechanical formalism. Indeed, formalism and settling into a groove can itself lead us into sin and block off the channels of grace. In all our self-examination it is essential that we begin by asking the Holy Spirit to show us the root difficulty which lies behind each action, to enable us to see beyond the sin to the cause of it. Not only that, but to see beyond it to the cure, to the grace of God, and to allow gratitude and joy in the experience of forgiveness to be the basis of our continuing sorrow. Sorrow and joy go hand in hand for the Christian is *peccator simul justus*, a sinner who is yet justified.

It was stressed in Chapter 2 that self-knowledge is an important aspect of prayer, and that personal spiritual guidance can be invaluable in deepening this self-knowledge and growing in the Spirit. A central element in our self-knowledge and our prayer must be the awareness of sin and the consciousness of reconciliation in Christ. Our lives need to be marked by an ever-deepening *metanoia*, that transformation of consciousness in God which is weakly, if at all, indicated by the English word 'repentance'. *Metanoia* is the constant renewing of the Christian consciousness. We need therefore to be thinking how this renewed consciousness can be nourished, and what are the ways in which penitence in prayer and life can be sustained in the future. The shape of confession is changing, and it is likely that, while the old formal structure of 'the box' will not disappear entirely, more and more confessions will be of a 'face-to-face' informal kind. It seems likely too that more Christians will find that some kind of group experience will help them both in self-examination and in the experience of forgiveness. In the early Methodist movement there was a strong sense of penitential discipline. In 1738 John Wesley provided questions to be asked for those seeking admission to the band meetings.

> Do you desire to be told your faults? . . . all your faults, and that plain and home? . . . that every one of us should tell you, from time to time, whatsoever is in his heart concerning you? Do you desire that, in doing this, we should come as close as possible, that we should cut to the quick?

At every class meeting the members were asked what sins they had committed since the previous meeting and even what temptations and thoughts they had experienced. Today more people are finding value in a similar kind of group support and group guidance, and this may well involve some kind of confessional discipline. It may also help us to understand elements in ourselves which are unclear, to become aware of areas of sin of which we were previously not aware, and therefore could not confess. We know from depth psychology that so much in our personalities is hidden and unknowable, and how vital it is that we achieve a healthy relationship between the conscious and unconscious in ourselves. This is not an alternative to confession, but it is a necessary complement to it.

We need too to be aware of the danger of a kind of pseudo-virtue, where we keep our rule of life, go to confession, receive the sacraments, fulfil all our duties, and yet somehow at the cost of our humanity. Religious people can be very depressing, very dull, over-intense and boring about the wonders of their faith. Again, one of the greatest values of a 'soul friend' or spiritual guide is the ability to help us laugh at ourselves, relax, not take ourselves too seriously or too piously, and the ability to see when even the discipline of confession may simply be reinforcing our immaturity and false piety. Another important area is that of the corporate dimensions of sin and the danger of becoming preoccupied with personal details at the expense of our social and political responsibility for maintaining structures of injustice. How can we best cultivate the spirit of penitence at this social, international level, and how can we create the necessary consciousness-raising conditions which will help us to see where we can act for change? We need to see how closely this links up with Christian penitence which can never be merely a private affair.

Most of all we need to see that the essence of sin lies not in the infringement of moral rules but in the fact that it separates us from God. And we can do worse than reflect on the words of the fourteenth-century *The Cloud of Unknowing:*

> Do thou . . . fill thy spirit with the ghostly meaning of this word SIN, and without any special regard unto any kind of sin, whether it be venial or mortal: pride, anger, or envy, covetousness, sloth, gluttony, or lust, What recks it in contemplatives what sin it is, or how great a sin . . . For all sins they think alike when the least sin separateth them from God and hindereth them from their ghostly peace.
>
> And feel sin a lump . . . and cry SIN, SIN, OUT, OUT!
>
> In the same manner shalt thou do with this little word GOD. Fill thy spirit with the ghostly meaning of it without any special regard to any of his works . . . or to any virtue that may be wrought in man's soul by any grace: not considering whether it be meekness or charity, faith or hope . . . for all virtues they find and feel in God . . . And because thou must always feel in some part this foul and stinking lump of sin as it were one and congealed with the substance of thy being: therefore shalt thou alternately mean these two words SIN and GOD . . . If thou hadst God, then shouldest thou lack sin; and mightest thou lack sin, then shouldest thou have God.

6
Prayer and conflict

> Do not bring us to the Trial, but deliver us from Evil. (Matt. 6.13)

> A pure heart penetrates both heaven and hell.
>
> THOMAS À KEMPIS

One of the most controversial aspects of new versions of the Lord's Prayer has been the replacement of the familiar 'Lead us not into temptation' by such phrases as 'Do not bring us to the time of trial' or 'do not bring us to the test'. The word *peirasmos* is the normal word for temptation, and it is possible that Jesus is urging us simply to pray that we might avoid such temptations, that God might preserve us. But the language conveys a stronger meaning. Biblical writers did not think much in terms of inner struggles between right and wrong, but in more concrete terms of 'testing' and 'trial'. Decisive moments were seen as tests from God, anticipating the final great trial, the revealing of the mystery of evil. So in Revelation 3.10 the Lord addresses the church at Philadelphia: 'I will keep you from the hour of trial (*peirasmos*) which is coming on the whole world.' The stress is on the testing of the chosen ones, and the thought is very close to that of 1 Corinthians 10.11–13. Paul points out that the trials of the past were recorded

> for our instruction, upon whom the end of the ages has come. Therefore let any one who thinks that he stands take heed lest he fall. No temptation has overtaken you that is not common to man. God is faithful, and he will not let you be tempted beyond your strength, but with the temptation will also provide the way of escape, that you may be able to endure it.

The prayer then is for fidelity in the decisive hour, for 'if those days had not been shortened, no human being would be saved' (Matt. 24.22). Of course, temptations are inevitable, and the Bible sees the trial of man as the prelude to his glory. 'When he has tried me', said Job, 'I shall come forth as gold' (Job 23.10). The trials and the testing of faith produce steadfastness (Jas. 1.2). Trials purify and reveal faith as genuine (1 Pet. 1.6, 7). God places people in situations of trial where they may fall, situations which may be disastrous: but the purpose is not disaster but triumph.

So we pray that the hour of trial may not lead us to destruction, and the second half of the petition 'Deliver us from evil' reinforces the sense. Jesus prayed not that his followers should be taken out of the world, but that they should be kept from 'the Evil One' (John 17.15). So we are not praying for deliverance from conflict, but rather that we may be victorious. Conflict as such is not only inevitable but also a necessary part of the life of faith. One of the most powerful expressions of spiritual conflict in the Bible is the picture of Jacob wrestling with the angel, that is, with God (Exod. 32.24–32). Jacob was left alone and 'a man wrestled with him until the breaking of the day'. Through the conflict Jacob realized that his combatant was God, and he called the place of conflict Peniel because 'I have seen God face to face and yet my life is preserved'. Eugène Delacroix, who painted the mural of Jacob's struggle in Saint-Sulpice, saw the conflict as a symbol of the ordeal and torment which is involved in discovering the truth about the universe. Jacob wrestles and prevails, he is not crushed, but he is wounded. God remains elusive, and Jacob, at the end of the struggle, still does not know his name. So there is discovery and revelation and blessing, but they are combined with bafflement, mystery, and wounding. Through the conflict, Jacob is strengthened. He does not know the name of God, but he does receive a new name for himself, and through this self-knowledge and self-strengthening there is a revealing of God.

Conflict is essential but there lies in the conflict the terrible possibility of faithlessness and betrayal, and it is from this that we pray for deliverance. The Evil One is described in the Bible as Satan and the Devil. But Satan originally meant an adversary, one who appears at 'the time of trial' to prosecute, one who opposes. So in the Old Testament the angel of the Lord appears as the adversary, the satan, of Balaam, standing across his path (Num. 22.22). Originally Satan himself was one of the sons of God, but his particular role was that of adversary, as in the Book of Job (1.6–12). Again the word devil, *diabolos*, is defined in the Old

Testament as an adversary. Thus Psalm 108.6: 'Let his adversary stand at his right hand'; or Zechariah 3.1: 'His adversary stood on his right hand to oppose him'. In addition to the specific theme of the adversary in court, the Bible uses a number of symbols for the forces of evil which stand in opposition to God, and foremost among these is the symbol of the dragon.

The dragon is a fantastic, mysterious, large, destructive creature, and stands for the forces of destruction. God, we are told in the creation narrative, made great sea monsters (Gen. 1.21) including dragons, leviathans and serpents. Some of them lived in the sea, others on land or in the deserts, the home of jackals and ostriches, the place of demonic conflict and struggle. These monsters were meant to praise the Lord (Ps. 148.7) but had tended to become hostile to God and men, terrifying and crushing people, and swallowing them up. In the Bible too the dragons take possession of the imperial powers of Egypt and Babylon in the Old Testament, and of Rome in the New Testament. Pharaoh is the great dragon (Exod. 29.3, 32.2), Nebuchadnezzar is also compared to a dragon (Jer. 51.34) while Rome is seen in Revelation as a red dragon with seven heads and ten horns (Rev. 12.3). Scripture also portrays the dragons as wilderness monsters, howling in the waste places (Job 30.29; Isa. 13.22), haunting the deserts, threatening the pilgrim church of the wilderness. So Psalm 91, a psalm used for centuries during the Sunday night Office of Compline and daily in the monastic Office, is a prayer for deliverance from dragons and all hostile powers.

We have seen in an earlier chapter how the theme of deliverance from evil powers into the freedom of the Kingdom of God is central to the Christian liturgy of Baptism. But it is also central to the Gospel itself: 'deliver us from evil' is what the Gospel is about. St John says that 'the whole world is in the power of the evil one' (1 John 5.19); in other words, evil is present everywhere, evil is endemic, evil is embodied in the very structures of the fallen world. So the ministry of Jesus is one of deliverance, setting people free from the oppression of evil forces. 'Satan' and 'Beelzebub' in the New Testament are seen as more than personal forces of evil; they are names for warped institutions. Behind the powers of the world are *angeloi*, *daimoniai*, *archai*, *exousiai*, the 'world rulers of this present darkness', the 'rudiments of the world' (1 Cor.

2.6–8; Eph. 6.12; Gal. 4.3; Col. 2.8). Christ, according to the New Testament, has conquered the powers and Paul in Romans 8 looks forward to the liberation of the whole created order. And it is through the Cross that the victory over the powers is brought about.

Yet the Cross itself was the culmination of a trial. St John in particular sees the ministry of Jesus as a kind of trial. The death of Jesus was the direct consequence of this ministry in which the powers of evil were confronted, the demons cast out, and the Gospel preached to the poor. The Christian belief is that the death of Jesus was not a tragedy, which was later undone by the Resurrection, a destruction followed by renewal. The death of Jesus is itself the victory over death: the Resurrection is in a sense already present in the death. As one of the Eastern Orthodox Lent Offices expresses it, the Cross 'sheds forth the rays of the resurrection'.

> Rejoice, the wood of the cross, wood three times blessed and deified, light of those who are in darkness; you anticipate in your splendour the rays of the resurrection of Christ, corresponding to the four dimensions of the world. (Orthodox Matins, Third Sunday of Lent.)

So the Cross is itself the victory, the despoiling of the principalities and powers, the destruction of death by death. By the power of Christ's death there occurs the undermining of the deathly reality of hell, for hell is the truly definitive death, fed and nourished by sin. The Cross plunges a piercing nail into hell. So, in the Orthodox office cited above, hell is made to speak in groaning terms: 'O my servants, O my powers, who has driven this nail into my heart? A lance of wood has pierced me by surprise, and I am broken.' Or, as St John Chrysostom put it in his Easter Sermon, 'Death tasted of life and was vexed.' When that sermon is read on Easter morning, the Greek Christians hold their paschal candles high and trace crosses in the air as they shout out the word Epikranthi!—Vexed!

The Cross then is seen by Christians not as an experience of tragic defeat but as one of victory over the powers of evil, a victory which we take to ourselves in prayer. Of course, the experience of crucifixion must have involved dereliction and alienation. In a sense, then, there is tragedy in the Cross, for it is the entry of God into a godless order, to undergo trial and judgement there. The cry of Jesus 'My God, my God, why have you forsaken me?' was a terrible sharing in the isolation and desperation of the human condition. It was, in Kierkegaard's phrase, a night of the Absolute. The Cross stands for the infinite distance between God and man, between God and God.

And yet from that Cross flowed life and prayerfulness. According to St John Chrysostom, the church was born out of the wounded side of Christ, and earlier Origen had written of 'the streams of the New Testament' springing from the wounded side of Christ. Hippolytus too compared the fourfold Gospel to the four streams of Paradise, and he says that streams of living waters flow from Christ's crucified body. Irenaeus is even more explicit: 'The church is the fountain of the living water that flows from the heart of Christ to us.' And this kind of language, linking the Cross with the sources of spiritual nourishment in the church, is common in the great spiritual writers. They see the sacraments of the church and its life of prayer as having their origin in the crucified God. 'This blood', wrote St Bonaventure, 'which flows from its source in the secret recesses of his heart, gave the sacraments of the church power to confer the life of grace, and for those who already live in Christ was a draught of living water welling up to eternal life.' The Cross, he insists in his devotional study *The Mystical Vine*, was supremely the death and resurrection of love.

> You cannot be ignorant of the fact that if the heart receives one wound it dies entirely, and becomes in a certain way insensible. The first wound alone was the cause of death to the heart of my dearest Lord Jesus. The heart of Jesus my bridegroom had received love's wound: it also received love's death.

It was love which wounded the heart of Jesus, love which shaped the Passion. Christ was wounded so that we might see behind the visible wound the invisible wound of love. St Bonaventure was typical of many writers who had seen in the wounds of Christ the source of a spirituality of union. So St Bernard of Clairvaux, writing on 'the richness of God's mercy in the open wounds of Christ', says: 'His body's open wounds lay bare the secrets of his heart, that mighty mystery of love . . . Never, O kind and gentle Lord, hast thou more clearly shown thy inmost heart than through thy wounds.' The fourteenth-century *Book of the Poor in Spirit* similarly speaks of 'the wounds of Our Lord from which all grace flows', and the *Imitation of Christ* advises us to 'love to dwell within the sacred wounds'. Christ was wounded for our transgressions, bruised for our iniquities, yet behind the physical suffering was a deeper suffering, the suffering of God's love, redemptive suffering.

'If God had been there, he wouldn't have let them do it', complained the small boy in Richard Jefferies' novel *Bevis.* But the essential Christian truth is that God was there, God was in Christ, in the suffering. The wounds of Christ are the way to union with God because the Cross is the centre of all Christian life and all Christian prayer. In fact it is true to say that the wounds of Christ *are* prayers. When he suffered he threatened not but committed himself (1 Pet. 2.23). In this wounded man we see our own way to the Divine love. We love him because he loved us first, and out of his heart, wounded by love, flowed rivers of living water. The New Testament compares Christ to the serpent with healing properties. To heal the victims of the serpent, Christ became like a serpent: the healer is himself wounded, the shepherd is stricken for the flock. The suffering servant is lifted up like the serpent in the wilderness so that we may be healed through his pain.

It is because of this central conviction about the victory and healing achieved by Christ's death that the Christian spiritual tradition contains a strong emphasis on sharing in and devotion to the Passion. It is particularly striking in the mystics of the Middle Ages. For example, Eckhart:

> On the Cross his heart burnt like a fire and a furnace from which the flame burst forth on all sides. So was he enflamed on the Cross by his fire of love for the whole world.

Or Julian of Norwich:

> With a glad countenance Our Lord looked at his side, rejoicing as he gazed, and as he looked, I, with my limited understanding, was led by way of the same wound into his side. There he showed me a place fair and delightful, large enough for all saved mankind to rest in love and peace.

Or Tauler:

> He gave us his heart all wounded that we may abide therein until we are wholly cleansed and without spot; until we are made like unto his heart and rendered fit and worthy to be led with him into the divine heart of the Father.

And in similar vein speak Henry Suso, Catherine of Siena, Ruysbroeck, Thomas à Kempis, and many others.

Christian prayer then both finds its source in the Cross and also involves a sharing in the Cross, and this involves the sharing of pain and anguish. Sometimes we are privileged to share, in a very intense way, the alienation from God and the darkness which covered the earth at the crucifixion. The Cross of Christ is not a problem to be understood, but a mystery into which we enter. In a sense the whole of Christian life is an experience of being plunged inwards to a deep yet increasingly simple and silent way of praying, with a strong sense of dwelling within the love of God and within the mystery of the Passion. This way of prayer is called contemplation.

Essentially contemplation is a way of looking at God, a gazing in wonder, a prayer of attention, and waiting upon God. Its central marks are stillness, simplicity, silence, and darkness. Ruysbroeck describes it as 'the simple staring with open heart into the divine brightness'. Many spiritual writers speak of a penetration into the mystery of God's Being as if through a cloud. In the movement towards contemplative prayer the spiritual writers often speak of the experience of darkness, and St John of the Cross specifically calls the transition 'the dark night of the soul'. In *The Ascent of Mount Carmel* he explains the use of this term:

> There are three reasons why we may say that this journey which the soul makes towards union with God is called 'night'. First, as concerns the point from which the soul sets out, its desires must be deprived of the delight of all the worldly things which it possessed, by being denied them. This negation and privation is as it were night for all the natural senses of man.
>
> Second, as concerns the means or way by which the soul must

> travel to reach this union, which is faith. This also is darkness to the understanding and as night.
>
> Thirdly, as concerns the goal to which the soul travels, which is God. He too is no more and no less than a dark night for the soul in this life. These three kinds of night must pass through the soul or rather the soul must pass through them and reach divine union with God.

The dark night is often wrongly used as a synonym for dryness or any type of desolation of spirit. St John however is quite clear that this is no passing phase, but is a definite and irreversible crisis point in the evolution of the spiritual life. He gives three signs by which the praying Christian can recognize the onset of the transition to contemplative prayer. First, the person finds that he can no longer meditate or use his imagination or enjoy doing so as he once did. Instead there is dryness. Secondly, he derives no benefit from the use of the senses or imagination generally. Thirdly, the most certain sign is that he still wants, and loves, to be alone with God, and to remain in 'loving attention' to God without any particular considerations.

St John of the Cross insists that once this stage is reached it is essential to make progress 'in a manner altogether contrary' to that previously followed. In the time of prayer now there will be no conscious activity except the bare intention to pray. The person simply remains in tranquillity and quietness. There is no question of ceasing to pray, but there should be no attempt at discursive meditation or attempts to make acts of devotion.

> The way in which souls should behave in this night of the senses is that they should not concern themselves at all with discourse and meditation, for it is no longer a suitable time for such things. Let them leave the soul in tranquility and quietness, even though it may seem clear to them that they are doing nothing and are wasting time.

St John is very critical of spiritual directors who do not understand what is happening and simply urge the person to greater and greater effort. He calls them 'spiritual blacksmiths'.

In contemplative prayer we usually experience a deepening of our love and an increased desire for God, even when there is no clear vision and when darkness prevails. Yet we are able to spend quite long periods in silent attention, nourished and strengthened by a powerful sense of God's presence within. So St John of the Cross says: 'Contemplation is nothing else but a sweet, tender and loving infusion of God which, if we oppose no obstacle, inflames the soul in the spirit of love.' Ruysbroeck in the fourteenth century described the experience well.

> We feed upon his immensity which we cannot devour, and we yearn after his infinity which we cannot attain; and so we cannot enter into God, nor can God enter into us, for in the untamed fury of love we are not able to renounce ourselves . . . In this storm of love our activity is above reason and wayless.

This deepening of love is an essential feature of contemplative prayer, and it is in the flowering of love in daily life that the fruit of contemplation is shown. Through contemplative prayer, love may be purified and set free. 'In the evening they will examine thee in love', says St John of the Cross.

Love in fact is the synthesis of contemplation and action, and it is in the flowering and abundance of love that we see the results of the contemplative path. We see in the lives of the great contemplatives, such as St John of the Cross and St Teresa of Avila, this overflowing of love into every part of life. In St Teresa we see particularly how contemplation brings about an integration of life so that she can pass immediately from the sublime to the apparently trivial. For prayer and love to her are very, very simple. She says that 'love alone, however manifest, leads to union with God', and she looks for the effects of prayer in loving service of one's fellows. And love is the heart of the prayer itself: 'If you would progress a long way along this road, the important thing is not to think much, but to love much. Do then whatever arouses you to love' (*Interior Castle*, Chapter 1). St John too writes of God's relationship to man as that of a loved one to his lover. He says in *The Living Flame of Love* that 'there is in fact a mutual interchange of love between the soul and God in the conformity of the union . . . wherein the goods of both, that is, the Divine essence are possessed by both together'.

Another vital aspect of contemplative prayer is that of listening.

This way of prayer has an essentially passive dimension. St Teresa used the analogy of the 'four waters' to represent four stages in prayer. First there is the bucket when there is a good deal of activity and effort. Then comes the water wheel and conduits where less action is needed, and finally come the waters of the stream, followed at last by natural rainfall which she sees as the symbol of contemplative prayer. So the amount of effort is reduced, and we seek merely to remain in a condition of attention to God.

What then of the darkness of which the mystics speak so much? Of course, not all darkness is indicative of spiritual progress. Some darkness in prayer is due to sin, some is the result of depression or is of physiological origin. But the darkness of which the mystics speak is the creative darkness of entering into the mystery of God.

> O dark dark dark, They all go into the dark ...
> I said to my soul, be still and let the dark come upon you
> Which shall be the darkness of God ...
> I said to my soul, be still and wait without hope,
> For hope would be hope for the wrong thing; wait without
>   love ...
> Wait without thought for you are not yet ready for thought.
> So the darkness shall be the light, and the stillness the dancing.
>
> T. S. ELIOT, 'East Coker'

What is happening in the dark night is, from the human point of view, the result of a change in the seat of control within the person. In the earlier period of prayer, the conscious ego was in control. But now the ego is set free, and the focal point of the personality moves to the centre. And it is there, at the centre of consciousness, that there may occur the encounter with God. The 'darkness and nakedness and nothingness' which mark this encounter is described in the writings of Ruysbroeck. 'In this darkness he is enwrapped', he says of the soul. 'The abysmal waylessness of God, so dark and so unconditioned that it swallows up in itself every divine way and activity.' He goes on:

> And the abyss of God calls to the abyss ... This inward call is an inundation of the essential brightness, and this essential brightness, enfolding as in an abysmal love, causes us to be lost to ourselves and to flow forth from ourselves into the wild darkness of the Godhead ...

> In the abyss of this darkness in which the loving spirit has died to itself there begins the manifestation of God and eternal life.

Similarly, Walter Hilton in *The Scale of Perfection* says that 'whoever loves God dwells in light' but must remain for a while in 'a night pregnant with good', a glowing darkness.

> Therefore wait for God's grace, persevere and do not overtax yourself... Understand that when you desire Jesus and wish to think of nothing but him, but cannot do it properly because of worldly thoughts crowding into your mind, you have in fact left the false daylight and are entering this darkness.

Hilton sees the night as simply a complete withdrawal of the soul from earthly things by an interior desire to love, see and know Jesus.

But it is in *The Cloud of Unknowing*, also from the fourteenth century, that we see most fully developed the theology of dark contemplation. The author of the *Cloud* belongs to a long tradition stretching from Gregory of Nyssa and Pseudo-Dionysius to the Rhineland mystics and St John of the Cross, the tradition which stresses that we can know more about what God is not than about what he is. The symbol of the cloud dominates the book, but the cloud is not up in the sky, remote from our souls. The cloud is within us: we are to direct our eyes into the depths of our own beings. There, rejecting and laying aside thoughts and concepts, we come to a knowledge of God through love: 'For of all other creatures and their works, yes, and of the works of God's self, a man may, through grace, have full knowledge, and he can think well about them: but of God himself no man can think.'

No amount of thinking can bring us to God. So in contemplative prayer we should think of nothing. Forget, forget, abandon all rational thought beneath the cloud of forgetting: this is the message of the author. If we empty our minds of all images, we will allow the 'blind stirring of love' to rise in our hearts. This love will pierce the 'cloud of unknowing' and bring us to a knowledge which is beyond that of the reason, a higher knowledge. Thoughts are a barrier to this knowledge, and so the advice given to those troubled by the persistence of thought is 'Tread him fast down with a stirring of love'. In his later work *The Epistle of Privy Counsel* the author speaks of 'a naked intent stretching unto God'.

Again it is love which is central to this teaching about contemplation. 'By love he may be gotten and holden, but by thought never'. *The Cloud* is emphatic that knowledge of God comes through love: 'And therefore lift up thy love to the cloud. Or rather (if I shall say thee sooth) let God draw thy love up to that cloud; and strive thou through the help of his grace to forget all other things.' The human side of the work of contemplation is forgetting, the removal of obstacles. It is God who is, in the words of *The Epistle*, 'the chief stirrer and worker'. Yet this knowledge which comes through love is a dark knowledge. It is obscure, knowledge from a cloud. This is how *The Cloud* speaks of it.

> For at the first time when thou dost it, thou findest but a darkness, and as it were a cloud of unknowing, thou knowest not what, saving that thou feelest in thy will a naked intent unto God. This darkness and this cloud, however thou dost, is betwixt thee and thy God, and hindereth thee, so that thou mayest neither see him clearly by light of understanding in thy reason, nor feel him in sweetness of love in thine affection. And therefore shape thee to bide in this darkness as long as thou mayest, evermore crying after him whom thou lovest. For if ever thou shalt see him or feel him, as it may be here it must always be in this cloud and in this darkness.

So the soul, filled with love, is plunged into the darkness of the cloud, where it cannot see clearly or even feel sweetly. Yet the author holds that to be in this dark cloud is a wonderful grace of God although it can bring with it great suffering. The suffering arises because the cloud prevents clear vision of God, and the senses crave for knowledge but cannot find it. It is a state of deprivation: in the words of St John of the Cross, it is as if 'a thick and heavy cloud is upon the soul, keeping it in affliction, and, as it were, far away from God'. In spite of this, *The Cloud* holds that it is a 'high and wonderful cloud' because the person in the cloud is in fact nearer to God than anyone else alive. This darkness leads to God as nothing else does. The night is 'more lovely than the dawn' in St John of the Cross's words.

The mystics who speak of the cloud and of the darkness are

referring to the darkness of faith. Gregory of Nyssa speaks of how Abraham 'after he had purified his mind of all such concepts . . . took hold of a faith that was unmixed and pure of any concept'. And it is this pure faith which is central to the teaching of *The Cloud of Unknowing*. It is only in the obscurity of faith that the person can grasp the transcendent God, for God is darkness to the mind of man, blinding the mind. For faith is not the same as reason or rational belief. Rather does the light of faith darken the intellect, which seems to be filled with nothing. Yet through faith comes a more intense vision which can come in no other way.

Yet, the mystics insist, there is no growth in contemplative prayer without the experience of suffering. For the deepening of love brings with it a sense of the transitoriness of human thought and the weakness of the intellect. The spiritual guides warn constantly against the idolatry of mind and concept. 'Try to make your understanding deaf and dumb,' wrote Evagrius, 'and so you will be able to pray.' It is through love that we come to know God, not through thought and speculation. But this deepening of love brings with it also an intensified sense of temptation and spiritual struggle. It is a real sharing in the passion of Christ.

Contemplative prayer is thus a sharing in the darkness of mystery, the darkness in which God reveals himself. But contemplation can be abused so that it becomes a means of spiritual self-indulgence. Nowhere is the abuse of contemplation attacked so fiercely as in the writings of Ruysbroeck, and his critique is highly relevant today when 'mysticism' is often sold as a commodity on the spiritual market. Chapter 4 of his *Book of Supreme Truth* is entitled 'Of the men who practise a false vacancy'. These men, he says, are 'turned in upon the bareness of their own being' and not upon God. They are 'so simply and so idly united with the bare essence of their own souls'. They neglect the common life and the sacraments for they believe themselves to have 'passed beyond all these things' and to be superior to them. They 'will endure no contradiction'. But, Ruysbroeck points out, their contemplation is false, for they are absorbed in themselves.

> And the onefold simplicity which they there possess they take to be God because they find a natural rest therein. And so they

> think themselves to be God in their simple ground; for they lack true faith, hope and charity.

Ruysbroeck returns to the theme of this 'natural rest' in his book *The Adornment of the Spiritual Marriage.* In Chapter 66 he describes the characteristics of this state.

> It is a sitting still, without either outward or inward acts, in vacancy in order that rest may be found and may remain untroubled. But a rest which is practised in this way is unlawful; for it brings with it in men a blindness and ignorance and a sinking down into themselves without activity. Such a rest is naught else than an idleness into which the man has fallen and in which he forgets himself and God and all things in all that has to do with activity. The rest is wholly contrary to the supernatural rest which one possesses in God.

Ruysbroeck sees that this natural rest leads to spiritual pride and self-sufficiency. These people are 'wholly attached in their desire to inward savours and the spiritual refreshment of their nature. And this is called spiritual lust'. They are, in his view, 'the most wicked and vile of all men living'.

Contemplation then can be abused, and there are a good many examples in the present day of bogus contemplative movements which promote the 'false vacancy' of which Ruysbroeck wrote. 'The Devil', as *The Cloud* stressed, 'has his contemplatives.' But true Christian contemplation, the quiet, loving waiting upon God in silence and darkness, is a vital aspect of Christian prayer. And this contemplation is not reserved for specialists or for those with extraordinary vocations. It is for all Christians who are truly seeking a life hidden with Christ in God.

The darkness, as we have seen, is not the periodic state of desolation or despair, but rather the normal and necessary experience of the mystery of God through faith. However, it is important to remember that desolation and despair are characteristics of most Christian lives at some point. Prophets and saints have often been deeply troubled people. To take two examples from the Old Testament, we find much spiritual anguish in the writings of Jeremiah and Job. Jeremiah's prayer was full of anguish and of struggle with depression and bitterness. Jeremiah carried with him in his ministry a terrible sense of his unworthiness (1.6) and even of failure (15.10–11). He was persecuted by his relatives and friends (11.19). As a result he was driven in upon himself and experienced deep depression and misery, so that he wished he had never been born (15.10; 20.14–18). He felt that his wound was incurable (15.18). Out of his experience came violent aggression against his enemies on whom he calls down curses and urges God to be merciless (17.18; 18.21ff). Yet he was compelled to continue.

> I am reproached and mocked all the time
> for uttering the word of the Lord.
> Whenever I said, 'I will call him to mind no more,
> Nor speak in his name again',
> Then his word was imprisoned in my body,
> like a fire blazing in my heart,
> And I was weary with holding it under,
> And I could endure no more. (10.8–9).

Again, in Job we see the good man who became the victim of appalling tragedy, including the loss of his family and physical sickness, so that he became reduced to loneliness and despondency.

> So now my soul is in turmoil within me,
> And misery has me daily in its grip.
> By night pain pierces my very bones,
> And there is ceaseless throbbing in my veins.
> My garments are all bespattered with my phlegm,
> Which chokes me like the collar of a shirt.
> God himself has flung me down in the mud,
> No better than dust or ashes. (Job 30.16–19)

Job's advisers try to console him, but without success. Job, who has given good advice to others in trouble, cannot see through his own distress.

> Think how once you encouraged those who faltered,
> How you braced feeble arms,
> How a word from you upheld the stumblers
> And put strength into weak knees.
> But now that adversity comes upon you, you lose patience;

It troubles you and you are unmanned.
Is your religion no comfort to you? (4.3–6)

Eliphaz indeed puts a sound and orthodox argument for committing oneself to God in the midst of trouble, but it cuts no ice with Job who is at the end of his tether. He is broken, he hangs over the abyss. Bildad is no more successful when he points Job to past history, while Zophar accuses Job of sin. Job is quite unhelped by these arguments and consolations, for God has hidden his face (13.24). And yet he turns from his well-meaning comforters to God who is present in the midst of his darkness.

The experience of being forsaken by God is common in prayer and in the Christian life in general. In fact some have suggested that doubt and uncertainty are the marks of our age, and that our spirituality must somehow incorporate them into itself. All spirituality must learn to cope with doubt and confusion, and prayer which is true can never be cosy and secure. For it is a groping towards God, and the way forward is often marked by danger and the possibility of becoming unhinged and lost in space. Like all journeys the journey of the inner life has its dangerous paths. Yet we do not pray in order to provide ourselves with defences against danger, but in order to face the danger through the power of the God who has been there first, who has cleansed the waters and harrowed hell. Yet there is an inescapable element in prayer which can best be described as 'wailing', that agonized crying out to the God who seems to have withdrawn. Nietzsche speaks of this condition in *Thus Spake Zarathrustra*. Man is abandoned and isolated, isolated from God. He cries out in desperation.

Who still warms me, who still loves me?
Offer me hot hands!
Offer me coal-warmers for the heart!
Spread-eagled, shuddering,
Like a half-dead man whose feet are warmed—
Shaken, alas! by unknown fevers,
Trembling with sharp icy frost-arrows,
Pursued by you, my thought!
Unutterable, veiled, terrible one!
Huntsman behind the clouds!

Struck down by your lightning-bolt,
You mocking eye that stares at me from the darkness—thus I lie,
Bend myself, twist myself, tortured,
By every eternal torment,
smitten,
By you, cruel huntsman,
You unknown—God!

God is seen in this desperate passage as 'unutterable, veiled, terrible one', as a huntsman, a mocking eye penetrating from the darkness. And this sense of abandonment and alienation, of distance between man and God, is one of the facts of the human condition which we must recognize and face in our prayer. At times our prayer will simply be the willingness to abide with uncertainty, with bafflement, with the experience of God's absence.

This experience of God's absence is a familiar one to the writers of the Bible: they speak of God as having turned his back and as being silent. But today the experience is in a sense more terrible because there is a widespread loss of hope and sense of sterility, a sense of the uselessness of human effort and of the power and supremacy of the machine. This absence of hope is worse even than despair, for despair is at least conscious. Despair has a vital role in prayer, it is dynamic and desperate. But the loss of hope is merely cold and dead, lifeless, inactive, producing nothing, saying nothing, aware of nothing. It is a void, it is the ultimate cold. Yet it is in this situation of the apparent 'eclipse of God' that hope really comes into its own. For the prayer of hope is not a cosy security but a response to the silence of God. It is a refusal to give in to the seemingly hopeless situation. It is the conflict of man with God, the refusal to abandon vision. It is the opposite of resignation and acquiescence, and as such it is a vital aspect of prayer. It is a clinging to the vision of the Kingdom in spite of the evidence to the contrary. In hope we wait in the dark, like watchmen awaiting the dawn.

Christian hope therefore is hope 'in spite of ...' A contemporary Latin American song expresses it well:

Since he came into the world and into history;
broke down silence and suffering;
filled the world with his glory;
was the light in the coldness of our night;

was born in a dark manger;
in his life sowed love and light;
broke hardened hearts
but lifted up dejected souls;
So today we have hope;
today we persevere in our struggle;
today we face our future with confidence
in this land which is ours.

And so in spite of the threats to hope, in spite of the terrible concentrated power of evil and oppression, Christian hope is always light out of darkness, and never a glib and naive optimism. Out of the deep we call to the Lord (Ps. 130.1).

All prayer, because it is faith in the mystery of God and a sharing in that mystery, contains the dimension of darkness. But from time to time the darkness becomes one of personal pressure to the point of what seems to be the total eclipse of God. Everything goes dark. The experience of deep depression is like this: everything seems utterly hopeless, and God has gone too. Life becomes a series of pointless events, and one wants to withdraw from them all, curl up, and die. Weariness sets in, and one feels utterly desolate, desperately alone, and isolated. The last thing we feel in depression is that we are made in the image and likeness of God: we feel rather that we are utterly useless, hopeless, desperate, and empty. This experience of depression is real, not a fantasy, and it is essential that we accept it. It is useless to struggle against it, or regard it as a sin, or to feel that we are too good to get depressed. Some of the most committed and saintly Christian people experience deep, dark depression, and grow through, and from, the experience.

Now depression, of course, affects the life of prayer. Our prayer in the darkness is hardly likely to be cheerful and filled with exultation, and much of it seems dead and meaningless. It is important to keep before one's eyes during this period of apparent loss of hope the truth that we *are*, in spite of everything to the contrary, children of God, made for glory, and of infinite value. On the other hand, our prayer will inevitably reflect our mood, and we will probably identify with the Psalmist in his moments of desolation more than those of triumphant praise. There is a solidarity in desolation as in worship generally. So to maintain a life of prayer in the midst of gloom is essential even if the prayer simply seems to be a case of abiding in darkness. 'Keep your mind in hell, and despair not' was the advice of the Eastern teacher Staretz Silouan.

Prayer and sickness are closely related at a superficial level because many people tend to regard the sick as being in peculiar need of prayer when they apply this attitude to no one else. Many lists for intercession include only the sick. But at a deeper level also prayer is related to the experience of pain and suffering. To begin to make progress in prayer is to become more sensitive to the pain of others and to our own inner pain, for all Christian prayer is, to some extent, a sharing in the Passion of Christ. It shares in the process of cleansing and purification of the heart from all that might obstruct the Holy Spirit. In particular, those called to any kind of pastoral ministry must share in the experience of being wounded, for only the wounded can heal. By *our* stripes *they* are healed. Dietrich Bonhoeffer held that it was the fact that Christians range themselves with God in his suffering which distinguishes them from heathen. Man is called to participate in the sufferings of God. In the second century St Ignatius said the same.

> Suffer me to attain to light, light pure and undefiled; for only when I am come thither shall I be truly a man. Leave me to imitate the passion of my God. If any of you has God within himself, let that man understand my longings and feel for me, because he will know the force by which I am constrained.

It is when we are confronted by sickness and by our own inability to *do* anything that the real crisis of contemplative prayer occurs. For the apparent inability to do anything is in fact a real inability: there *is* nothing we can *do*. We can only pray with an intensity of love, in the midst of silence and darkness. To pray in the midst of suffering is to accept that God is in the deepest region of hell, and we remain there with him. Often the prayer which comes from the heart of sickness is a very passive prayer in which we lean very heavily on the prayer support of others within the Body of Christ (1 Cor. 12.26). It may be that only through prolonging and intensifying the sense of our own helplessness and reliance on others can God teach us important lessons about ourselves and our limitations. A physical illness in which one is reduced to a state of great weakness and apparent uselessness can be a time of grace and renewal. But often it does not seem like this at the time, only a time of disintegration and failure. 'Where were you, my God, whilst my heart was tormented?' asked St Catherine of Siena. God replied, 'I was in your heart.' In such physical sickness, a physical-based prayer is valuable. Simply to hold a crucifix or a rosary may be the best and simplest prayer we can offer.

Through physical, as through mental, suffering a real inner healing of the spirit may occur; and it is inner healing which is the primary concern of intercessory prayer. When we pray for others we seek to bring their deepest needs within the sphere of the healing work of Christ. It is not our love or our peace which we are seeking to impart: rather we are seeking to be ministers of healing and reconciliation through the power of God which is released through the prayer of intercession. We align ourselves not only with the suffering of God but with the redemptive power which flows from that suffering. Intercession thus is more than a mere recital of names: it is a literal standing between, an act of reconciliation, a sacrificial, priestly work in which Christ allows us to share. Intercession for healing of the sick and troubled is therefore a ministry of the greatest importance and one demanding a strong sense of discipline and responsibility.

What we are seeking to do in intercession for the sick is to become involved in a process of reversal of the destructive forces of evil in the world. Intercession cannot be separated from the other aspects of prayer with which we have been concerned. It is, for example, closely linked with self-knowledge and purity of heart. One of the Fathers once said that 'he who knows himself is greater than he who can raise the dead', and it is certainly true that the deepening of one's own inner knowledge and inner purity is of benefit to those for whom one prays. But to deepen love is to deepen suffering, and there is in intercession an intimate involvement in the pain and anguish of others. How intercession 'works' is often beyond our understanding, though, at the human level, we can gain some clues from depth psychotherapy. Jung held that healing through faith sprang from an *unconscious* relationship, a relationship based on response to a need of the soul. When this need is awakened in someone through the ministry of another in whom it is alive, there occurs an influx of a new stream of energy, and the centre of the personality becomes anchored in new ground. It may be that something like this occurs in intercession which acts at this unconscious level to bring about healing and newness of life.

It is the experience of those involved in the ministry of healing that the most remarkable physical transformations occur. But not all healing is physical. The saintly Padre Pio was a great healer, but his own hands, feet, and side were marked by open wounds for over fifty years, wounds which brought him into an intimate union with the Crucified. Once a man came to Padre Pio and told him that he was going blind, and asked for healing. Pio replied, 'My son, there are many people who sin with their eyes.' The man replied, 'Oh Padre, for them I would gladly give my sight.' He did go blind, but who would dare to say that no healing occurred? Often the strength drawn from the physical wounds is itself a healing power in the world. Prayer may heal at a different level from the physical, at the level of undermining the reality of evil in an individual. For the effect of prayer is to transform the human person into a home for the divine presence. This is how St John Chrysostom sees the use of the Prayer of Jesus, and he makes the closest association between this prayer and the ministry of deliverance.

> The name of the Lord Jesus Christ as it descends into the depths of the heart will subdue the snake which controls its pastures, and will heal and revive the soul. Continue constantly in the name of the Lord Jesus that the heart may swallow the Lord and the Lord the heart, and that these two may be one. However, this is not accomplished in a single day, nor in two days, but requires many years and much time. Much time and labour are needed in order to expel the enemy and instate Christ.

The work of intercession therefore is a true ministry and the most effective form of Christian action, working at the deepest level of reality.

Father Francis MacNutt in his valuable study *Healing* speaks of four basic prayer methods which we must understand in order to exercise a complete healing ministry. The first is *prayer for repentance* where there is personal sin causing the sickness. Forgiveness of sin is intimately connected with physical and spiritual health, and a good deal of sickness is due to, or affected by, the fact that we are not right with God or with our fellow human beings. In Jesus' teaching on prayer there is a strong emphasis on the place of forgiveness. 'When you stand in prayer, forgive whatever you have against anybody' (Matt. 11.25). The refusal to forgive is one of the most serious barriers to prayer and health. And so we need to pray for forgiveness and for the ability to forgive others, both in ourselves and in others. The Sacrament of Reconciliation has an important place in the ministry of healing.

Secondly, there is *prayer for inner healing*, or 'healing of memories'. If prayer really works at a deep level, we should expect that it operates at the level of the deep emotional wounds which most of us have experienced, and which can, if they are not faced, dominate our lives and prevent us from making progress in the Christian life. If healing is to take place, these wounds and painful memories from the past must be healed. Prayer for inner healing is a prayer that God would free us from the effects of these past wounds, and would heal them.

Thirdly, there is *prayer for physical healing*, the kind of healing of which we naturally think, but which is in fact only one level of it. Physical healing undoubtedly does occur through prayer, but it is essential that we pray that God's will may be done, that God would heal in his way.

Finally, there is *prayer for deliverance*. This is sometimes called exorcism, but because this term has been so misunderstood and misused, many prefer to speak of it as the ministry of deliverance. It is a prayer for the setting free of individuals, communities and places from the oppression of evil forces. It is a demanding and important aspect of healing prayer, but one which should not be entered into without careful spiritual preparation. To enter into a discussion of this field of ministry is beyond the scope of this book, but readers are referred to some of the books listed in the bibliography.

Associated with all these forms of prayer for healing may be the laying on of hands and anointing with oil. Although laying on of hands is used sacramentally in confirmation and ordination, its wider and more informal use is common within the context of prayer for healing. From the time of the Bible until now the Holy Spirit uses the hands of Christian people—not only priests—to convey grace and strength. It would be wrong to treat such a ministry as a kind of pseudo-sacrament, and equally wrong to neglect or despise its use. Laying on of hands can occur within the framework of the sacraments, but it can also be an important element in private prayer. In the Old Testament, during the consecration of levites, the whole people laid their hands upon them (Num. 8.10), and Moses laid hands on Joshua to set him apart as the leader of the people (27.18–20). On one occasion in the Old Testament the action is used as a blessing, in the case of Jacob laying his hands on the two sons of Joseph (Gen. 48.14–20). In the Gospels we find Jesus using the laying on of hands both in blessing (Mark 10.12,16) and in healing (Mark 5.23, etc). The early Christians certainly used the laying on of hands to convey the gift of the Holy Spirit.

In the tradition of the church there are many instances of the laying on of hands by lay people, and this practice, which seems to have been common in the early church, has recently become widespread again through the Charismatic renewal. It is best seen as an active form of prayer. St Augustine once described it simply as 'prayer over a man'. On the other hand, the sacrament of anointing involves more careful preparation and is not an act which is frequently repeated. The holy oils which are blessed each year on Maundy Thursday are oils which are to be used in the context of prayer. There are three oils, those of catechumens, chrism and healing, each with its special place. The oil of catechumens is strictly for use on non-Christians, that is, on those who are not yet baptized: it is an oil associated with prayer for deliverance from evil (the baptismal exorcism) and with strengthening. The chrism is the baptismal oil itself, for it is from chrism (oil: hence Christos, the Christ or anointed One) that we derive the term 'Christening'. The oil of healing is that oil which is used to anoint the sick and the dying.

While the oil of healing is usually associated with prayer in relation to physical and mental sickness, it should be emphasized that all anointings, including those within the baptismal liturgy, are concerned with deliverance from evil and oppression, and with the imparting of the healing power of the Spirit; and that all anointing is part of a liturgy of conflict with the powers of evil. In considering the element of conflict in prayer therefore the anointings have a special, though neglected, place. The oil of catechumens was originally used on those who were preparing for Baptism and were therefore part of the catechumenate. Today, as infant Baptisms decline in many parts of the church, the revival of a modern style of catechumenate may well restore it to its former importance. It was, and is, used to anoint candidates, and it follows an exorcism, or prayer for deliverance. In the early church the act was preceded by prayer and fasting in which the whole Christian community took part as well as the candidates. So Justin Martyr writes:

> As many as are persuaded and believe that these things which we teach and describe are true, and undertake to live accordingly, are taught to pray and ask God, while fasting, for forgiveness of their sins; and we pray and fast with them.

Then comes the exorcism, a prayer that the candidate might be delivered from the power of darkness. It is probably to the recently baptized who have experienced the liturgy of deliverance that St Peter addresses these words in his First Epistle:

> You are a chosen race, a royal priesthood, a holy nation, God's own people, that you might declare the wonderful deeds of him who called you out of darkness into his marvellous light. Once you were no people but now you are God's people; once you had not received mercy but now you have received mercy. (1 Pet. 2.9–10)

The use of oil in connection with the exorcism goes back to the second and third centuries. St Cyril reminded his congregation at Jerusalem that 'when you were stripped, you were anointed with exorcised oil'. Today in the modern Roman rite of Baptism the candidate is anointed with the words: 'We anoint you with the oil of salvation in the name of Christ our Saviour; may he strengthen you with his power who lives and reigns for ever and ever. Amen.'

The anointing with chrism after Baptism has, since the splitting up of the rite in the west, become associated with Confirmation. This too is very ancient. So the third-century document *The Apostolic Tradition* says that the candidate, as he comes up from the water, 'shall be anointed by the presbyter with the Oil of Thanksgiving', and soon afterwards he is led to the bishop who anoints him again before giving him the kiss of peace. In contrast to the pre-baptismal oil of deliverance, this is an oil associated with thankgiving and celebration, with the receiving of the fullness of God's spirit, and with entry into the priestly body of the church. Taken together, the oils used in Baptism symbolize and effect the twofold power of deliverance and strengthening in Christ. So the baptismal liturgy is a microcosm of the entire Christian life of conflict with evil and putting on of the Christ-life.

What of the oil of healing? The restoration of anointing to the local church as a normal part of its prayer and liturgy is of the greatest urgency. For too long anointing was associated with the onset of death, and it was therefore termed 'extreme unction' and seen as part of the 'last rites'. Of course, there is an important place for anointing of the dying, but it has a much wider role than this. The new Roman order for anointing the sick makes this clear.

> Through this holy anointing and his great love for you, may the Lord help you with the power of his Holy Spirit. Amen.
>
> May the Lord who freed you from sin heal you and extend his saving grace to you. Amen.

The prayer used at the blessing of the oil makes its role in healing even more explicit.

> Lord God, all-comforting Father, you brought healing to the sick through your Son Jesus Christ. Hear us as we pray to you in faith, and send the Holy Spirit, the Comforter, from heaven upon this oil, which nature has provided to serve the needs of men.
>
> May your blessing come upon all who are anointed with this oil, that they may be freed from pain, illness, and disease and made well again in body, mind and soul.
>
> Father, may this oil, which you have blessed for our use, produce its healing effect, in the name of our Lord Jesus Christ.

The change in emphasis and expression in the revision of the rite of anointing was quite deliberate: in fact Pope Paul VI specifically stated that the sacramental formula was modified in order to express fully the effect of the sacrament.

The use of oil for healing goes back to the Gospel period when the disciples of Jesus went preaching repentance, casting out devils, and anointing the sick (Mark 6.13). In the early church the oil which was blessed by the bishop was taken home by the people and used when anyone in the household was sick. Lay anointing was common although the blessing of oil was reserved to the bishop. However lay anointing was suppressed in the ninth century, and in the twelfth century it came to be seen as the sacrament of the dying. Today we are seeing the renewal of this sacrament and its restoration to a central place in the church's life of prayer.

Prayer then has a crucial role in healing, and in intercessory prayer we are helping to release into a situation of suffering the powers of healing love. In the sacramental use of anointing we are deeply involved in the healing of man both physically and spiritually. But this is not to deny the essential place of prayer in relation to death, and the central place of death in Christian spirituality. Prayer and dying are clearly close if only because they accompany each other through life: all life is involved with the process of dying, and in Christian understanding all life is prayer. Throughout our lives there is dying and the birth of new life through death, and this is as true at the spiritual level as at the physical level of tissues and cells. And the facing of the reality of death in daily living is central to New Testament spirituality: he who seeks to save his life will lose it. It has been said that the best way to live is to die every night, and that one of our chief dangers is that of clinging to our past and seeking to preserve it against the harsh spiritual facts of new life through death.

If this is so then it follows that to prepare ourselves for death by living lives of self-abandonment is the best preparation for our pastoral ministry to the dying. The Christian who has at least begun to face death in himself can begin to enter into the experience of the dying person with sensitivity. Dr Cicely Saunders, the pioneer of the hospice movement, wrote of a dying patient whom she asked what he looked for in those who were caring for him. He answered, 'For someone to look as if she is trying to understand me.' And understanding must involve the understanding of the person's need to prepare for death. The refusal, or inability, of many doctors to tell the truth to dying patients, a fact which emerges very clearly from a number of recent studies, is therefore worrying. For the onset of death is too important for the Christian to be deceived about it. Many dying people, of course, do know the truth, and need the opportunity to express it and have their insight confirmed. The Christian has a vital contribution to make here in trying to help people to face death and in holding them before God during their period of dying. But he must also recognize that to do this demands a real facing of that terrible reality in his own life, and that his own prayer will be deepened by the insights of the dying.

Prayer alongside the dying will usually be a silent kind of watching. 'Watch with me' is its most accurate slogan, for its principal marks should be respect for the dying person, and attention to his agony and distress. It is a deeply contemplative form of prayer. We need to listen to and learn from the prayer of the dying, as indeed from elderly people in general. Jung held that in the second half of life the unconscious spontaneously invades consciousness. The onset of middle age brings difficulties and opportunities in prayer life. We often make the mistake of seeing the ageing process in entirely negative terms, as decline and loss of function. Of course, growing old does involve the shrinking of the number of functional brain cells, and it has effects on intelligence, memory, and so on. But the positive contribution of the old to the praying life of the Body of Christ needs strong emphasis. In many parishes in fact it is the obscure prayer life of a few old people which is the spiritual mainstay and source of strength. And as death draws near this prayer may grow in silence, simplicity, and confidence.

So we are to share in the prayer of the dying. But prayer also is needed at the time of death, and after death as we continue to hold the departed in our prayer and in the pleading of the Sacrifice of the Mass. The liturgy of Christian burial needs to express the faith in the resurrection. For death is the last enemy to be destroyed, and Christian prayer is living prayer, prayer which is a sharing in the risen life of Christ. But that experience of being risen in Christ comes only through the experience of dying: light comes through the sharing of darkness. That is the meaning of dying daily: every day we do 'die a little' and so prepare for the final conflict. True prayer should help us face, and not evade, that conflict, by enabling us to live as we shall eventually die. In Blake's words:

> Man was made for joy and woe,
> And when this we rightly know,
> Thro' the world in safety go,
> Joy and Woe are woven fine,
> A Clothing for the soul divine.

7
Prayer and progress

> For the Kingdom, the Power and the Glory are yours, now and for ever. (Matt. 6.13 (in some versions))

> You are not here to verify,
> Instruct yourself, or inform curiosity
> Or carry report. You are here to kneel
> Where prayer has been valid.
>
> T. S. ELIOT, 'Little Gidding'

The way of prayer is a way of progress: progress to and in God; progress in holiness; progress towards the Kingdom; progress in communion, and in penitence; progress through conflict. Prayer, like the church, is always on the move. But this theme of the moving church, the pilgrim church, a people on the march, has to a great extent been eroded by the emergence of 'established churches'. Now the church and its buildings seem to represent permanence and stability rather than transition, the static rather than the changing, property rather than poverty. Also today we tend to see churches as meeting places for worship and other activities rather than as places sanctified by and for prayer. We have a functional view derived from our functional society. Often churches are locked most of the week so that people could not use them for prayer if they wished. In the Middle Ages, when the great cathedrals were built, it was assumed that worship was the most vital of all human activities. Now in a culture which has forgotten the meaning of worship but which, at many points, searches for 'signals of transcendence', the church building should witness to a reality which is in time and space but also moves beyond them. It should excite and inspire the movement of prayer, raising our spirits by the symbols of glory.

The consecration of sacred places and the central importance given to them by Christian tradition derives from the basic doctrines of Creation and Incarnation. It is because the created world is holy and good, but also twisted and disfigured, that certain places are set apart as redeemed areas, liberated zones, reclaimed from the forces of evil. The church is a redeemed part of the creation, not as a refuge from the unredeemed world, but rather as a foretaste of its redemption to come, when the creation itself shall be freed from decay and enjoy the glorious liberty of the children of God (Rom. 8). Again it is within the church that the Incarnate Word, Jesus Christ, is present in the Eucharistic action and in the sacrament reserved. It is in fact the Eucharist which constitutes the church. All church buildings are built around an altar at which Christian people gather to celebrate the Eucharist together. There too, in churches of the Catholic tradition, the sacrament is reserved in a tabernacle or similar structure for the adoration of the people and the communion of the sick.

There is thus a sense in which Christ is present in the church in a particular, though not exclusive, manner. The Incarnation again is the pattern. Christ's presence in Galilee did not mean that the universal presence of God in creation and within human beings was in any sense diminished. The sacramental presence of Christ in the powerful and concentrated form of the Holy Sacrament does not mean that we are denying his presence elsewhere. The particular does not deny the universal, nor the universal the particular, and we need to re-emphasize the real and particular presence of Christ in the church building, consecrated and sanctified by the Holy Spirit and containing the Eucharistic Bread of the Presence. There is a special power and strength which flows from the sacrament, and which makes the church an important place of, and aid to, prayer. God has given us churches and blessed them with his Eucharistic presence in order to aid our prayer and provide us with additional grace. We should not despise them, or despise those who use them, by some glib comment about finding God in the world. Of course, we should find God in all things and in all places; of course, the world is a sacrament. But the whole point of the sacraments and of the setting apart of certain places as sacramental places is to enable us to make progress in that ability to see the whole world as sacramental. That ability does not come suddenly or easily.

To use the church for private prayer on weekdays and perhaps at night is therefore both valuable and sensible. In fact, in many places today, the church may be the only place where silence and solitude are possible. This raises the problem, particularly in cities, of locked churches. Often churches which are left open are safer than those which are locked since the presence of people, praying and visiting, is usually a better deterrent to vandalism than locks and bolts. Encouraging a group of Christians to make use of a church building and to pray in it is an important area of pastoral ministry. But if it is unavoidable that a church should be locked, then keys can, and should, be made available to those people who wish to use the church for the purpose for which it was built. The work of prayer is what churches were made for, and a church which is not prayed in is a scandal and should be pulled down.

In a society which overvalues production and profit and judges activities in terms of these qualities, it is essential that church buildings continue to witness to the value of adoration and prayer as ends in themselves. Yet buildings, even consecrated buildings, are not the only places for prayer. In the New Testament and in the early history of monasticism the desert, the literal physical desert wastes of Egypt, constituted the place above all others for encounter with God and the self, the place of spiritual conflict and spiritual progress. What can we say today about the place of the desert in the growing Christian life?

The desert in Christian spirituality means the place of solitude and emptiness, the place where we are stripped and simplified. It is not surprising that many generations of Christians have found the literal desert wastes to be the ideal setting for contemplation. Thomas Merton once defined contemplation as 'the preference for the desert'. From very early times God has confronted people in the desert. The spiritual history of Israel is a desert history (cf. Deut. 32.10; Amos 5.25; Exod. 3.2).

> It is the persistent recollection of this historic experience of the Sinai desert amid the annual festival enactment of the conversion of dryness into fertility that has given the scriptural texts the extraordinary complexity and potency which was to survive in varied impulses into Christian history. (George H. Williams, *Wilderness and Paradise in Christian Thought*, 1962, p. 5)

The desert has a prominent place in the New Testament as in the Old. It is there that John the Baptist preaches the need for *metanoia*, transforming of consciousness, and it is there that Jesus experiences conflict and temptation, struggles with his identity and his mission, and prepares himself for the *exodus* to Jerusalem. It was in the desert that the early Christians sought the path of union with God and wrestled with evil. Of the desert St Jerome wrote:

> O desert enamelled with the flowers of Christ. O solitude where those stones are born of which in the Apocalypse is built the city of the Great King ... How long will you remain in the shadow of roofs, in the smoky dungeons of the cities? Believe me, I see here more of the light.

So in all ages of the church the desert has drawn people in search of God and of themselves. In our time Carlo Carretto wrote of the Sahara as the place where he learnt to pray, and from his desert experience he was driven to share the gift of prayer with his friends. The early desert fathers saw withdrawal into the desert (*anachoresis*) as the first stage of a long process of achieving loving attention to God. It was a first stage but a necessary one. It had the effect of removing external distractions and making the cultivation of physical silence possible. So for the monk the simple cell became the framework of prayer and growth. St Anthony explained:

> Fish, if they tarry on dry land, die: even so monks that tarry outside their cell or abide with men of the world fall away from their vow of quiet. As fish must return to the sea so must we to our cell; lest it befall that by tarrying without, we forget to watch within.

But the desert is not simply a place for monks: it has a vital place in the spiritual life of all Christians.

What is the essential point of desert experience? Why is it that, in the words of St John of the Cross, 'the best fruit grows in land that is cold and dry'? The essential fact to grasp is that in the desert we live by trust and by naked faith. All props, all non-essentials, all luxuries, are taken away. The desert road is one of solitude and emptiness, and it exhausts the soul. It is the place both of sterility and of the divine presence, of demons and of the encounter with God.

In the desert we are deprived of those things which prevent us from seeing ourselves and reality in nakedness and simplicity, freed from disguises and false appearances. We are reduced to a simplicity of life and set free from attachments which obstruct our path. So we begin to see more clearly, perhaps too clearly for comfort. The desert therefore will be a place of pain and anguish, but it will also lead to greater clarity, greater insight, greater stillness of soul. In the wastes of the desert the voices of the world can be heard more distinctly and in their true perspective, and we can begin to move more close to the heart of things.

What does the desert mean in today's world? It is unlikely, for most people in the west, to mean a literal desert. It must mean solitude, silence, withdrawal. It stands for the perpetual need in prayer to leave the strife and tumult and retire to the solitary place. So we may leave our ordinary place of life and work and seek a quiet retreat in the country for a 'desert day'. We may find our desert in the city in some hidden corner. Here the city church which is open can provide a desert for many travellers, and can exercise a vital ministry simply by being open and being there.

However there are some Christians who are called to the life of the desert as a permanent way of discipleship. They are called hermits or solitaries. They spend much time alone, though they are never really alone. They are deeply involved in humanity, involved with its anguish and pain. They are 'watchmen upon the walls' at the point where evil and the paschal mystery meet. 'My life is with my neighbour', said St Anthony, the first great Christian hermit. So the solitary, through his prayer and his penitence, embraces the world which he seems to have left. He testifies to a solidarity between people and within the human family, a solidarity which is unexpected and mysterious and whose basis lies in prayer.

The existence of the solitary vocation exposes at its most painful point the problem of the value of prayer. To those for whom prayer is merely functional, an aid to work, the solitary's life is wasted: it is indeed waste itself. For the solitary sees prayer as an end in itself. And yet the solitary merely poses a question which needs to be answered by every Christian, and he lives a life which, in some degree, must be lived by all of us. In particular, the witness of the solitary is vital in a culture which seeks to devalue the human person and see human beings as being important only for what they produce. It is only a society in which people possess an interior solitude which can be held together by love. Thomas Merton constantly stressed this need for solitude and he pointed out that in reality all men are solitary. What is important is that they should become aware of this dimension. It is this awareness which people have found in the isolation of the desert, and to which the solitaries in their desert bear special witness.

The solitary life paradoxically must begin from the firm belief that human beings are a solidarity, that they are not isolated units but one body in Christ. There is no solitude without communion, man is not an individual but a person, and persons are made for communion. So, in James Baldwin's words, 'whoever debases another debases himself', and, conversely, whoever seeks purity of heart will inevitably affect and involve others in his quest. So Father Congreve, the nineteenth-century Anglican monk, could say that 'perhaps none have realised as intensely the saving mystery of fellowship, the love of brethren, as those whom God has called to live by prayer in the greatest solitude, even in the continual contemplation of the hermit'. The solitary seeks not only to grow closer to God and to humanity, but also to work at a healing level to combat the forces of evil in the world. 'The solitary life', wrote Thomas Merton, 'is an arid, rugged purification of the heart.'

But for those, the majority, who are not called to the solitary life, the practice of solitude has an importance for prayer, as we saw earlier. It was central to the ministry of Jesus, and through the centuries the great spiritual teachers and guides have insisted on solitude as a necessary condition of growth in inner silence and prayerfulness of spirit. As Eckhart said, 'You must depart from all crowds, and go back to the starting point, the core out of which you came.'

To withdraw, even for a short time, into solitude is to disengage oneself from the oppression of words. Our age is one which is marked and disfigured by the corruption and dehumanizing of language. We live under the constant onslaught of words from advertisements and from propaganda, and the clichés and slogans of the consumer technocracies. Words by the million wash over us in a wave of meaninglessness. But the recovery of meaning and of resistance to this oppression derives from the practice of inner silence. Out of silence and solitude comes *diakrisis*, discernment, discrimination. Yet the solitude also bears within it conflict and struggle. As St Anthony expressed it, 'Who sits in solitude and is quiet has escaped from three wars: hearing, speaking, seeing: yet against one thing shall he continually battle: that is, his own heart.' The battle in the heart, as we have seen, is more important than external battles, for the heart is the centre of life. In our attempts to make progress in prayer, then, it is vital that we find space for solitude and the practice of silence.

One neglected aspect of the hidden life in the world is that of prayer during the night, or 'keeping vigil'. The night is often a time of silence, one of the few times in many people's lives when uninterrupted silence is possible. The night is not always the right time for prayer, and for some it is emphatically the wrong time: if one is exhausted with the work of the day, the night time should be used for sleep and relaxation. But there are many for whom the night hours are ideally suited to prayer, and this might include prayer in church where a group might undertake a time of night adoration, or intercession. The night is for many a time of despair, of violence, of temptation, of sin, of suicide, and of broken hearts. It is all the more urgent that there are Christian people who see prayer in the night as part of their pastoral responsibility.

But for many, the time when lengthy and sustained solitude is possible is the time of retreat, and a rule of disciplined prayer should find time and room for a retreat, if possible, at least annually. What is a retreat? It is a time, lasting from two days to a week or longer, of concentrated, intense silence and prayer. All over Britain are retreat centres, some of them in monasteries and convents, but an increasing number being centres built specially for retreats: they are popular not only among churchpeople, but among the large numbers of 'unattached' seekers who are looking for a spiritual path and exploring the life of the spirit. In this time of retreat we withdraw physically to a place where silence is possible, and we seek, through silence and withdrawal, to grow in our Christian life. A retreat may be conducted as a group exercise, and often a group from a church or elsewhere will go into retreat together. But it may be 'private', a time when we are silent by ourselves—though, like private prayer, a 'private' retreat is still a sharing in the common spirituality of the Body.

A conducted retreat is one which is led and guided by someone, usually, but not necessarily, a priest. This will usually take the form of a series of addresses on a theme, or conducted meditations, or exercises in prayer. But much of the time will be spent in silence, and it is the silence which is the most important element in retreat. A private retreat is one in which the individual organizes his own programme of prayer and works out his own timetable. In both the purpose is the same: to deepen and nourish the life of the spirit by withdrawal and concentrated attention. Today, when so many people are unfamiliar with, and sometimes frightened of, silence, some conducted retreats are a mixture of silence and discussion, in an attempt to introduce people to silence gently and gradually. The very experienced retreat conductor and spiritual director Norman Goodacre has described some ways in which the traditional retreat can be modified to meet modern needs (*Experiments in Retreats*, Mowbrays 1970).

To go into retreat is not to 'opt out' of one's social responsibility, or to treat the life of the monastery or enclosed order as superior to that of the city streets. But at a time when many of us are, rightly, very active and busy, retreats are more, not less, necessary, so that we can balance our activity by contemplative insight and clear perception. Retreats are a sharpening of our perception, a purifying of vision, a training programme for the spirit. In retreat we seek to be able to go on serving the world with renewed strength without being dominated or swallowed up by it. So rest and activity both have a place there: rest, because we are tired, and rest is good and necessary for us; activity, because a retreat is more than a rest, it is an exercise, a discipline. If we are to grow in prayer we need that intense concentrated time of discipline.

However, the purpose of prayer in the solitary place is to enable us to pray in the streets. St Symeon the New Theologian, in the tenth century, was one of the first of the eastern saints to emphasize strongly that the fullness of the mystical life was accessible to those living in the midst of cities. Today the urban contemplative is more and more evident. St Anthony is coming back from his desert, for the age of Constantine is ended. Again, as in the early years, the church is a minority movement, a movement in growing conflict with the pagan world, and it needs all the contemplatives it can get. The desert is now in the midst of the city. So many Christians are struggling to find ways of living lives of contemplative prayer in the urban context. The example of the Little Brothers and Little Sisters of Jesus, the family formed by Charles de Foucauld to which reference was made earlier, has been followed by many who have sought this way of living the Gospel. The central task with which these Christians are concerned is the discovery of an urban spirituality, a form of Christian life-style which is viable and enriching for those living and working in the 'urban cores'.

The problems of urbanization which raise so many issues for pastoral action present the back-street church with questions about its *ascesis*, its inner spiritual discipline. In fact the French theologian Jacques Ellul has argued that because the city is a place of non-communication, we are not asked to preach but rather to pray (*The Meaning of the City*, Eerdmans, 1971, p. 124). Christians in Latin America have responded to the problem of size and lack of community in cities by creating 'communidades de base' or basic communities which read the Gospel together, celebrate their faith, and deepen their spirituality. In the churches of the United States and Britain too the challenge of urban crisis is increasingly being seen in the context of prayer and spiritual struggle. As a recent document from the Roman Catholic Church in the USA has expressed it:

> It is here, at the core, that one discovers that history is created, if not by the spiritually mature, then by the spiritually deformed and degenerate. It is here, at the core, where prayerful hands become clenched and the presence of God is most discernible in rage. (*Hear the Cry of Jerusalem*, National Urban Pastoral Statement, 1978)

These writers argue strongly that the modern city is the new desert, the place where human life is not sustained but only preyed upon. The city has been abandoned, and only the wretched and the weak are its inhabitants. In the city one sees a conspiracy against God's poor, and 'there are no angels to weep with its people'. The city, marked everywhere by the sense of powerlessness of most of its occupants, has become a culture enchanted with the demonic, a culture with the classic desert temptations to idolatry.

The ministry in cities is thus a ministry marked by exorcism and contemplation, by the casting out of demons and that close attention to the signs of God's presence which is the basis of prophecy. The consecration of places to the glory and service of God presupposes a world in which all things are not yet so consecrated. Just as buildings and places can be centres of holiness, justice and the peace of God, so buildings and places can be centres of evil and destructive forces, exercising a disturbing and malign influence on those who go there. Christian prayer has always contained petitions for deliverance of such places from the hostile influences which stand in the way of spiritual renewal. Thus the ancient Compline prayer: 'Visit, we beseech you, O Lord, this place, and drive far from it all the snares of the Enemy. Let your holy angels dwell here to keep us in peace, and may your blessing ever be upon us.' Part of the urban crisis is the concentration of injustice and cruelty: houses which are used to exploit and dehumanize their occupants; street corners which are used to sell racist literature and to incite racial violence; slum properties which serve only to degrade their owners. These are some of the places which stand in need of deliverance. The Christian community in the urban cores must see its role as one of commitment both to prayer and politics, to contemplation and struggle for justice.

Because God works in and through the specific and the particular, part of the Christian tradition of prayer involves movement from one place to another—pilgrimage. A pilgrimage is a deliberate, planned, prepared visit by an individual or a group to a place which has been used by God to give grace and blessing. Of course, the whole of the Christian life is a movement, a pilgrimage, for we are

> seeking Jerusalem, dear native land,
> through our long exile on Babylon's strand.

All Christian prayer is the prayer of a people on the march, a travelling people. It is the prayer of movement. St Augustine expressed it well in his contrast between our present singing of 'Alleluia' and that of heaven.

> How happy will be our shout of Alleluia there—how carefree—how secure from any adversary, where there is no enemy, where no friend perishes . . . So, brethren, let us sing Alleluia now, not in the enjoyment of heavenly rest, but to sweeten our toil. Sing as travellers sing along the road, but keep on walking. Sing, but keep on walking. What do I mean by walking? I mean Press on

from good to better. The apostle says there are some who go from bad to worse. But if you press on, you keep on walking . . . So sing Alleluia and keep on walking.

The early British saints were great walkers, and the sites of their ministry at such places as Iona, Lindisfarne, and the towns of Northumberland and Durham have long been favourite places of pilgrimage. The ancient sites of the Christian churches at Glastonbury and Canterbury, or the medieval village of Walsingham, 'England's Nazareth', are centres of pilgrimage to which many thousands go in search of an enriching of their Christian lives.

A pilgrimage is different from a retreat, but, like a retreat, it can play a vitalizing and reviving role in the life of prayer. The decline of pilgrimages since the Middle Ages, when, as we know from Chaucer, they were hilarious as well as holy escapades, is partly to do with the fact that nowadays we have other ways of getting a holiday! For medieval Christians the pilgrimage was often the only holiday. But there is also a theological reason, and this is the realization of the holiness of all things and places. Yet that theological truth should not destroy the pilgrim spirit, merely correct its possible misuse: we do not go to Glastonbury or Walsingham because they are more holy, but because God has used them, and continues to use them, to communicate himself. A pilgrimage is always a joyful affair. Medieval pilgrimages usually started at inns, as Chaucer started at the *Tabard* in Southwark. But they are essentially acts of prayer and commitment, and of thanksgiving for the creation. To go on pilgrimage can deepen in us such commitment to serve God in all parts of his created world.

Another aspect of pilgrimage is the quest for a holy person, a charismatic figure, someone from whom we can learn wisdom and discernment. So in the early centuries eastern Christians sought out the monks of the Egyptian desert. So today many young people take the long and weary road to India in search of gurus. And yet the truth we seek is very close to us, however many journeys we need to undertake in order to find it. The purpose of pilgrimage is to realize that what we seek is within us, that God is closer to us than breathing. In order to find this simple truth we become explorers, and this may mean geographical explorers. In the particular place, on the particular plot of earth, here, we find God. In T. S. Eliot's words in 'Little Gidding':

> We shall not cease from exploration
> And the end of all our exploring
> Will be to arrive where we started
> And know the place for the first time.

In the exploration which is prayer, we do not go alone, but are part of a numberless company of fellow-disciples, living and dead. This is what we mean by the 'communion of saints'. The *koinonia* or solidarity of the people of God does not end with death. Many Christians have no qualms about asking the living for their prayers, but shrink back from asking for the prayers of the saints. The late S. J. Forrest wrote a poem about this fear.

> Oh Vicar, do not pray for me.
> You're only wasting time.
> I have no need of holy prayers
> To help me in my climb.
> I thought you were a sinner,
> But they tell me that you ain't.
> I will not let you pray for me
> In case you are a saint!

Of course it is possible that we might make devotion to, and prayer to, the saints a substitute for devotion to Christ. But that is hardly a serious danger in the twentieth century! It is far more probable that we might be tempted to isolate Christ from his Body, to seek to worship a lonely Christ in an isolated and remote heaven, ignoring the common life which surrounds both him and us. Probably one of the main factors which has led to the revival of pilgrimages in our day has been the recovery of a sense of solidarity with the saints of the past, and the sense of their continued presence and power in certain places. T. S. Eliot wrote in *Murder in the Cathedral*:

> For wherever a saint has dwelt, wherever a martyr has given his blood for the blood of Christ,
> There is holy ground, and the sanctity shall not depart from it,
> Though armies trample over it, though sightseers come with guidebooks looking over it;

From where the western seas gnaw at the coast of Iona,
To the death in the desert, the prayer in forgotten places by the broken imperial column,
From such ground springs that which forever renews the earth ...

But the communion of saints is not something which is determined by geography, however much certain places may figure in our relationship with the saints of the past. The daily worship of the church everywhere takes place in the company of 'angels and archangels and the whole company of heaven'. Our prayer is aided by their prayers, and we should ask for their help and support.

In this solidarity of the Body of Christ, the church has given a place of central importance to Mary, the Mother of Jesus. One of the commonest prayers of the church is the Hail Mary, said by millions of Christian people every day.

Hail Mary, full of grace, the Lord is with thee. Blessed art thou among women, and blessed is the fruit of thy womb, Jesus.
Holy Mary, Mother of God, pray for us sinners now and at the hour of our death. Amen.

The Virgin Mary is the Christian prototype of all little people. In the Bible, virginity stands for the impossible. It meant humiliation, failure, barrenness, futility; the virgin had no future and was despised for her emptiness and waste. But, as Pope Paul VI stressed in his Encyclical on Mary, *Marialis Cultus* (1974), Mary stands for the truth that God 'vindicates the humble and oppressed, and removes the powerful people of the world from their privileged positions'. In the same vein, the nineteenth-century Anglican priest Thomas Hancock called Mary's song Magnificat 'the hymn of the universal social revolution'. So Christian prayer and spirituality is full of praise to Mary, as illustrated by the Orthodox hymn.

Rejoice, for thou art the source of joy,
Rejoice, for thou art the salvation of the fallen Adam.
Rejoice, for thou hast dried the tears of Eve.
Rejoice, O sublimity inaccessible to the thought of man.
Rejoice, O depth unfathomable even for the eyes of angels.
Rejoice, for thou art the throne of the King of Majesty.
Rejoice, for thou bearest him who bears the universe.

Rejoice, O Star that heralds the coming of the Sun.
Rejoice, O Womb in which God becomes man.
Rejoice, thou by whom man has been renewed.

Mary is seen in Christian tradition as the New Eve, the woman clothed with the sun, the God-bearer (*Theotokos*, a title bestowed on her at the Council of Ephesus in 431). She is the one

whose name
All but adoring love may claim.

Far from being the meek and gentle, passive lady of corrupt piety, or the symbol of family stability of some church devotions, Mary is a figure of vitality and mystery, standing as she does at the point of intersection of the timeless and time, at the point where the powers of the age to come create confusion in the world. Donne expressed well the incredible wonder of her role in redemption.

Ere by the spheares time was created, thou
Wast in his minde, who is thy Sonne and Brother;
Whom thou conceiv'st, conceiv'd, yea thou art now
Thy Maker's maker, and thy Father's mother;
Thou hast light in dark; and shutst in little room,
Immensity cloysterd in they deare wombe.

Of course, there have been, and still are, false and unhealthy forms of devotion to Mary. Anglicans seem to be peculiarly inclined to isolate devotion to Mary from the rest of Christianity, seeing it as something reserved for places like Walsingham, and for certain feasts, and to be ignored throughout the rest of the year and elsewhere. More common is the type of person who treats Mary as a kind of ideal, and unreal, woman, a mother-substitute, a sentimental mixture of pseudo-chivalry and sexual projection. For some, devotion to Mary seems to be polemical, part of one's propaganda, a way of making a point. All these are dangers and aberrations, but they should not blind us to the important place of Mary and of Marian devotion in Christian prayer. Such devotion should be marked by theological perspective, an understanding of Mary's place in the scheme of redemption, and natural spontaneity, avoiding the artificial and precious.

In our prayer then we are in union with Mary who bore the

Word of God in her body. We too seek through our prayer the union between the Word of God and our own lives. So Mary is the archetype of the church, the first member of the redeemed community. Everything she now is, we will be. As the Preface to the Mass of the Assumption put it, Mary is 'the beginning and the pattern of the church in its perfection, and a sign of hope and comfort for God's people on their pilgrim way'. Christian spirituality suffers if it loses what the Swiss theologian Hans Urs von Balthasar has called 'the marian principle'.

> Without mariology Christianity threatens imperceptibly to become inhuman. The Church becomes functionalistic, soulless, a hectic enterprise without any point of rest, estranged from its true nature by the planners. And because, in this mainly-masculine world, all that we have is one ideology replacing another, everything becomes polemical, critical, bitter, humourless, and ultimately boring, and people in their masses run away from such a church. (Hans Urs von Balthasar, *Elucidations*, SPCK 1975, p. 72)

A true Marian element in our prayer should have no overtones of male superiority and female passivity, but rather should help to restore to spirituality the feminine dimension which is often missing.

Christian prayer, as we have seen, is the prayer of the entire Body of Christ throughout the universe. When we pray, we pray with the church. The formal way in which this solidarity is expressed in the daily routine of prayer is through the Divine Office, and it is essential to devote some space to this. An Office is simply a structured form of prayer containing psalms, scripture readings, and prayers. While many Christians have been fearful and suspicious of this way of praying, seeing it as the enemy of informality and homeliness, others have found that it gives them the needed discipline and structure which aids freedom rather than stifles it. The idea of some set form of Office in fact is based on a realistic assessment of human beings and of our prayer potential. We do not always pray with spontaneity and ease, nor should our prayer depend on the way we feel. Prayer which is so based on feelings is unstable and lacks depth. The Office is an objective form of prayer which is independent of our feelings, although of course it is often accompanied by, and arouses, deep feelings and emotion. It is a sharing in the prayer of the whole church.

The idea of a daily Office can be traced back to the recital of the 'Hear, O Israel' (Deut. 6.4) twice daily, and the three hours of prayer in Judaism, first attested in Daniel 6.11. Here there was a daily pattern of prayer—in the morning, at about three in the afternoon, and in the evening ('at the time of the evening sacrifice': Ezra 9.5; Dan. 9.21). By New Testament times the custom of praying three times a day seems to have been widespread (Acts 3.1; 10.3,30) The Didache enjoins the use of the Lord's Prayer three times a day (Didache 8.3), and vigils, the extension of evening prayer through the night, were held in apostolic times (2 Cor. 6.5; 11.27).

It is Tertullian who explains how the observance of the three hours of prayer corresponded with the principal divisions of the working day which were marked by the ringing of the city bells. But it is from the fourth-century writer Prudentius that we derive detailed evidence of Office hymns for the various hours, and extracts from Prudentius' hymns are found in most western breviaries. In the fourth century the communal recitation of the hours was established in the monasteries, from which they spread to the church at large. It is clear from the writings of St John Chrysostom in the same century that Offices were said in local churches, for he cites the objection to lay participation: 'Is it possible that a man of the world, engaged in the business of the tribunals, can be interrupted three times a day to go to church for prayer?' In reply, he points out that it is possible to pray in private wherever one might be. It was not, however, until the ninth century that there was any uniformity in the pattern of the daily Office, and it came about through the influence of the Benedictine movement.

In the Rule of St Benedict the term 'Divine Office' is used to translate *de officiis divinis* in the sections on the ordering of the daily rhythm of prayer. *Officium* means a duty, as indeed did the Greek word *leitourgia* from which we derive liturgy. From the sixth century the sevenfold daily Office and the lengthy night Office was established within monasticism, and it was this monastic Office which formed the basis of the Roman Breviary and of our present western Offices. The fully developed Office consisted of the Night Office and the two major day hours, Lauds (Morning Prayer) and Vespers (Evening Prayer) and five lesser hours—Prime (6 a.m.), Terce (9 a.m.), Sext (12 noon), None (3 p.m.), and Compline, the late night service. These hours were associated with the natural rhythms of the day, and the lesser hours were given psalms which could be learnt by heart and recited without books in the fields, at work, or in the darkness of the cell. In support of the sevenfold Office St Benedict quoted Psalm 119.164: 'Seven times a day will I praise thee.' In fact, praise is central to the whole idea of an Office until the Reformation when instruction and 'edification' become more dominant. Yet the stress on praise as the primary purpose of the Office has remained central in Roman Catholic thought. The Encyclical *Mediator Dei* (1947) reaffirmed it. 'The Divine Office is the prayer of the mystical Body of Jesus Christ . . . he unites the whole community of mankind to himself . . . in singing this canticle of the divine praise.' Or again the Apostolic Constitution of Pope Paul VI by which the revised Roman Office was promulgated in 1970 begins by speaking of 'the Canticle of Praise, unceasingly hymned in heaven' which 'has been faithfully continued by his church throughout the ages, though in a variety of forms'. Towards the conclusion it expresses this wish:

> . . . let there resound throughout the church a magnificent hymn of praise to God, and let it be united to that hymn of praise sung in the courts of heaven by the angels and saints. May the days of our earthly exile be filled more and more with that praise which throughout the ages is given to the One seated on the throne and to the Lamb.

Nor is this view of the Office as an act of praise peculiarly Roman Catholic. A Baptist minister, Stephen Winward, in his introductory essay to *The Daily Office*, the ecumenical revision published in 1968, says: 'The primary purpose of the Office is to offer praise to God.'

This is not the place for an examination of the changing pattern of the Divine Office since the Anglican vernacular Office of 1549 onwards, the revisions of the Roman Breviary since 1568, and the major changes in both churches in the last decade. Nor is there space here to look at the possible adaptation of the Office, in its various forms, to the needs of busy Christians with little time. This is an urgent task which needs to be attempted. But a prior task is that of defending the principle of use of an Office at all. For many Christians, the idea of a daily Office is something peculiar to monks and nuns, and to those clergy who feel inclined to follow the monastic pattern. One of the tragic facts of recent years has been the number of parish clergy who have ceased to use any form of Office and whose spirituality has suffered to a serious degree. One reason for this is that for many the Office as they have known it has ceased to provide them with an adequate vehicle of praise and with adequate spiritual nourishment. But what of lay people? Is the Office not for the laity too? And in what form can it be prayed?

The value of an Office is its objectivity. It is a means by which we pray with the whole church, uniting our prayer with that of millions of other Christians living and dead. This is true whether one is alone or with a group, for the Office is essentially a corporate act. It is objective too in that it does not depend on our feelings, but gives our prayer life a regularity and a disciplined framework. Far from being difficult in a busy life, it is precisely what is needed: a short and set layout in which praise, Bible reading, intercession and other elements in prayer are held together in balance. Of course, the form of the Office, and the way in which it is used, are of the greatest importance, and we need to think in terms of a basic skeleton framework which can then be 'enfleshed' in our different situations. At its simplest a daily Office would consist of canticle of praise, use of the Psalms according to a plan, a short passage from the Bible, and time for intercessory prayer. There is an abundance of resources in the recent revisions of the Office to enable people in all ways of life to adapt the Office to their needs. In the building up of the Body of Christ, of mature Christians with lives of deep prayer, the spread of use of the daily Office is of the greatest value.

But the whole point of the Office and of set times and forms of prayer is to enable us to attain the state of habitual prayerfulness. Jesus taught his followers to pray *always* (Luke 18.1) and St Paul added 'without intermission' (1 Thess. 5.17). This continual prayer in the midst of life and activity should be our aim, but it needs to be nourished in order to develop. St Basil explained that such habitual prayer does not mean word-centred prayer but the integration of prayer with life: 'This is how you pray continually—not by offering prayer in words, but by joining yourself to God through your whole way of life, so that your life becomes one continuous and uninterrupted prayer.' Similarly many centuries later Thomas of Celano said of St Francis of Assisi that 'in his whole being he was not so much praying as himself transformed into prayer'. So the aim of our concentrated prayer time is to enable prayer and life to be unified. That is why St Anthony made the puzzling statement that no person who is conscious that he is praying is praying perfectly. Perfect prayer becomes as natural and unselfconscious as breathing. So St Isaac the Syrian in the seventh century:

> When the Spirit takes its dwelling place in man he does not cease to pray, because the Spirit will constantly pray in him. Then, neither when he sleeps, nor when he is awake will prayer be cut off from the soul; but when he eats and when he drinks, when he lies down or when he does any work, even when he is immersed in sleep, the perfumes of prayer will breathe in his heart spontaneously.

By praying some of the time we aim to be able to pray at all times, to attain uninterrupted consciousness of God in all situations. For the Lord, as St Teresa said, is among the saucepans. That does not mean that when we are washing the saucepans, we are consciously thinking of God: not only would that lead to the very fragmentation of mind which is the enemy of prayer, but it would also mean the washing up was done badly. The Vietnamese Buddhist monk Nhat Hanh, recalling the Sutra on Mindfulness, tells us rather that we should wash the dishes in order to wash the dishes. The key to such mindfulness is a unity of body and mind, a unity which the spiritual teachers of the east see to be closely connected with breathing. Hence the teaching about keeping the recollection of the Name of Jesus united with one's breath.

Prayer at all times requires discipline. It is helped and nourished by corporate worship, by the practice of silence, by mind control, and by the recitation of the Office. Through them we can slowly learn to move between the inner and the outer worlds, for, as Thomas à Kempis tells us in *The Imitation of Christ*:

> He who walks by an inner light, and is not unduly influenced by outward things needs no special time or place for his prayers. For the man of inner life easily recollects himself, since he is never wholly immersed in outward affairs.

It is in order to develop further this capacity to move from prayer to action, and from action to prayer, that the eastern church teaches the constant use of the Prayer of Jesus (see Chapter 2): 'Lord Jesus Christ, Son of God, have mercy on me a sinner.' This prayer stands at the centre of the spiritual tradition of the eastern church. From the fifth century onwards we learn of the prayer of invocation or 'remembrance' of the Name of Jesus. Its use grew out of desert monasticism with its stress on *hesychia* and on 'holding the mind in the heart'. The central idea is to incorporate prayer very deeply in the centre of the personality so that one prays continually. The Jesus Prayer thus is more than a use of words, it is the taking into one's heart the reality of the nature of Jesus. In the experience of thousands of Christians the use of this prayer has proved to be an effective way of attaining to that close union with God and man which is the aim of all prayer.

In prayer we are seeking to realize in our selves that condition of union with God and man. This book has considered some of the approaches to prayer and some of the disciplines which will help to nourish the life of prayer and enable it to flourish. But books have a limited aim and can themselves be a substitute for prayer. All prayer is movement, and the most that a book such as this can do is help that movement along. But prayer cannot be taught, cannot be contained, cannot be captured, and the moment we think we have captured it, we have lost it. For the meaning of prayer can only be discovered in the darkness of the life of faith. Tennyson caught the essence of this life well in *In Memoriam*.

> Our little systems have their day;
> They have their day and cease to be;
> They are but broken lights of thee,
> And thou, O Lord, are more than they.
> We have but faith: we cannot know,

For knowledge is of things we see;
And yet we trust it comes from thee,
A beam in darkness: let it grow.

Bibliography

This book has been an introduction to Christian spirituality and has treated most of the aspects of the life of prayer very briefly. The following books are strongly recommended for further reading.

Prayer and Spirituality: General

Abhishikatananda, *Prayer*. SPCK 1972.

Bernard Basset, *Let's Start Praying Again*. Sheed and Ward 1972.

Mark Gibbard, *Why Pray?* SCM Press 1970.

F. C. Happold, *The Journey Inwards*. Darton, Longman and Todd 1968.

F. C. Happold, *Mysticism*. Penguin 1963.

Martin Israel, *Precarious Living*. Hodder and Stoughton 1976.

Martin Israel, *Summons to Life*. Hodder and Stoughton 1974.

William Johnston, *Christian Zen*. Harper and Row 1971.

Adrian van Kaam, *Dynamics of Spiritual Self-Direction*. Dimension Books, Denville, New Jersey 1976.

Morton Kelsey, *Encounter with God*. Hodder and Stoughton 1976.

Andre Louf, *Teach Us to Pray*. Darton, Longman and Todd 1974.

A Monk of the Eastern Church, *Orthodox Spirituality*. Fellowship of St Alban and St Sergius and SPCK 1968.

Michel Quoist, *Prayers of Life*. Gill, Dublin 1963.

Simon Tugwell, *Prayer*. 2 vols. Veritas Publications, Dublin 1974.

Evelyn Underhill, *Worship*. Nisbet 1936.

Biblical Teaching

Donald Coggan, *The Prayers of the New Testament*. Hodder and Stoughton 1967.

Joachim Jeremias, 'Abba' in *The Central Message of the New Testament*. SCM Press 1965, pp. 9–30.

Contemplative Prayer

Raymond Bailey, *Thomas Merton on Mysticism*. Image Books, New York 1974.

John J. Higgins, *Thomas Merton on Prayer*. Image Books, New York 1975.

Mother Mary Clare, *Carmelite Ascent*. SLG Press 1973 (from Convent of the Incarnation, Fairacres, Oxford).

Thomas Merton, *Contemplative Prayer*. Darton, Longman and Todd 1973.

Thomas Merton, *Contemplation in a World of Action*. Image Books, New York 1973.

Spiritual Direction

Damian Isabell, *The Spiritual Director: A Practical Guide*. Franciscan Herald Press, Chicago 1976.

Kenneth Leech, *Soul Friend*. Sheldon Press 1977.

The Jesus Prayer

A. M. Allchin (ed.), *Theology and Prayer*. Fellowship of St Alban and St Sergius 1975.

Mother Maria, *The Jesus Prayer*. Greek Orthodox Monastery of the Assumption, Filgrave, Newport Pagnell, Bucks 1972.

Kallistos Ware, *The Power of the Name: The Jesus Prayer in Orthodox Spirituality*. SLG Press 1974.

Meditation

Daniel Goleman, *The Varieties of the Meditative Experience*. Rider and Company 1977.

Morton Kelsey, *The Other Side of Silence: A Guide to Christian Meditation*. SPCK 1977.

Klemens Tilmann, *The Practice of Meditation*. Search Press 1977.

Charismatic Spirituality

James Byrne, *Threshold of God's Promise*. Ave Maria Press, Indiana 1970.

D. L. Gelpi, *Pentecostal Piety*. Paulist Press, New York, 1972.

John Gunstone, *A People for his Praise*. Hodder and Stoughton 1978.

Kilian McDonnell, *The Holy Spirit and Power*. Doubleday 1975.

Prayer and Politics

John Pairman Brown and Richard L. York, *The Covenant of Peace: A Liberation Prayer Book*. Moorhouse-Barlow, New York 1971.

James Douglass, *Resistance and Contemplation.* Doubleday, New York 1972.

Albert F. Gedraitis, *Worship and Politics.* Wedge Publishing Foundation, Toronto 1972.

Thomas Merton, *Faith and Violence.* University of Notre Dame Press 1968.

Jurgen Moltmann, *The Church in the Power of the Spirit.* SCM Press 1977.

Sacraments and Prayer

R. F. Hoey (ed.), *The Experimental Liturgy Book.* Seabury Press, New York 1969.

Leonel L. Mitchell, *The Meaning of Ritual.* Paulist Press, New York 1977.

John A. T. Robinson, *Liturgy Coming to Life.* Mowbrays 1960.

John A. Robinson, *On Being the Church in the World.* SCM Press 1960.

Alexander Schmemann, *Of Water and the Spirit.* SPCK 1976.

Mark Searle, *Christening.* Kevin Mayhew 1977.

Sin and Confession

Joseph M. Champlin, *Together in Peace.* Ave Maria Press, Indiana 1975.

Monica Furlong, *Christian Uncertainties.* Hodder and Stoughton 1975.

Michael Scanlan, *The Power in Penance: Confession and the Holy Spirit.* Ave Maria Press, Indiana 1975.

Healing and Prayer

Francis MacNutt, *Healing.* Ave Maria Press, Indiana 1974.

Michael Scanlan, *Inner Healing.* Paulist Press, New York 1974.

Prayer Groups

John Gunstone, *The Charismatic Prayer Group.* Hodder and Stoughton 1975.

George McCauley, *The God of the Group.* Argus Communications, Niles, Illinois 1975 (obtainable in the UK from Argus Communications, 89 Railway Street, Hertford, Herts).

Robert Petitpierre, *Meeting for Prayer.* SPCK 1967.

The Divine Office

Sister Benedicta, SLG, *Liturgy Today: The Divine Office and the Eucharist.* SLG Press 1974.

Peter Coughlan and Peter Purdue (trans.), *The Liturgy of the Hours.* Geoffrey Chapman 1971.

Peter Coughlan *et al.*, *A Christian Prayer Book.* Collins.

The Divine Office: The Liturgy of the Hours according to the Roman Rite. 3 vols. Collins 1974.

Austin Flannery (ed.), *Making the Most of the Breviary.* Mayhew-McCrimmon, undated.

Ronald C. D. Jasper (ed.), *The Daily Office by the Joint Liturgical Group.* SPCK and Epworth Press 1968.

Ronald C. D. Jasper (ed.), *The Daily Office Revised by the Joint Liturgical Group.* SPCK 1978.

Morning and Evening Prayer from the The Divine Office. Collins 1977.

W. G. Storey (ed.), *Days of the Lord.* 3 vols. Herder 1965.

W. G. Storey, *Bless the Lord: A Prayerbook for Advent, Christmas, Lent and Eastertide.* Ave Maria Press, Indiana 1974.

Index